D1474876

SOUTHERN LITERARY STUDIES

Fred Hobson, Editor

FAULKNER

AND THE DISCOURSES OF CULTURE

CHARLES HANNON

LOUISIANA STATE UNIVERSITY PRESS   BATON ROUGE

DESIGNER: Barbara Neely Bourgoyne
TYPEFACE: Adobe Minion
TYPESETTER: Coghill Composition Co., Inc.
PRINTER AND BINDER: Thomson-Shore, Inc.

Portions of Chapter 5 first appeared in the essay "Race
Fantasies: The Filming of *Intruder in the Dust*," in
Faulkner in Cultural Context, ed. Donald Kartiganer and
Ann Abadie (Jackson: University Press of Mississippi, 1997),
and are reproduced by permission. Portions of Chapter 3
first appeared in the essay "Teaching the Conflicts as a
Temporary Instructor," *College Literature* 24.2 (1997): 126–41,
and are likewise reproduced by permission.

Library of Congress Cataloging-in-Publication Data
Hannon, Charles.
    Faulkner and the discourses of culture / Charles Hannon.
        p.   cm.—(Southern literary studies)
    Includes bibliographical references and index.
    ISBN 0-8071-2986-0 (alk. paper)
    1. Faulkner, William, 1897–1962—Criticism and interpretation.   2. Literature and
anthropology—Southern States—History—20th century.   3. Culture in literature.
I. Title.   II. Series.
PS3511.A86Z78453   2004
813'.52—dc22

                                                        2004011545

for Uma

CONTENTS

AA   William Faulkner, *Absalom, Absalom!* (1936; repr., New York: Vintage International, 1990).

BR   W. E. B. Du Bois, *Black Reconstruction in America, 1860–1880* (1935; repr., New York: Athenaeum, 1992).

DI   Mikhail Bakhtin, *The Dialogic Imagination: Four Essays.* Ed. Michael Holquist. Trans. Caryl Emerson and Michael Holquist (Austin: University of Texas Press, 1981).

FCF   Malcolm Cowley, *The Faulkner-Cowley File: Letters and Memories, 1944–1962* (New York: Viking, 1966).

FD   William Faulkner, *Flags in the Dust* (1929; repr., New York: Vintage, 1974).

ID   William Faulkner, *Intruder in the Dust* (1948; repr., New York: Vintage International, 1991).

KG   William Faulkner, *Knight's Gambit* (1949; repr., New York: Vintage, 1977).

LW   David Minter, *William Faulkner: His Life and Work* (Baltimore, Md.: Johns Hopkins University Press, 1980).

Rev   Albert Kirwan, *Revolt of the Rednecks: Mississippi Politics, 1876–1925* (Lexington: University of Kentucky Press, 1951).

SP   William Faulkner, *Soldier's Pay* (1926; repr., New York: Liveright, 1997)

TH   William Faulkner, *The Hamlet* (1940; repr., New York: Vintage International, 1990).

TU William Faulkner, *The Unvanquished* (1938; repr., New York: Vintage International, 1991).

WOA Herbert Agar and Allen Tate, eds., *Who Owns America? A New Declaration of Independence* (New York: Houghton Mifflin, 1936).

FAULKNER AND THE DISCOURSES OF CULTURE

Voice and Discourse in Faulkner

I listen to the voices, and when I put down what the voices say, it's right. Sometimes I don't like what they say, but I don't change it" (*FCF*, 114). When Malcolm Cowley transcribed this statement into his journal on October 26, 1948, he must have thought that Faulkner was describing the voices of inner genius. Faithfully adhering to his intuition, Faulkner had performed what Cowley, in the introduction to *The Portable Faulkner*, would call "a labor of imagination that has not been equaled in our time." Faulkner's fidelity to the voices he heard made sense to Cowley, who, beginning in 1940, had been true to his own inner convictions (this time critical) in the reassessment of Faulkner's achievement that made *The Portable Faulkner* possible, and that culminated, at the end of the decade, in Faulkner's being awarded the Nobel Prize.[1] As Faulkner had used the metaphor of voice to describe his representation of Yoknapatawpha and its people, Cowley describes his effort to re-present Faulkner to his American audience in terms of a lone voice that soon would be confirmed by others. It is every critic's dream, Cowley wrote, to "come upon an author whose reputation is less than his achievement and in fact is scandalously out of proportion with it, so that other voices will be added to the critic's voice, in a swelling chorus, as soon as he has made the discovery" (*FCF*, 3). For both Faulkner and Cowley, the metaphor of voice is related to the romantic trope of the Muse, who guides author and critic alike in the creation and evaluation of aesthetic material. For Faulkner the writer, these voices speak from a realm of the true ("when I put down what the voices say, it's right"); for Cowley the critic, they emerge from silence to confirm ("in a swelling chorus") one's sense of the true, and ultimately, one's sense of the world.

Faulkner and Cowley's joint understanding of voice as a vehicle of unitary truth and self-ratification differs radically from Mikhail Bakhtin's theory of dialogics, and from the theories of Marxist critics who have studied the process by which various languages of the social formation are inscribed upon the individual unconscious, and thus become one's "own." Bakhtin proposes that novelistic language is distinct from that of other genres because of its unique staging of *heteroglossia,* the multiplicity of variously inflected voices comprising any given culture. Novelistic language is "internally stratified," Bakhtin writes, into "social dialects, characteristic group behavior, professional jargons, generic languages, languages of generations and age groups, tendentious languages, languages of the authorities," and so on (*DI,* 262–63). To be sure, Cowley recognized as early as 1946 that the power of Faulkner's novels resides in their staging of the multiple voices to which the author was exposed as a youth. Faulkner based his work, Cowley writes in *The Portable Faulkner,* "on scraps of family tradition . . . ; on kitchen dialogues between the black cook and her amiable husband; on Saturday-afternoon gossip in Courthouse Square; on stories told by men in overalls squatting on their heels while they passed around a fruit jar full of white corn liquor." Cowley does not dwell upon the *aurality* of these sources, writing instead that the pattern of Faulkner's work "was based on what he *saw* in Oxford."[2] Yet each source in Cowley's list represents a different voice, a different socioeconomic (and, we might add, racial and ethnic) language, in Bakhtin's meaning of these terms. For Cowley, they are all refined into a single "pattern" through the mechanism of Faulkner's imagination. For Bakhtin, however, the power of novelistic language is precisely its ability to stage the conflicts that occur when such a variety of voices enter into dialogue with one another. Rather than resolving these conflicts through a single artistic vision, the novel retains the tensions that exist between a culture's different socioeconomic groups. The novel is thus more than the creation of the novelist; it becomes a record of the novelist's era—in particular, the tensions, conflicts, and struggles that divided (and sometimes united) that era's various social groups. Because Faulkner did not change the voices he heard (despite the fact that he sometimes did not like what they said), his novels embody the *heteroglossia* of his time: the voices of dominant groups seeking to achieve ideological supremacy, as well as the voices of dissent, resistance, and contradiction.

We often say that Faulkner "found his voice" as a novelist. It is a little painful to read his early poetry and discover that the writer of *The Sound and the Fury, As I Lay Dying,* and *Absalom, Absalom!* was once an imitative poet. As David Minter observes, "In his early poetry he drew, not on his knowledge of the hills, birds, and inhabitants of Mississippi, but on his knowledge of English poetry of the nineteenth century" (*LW,* 20). It was simply impossible for Faulkner to accomplish with poetry what he wanted to do as a writer. Overly influenced by the English Romantics and, later, by English, French, and American modernists, the "voice" of Faulkner's poetry remains tethered to a position of observation rather than one of individual experience. As a consequence, it speaks self-consciously from a world that is remote from the lived experiences of Faulkner himself and of his contemporaries.

For Bakhtin, such verse speaks from the "epic world": it is concerned with the "absolute past" rather than the present; it is stilted by its emphasis upon generic conventions. The result is that it constructs an impassable distance between the artistic object and the moment of artistic representation (*DI,* 13–20). "The epic world is constructed in the zone of an absolute distanced image," Bakhtin writes, "beyond the sphere of possible contact with the developing, incomplete and therefore rethinking and re-evaluating present" (*DI,* 17). By contrast, in the novel, "contemporaneity," "the present in all its openendedness" (*DI,* 19), becomes the object of representation, because novelistic language allows the conflicting voices of the social formation to confront one another over the "truth" of the present moment. To illustrate this essential difference between the "epic" world of Faulkner's poetry and the "novelistic" quality of his prose, we can compare his representation of field labor in one of his early "Mississippi Poems" to a related representation in his first Yoknapatawpha novel, *Flags in the Dust.* This comparison will show how Faulkner's obsession with English literary tradition, especially with the pastoral mode of the Romantics, limits the possibilities of "voice" in his early poetry; and how his practice as a novelist allowed him to "dialogize" the scenes of his earlier poetry, and thus represent more fully, in the novels, the *heteroglossia* of his time.

Here are the first two stanzas of poem V from "Mississippi Poems":

> He furrows the brown earth, doubly sweet
> To a hushed great passage of wind

Dragging its shadow. Beneath his feet
The furrow breaks, and at its end

He turns. With peace about his head
Traverses he again the earth: his own,
Still with enormous promises of bread
And clean its odorous strength about him blown.[3]

The pastoral quality of this scene is overpowering: the earth is "doubly sweet," and of an organic piece with the other elements such as the wind and, later in the poem, the "rumorous waters" (line 27). For the agricultural laborer in Faulkner's poem there is "peace about his head," for the day is "still," "clean," and abundant with the "promises of bread." The pastoral imagery of this poem constructs a world of classical antiquity which, like the epic world in Bakhtin's sense, "is walled off absolutely from all subsequent times, and above all from those times in which the singer and his listeners are located" (*DI*, 15–16). This "absolute past" delineates a world of unalienated laborers who, as in the poem's final lines, can "Furrow the brown earth, doubly sweet / To a simple heart, for here a man / Might bread him with his hands and feet" (lines 30–32). There is no parallel here between the agricultural labor performed by the man in Faulkner's poem and that performed by actual farm workers in 1920s Mississippi. Certainly there is little indication of the struggles and abuses these workers endured as a result of the terms of their contracts with lenders and landowners. Rather, Faulkner's studied effort to preserve the formal traditions of poetry (of rhyme, meter, syntax, and sound) constructs two impassible barriers or "distances" characteristic of Bakhtin's "epic" language: between the speaker of the poem and the object of his artistic representation (which results in a surplus of "literary" images and a dearth of realistic representations); and between the object of representation and the audiences of the 1920s that Faulkner might have hoped to reach (whether friends, family, lovers, or publishers). As Minter observes, "Poetry seemed to him—and as he practiced it, it was—all order and restraint" (*LW*, 41).[4]

In *The Marble Faun* (1924), Faulkner's first poem sequence, a similar "absolute past" is peopled with sprites and fairies, and the poem's central figure is cut off from the world these spirits seem to construct for themselves. As Minter notes, "the activities he observes, such as the freedom of the 'quick keen snake,' he cannot directly experience" (*LW*, 28). Above all, in these poems there is a reverence for the literary image that is lacking in novelistic discourse, not least because the dominant trope of the novel is not worship but laughter. "Laughter demolishes fear and piety before an object, before a world, making of it an object of familiar contact and thus clearing the ground for an absolutely free investigation of it," Bakhtin writes (*DI*, 23). The familiarity of the world of the novel "permits the author, in all his various masks and faces, to move freely onto the field of his represented world, a field that in the epic had been absolutely inaccessible and closed" (*DI*, 27). The object of artistic representation is thus "brought low" in the novel and is subjected to the scrutiny of parody and travesty (*DI*, 21); the author can treat it with scorn, can make fun of it and of his own attempts to represent it. An example of this is the apostrophe to the mule from *Flags in the Dust*, in which Faulkner literally enters the "field" of the present and parodies his earlier efforts (as in poem V of "Mississippi Poems") to represent the "contemporaneity" of his day with the worshipful language of the epic:

Some Cincinnatus of the cotton fields should contemplate the lowly destiny, some Homer should sing the saga, of the mule and of his place in the South. He it was, more than any one creature or thing, who, steadfast to the land when all else faltered before the hopeless juggernaut of circumstance, impervious to conditions that broke men's hearts because of his venomous and patient preoccupation with the immediate present, won the prone South from beneath the iron heel of Reconstruction and taught it pride again through humility and courage through adversity overcome. (*FD*, 313)

In poem V, Faulkner had tried *to be* that Cincinnatus or Homer of the agricultural South. Here, the novelist casts that effort as an impossibility in the present world (*should* contemplate, *should* sing) or at least as an effort that *this* novel's narrator is unwilling to undertake. Like the mule itself, the novelist assumes a "venomous and patient preoccupation with the immediate present."

Once we recognize that Faulkner's novelistic language is shot through with voiced conflicts of the 1930s South, his narratives begin to resonate in surprising ways. In the narration that precedes this passage on the mule in *Flags in the Dust*, for instance, we can hear several voices in conflict over the facts of property ownership in the postbellum plantation South. The narrator speaks of the "*Sartoris* place," where "*Sartoris* cotton" is farmed by sharecroppers. Yet, these workers have recently finished picking "*their* cotton" and are bringing "*their* cane" to make "*their* winter supply" of molasses (*FD*, 313; emphases added). Possession is utterly confused in this scene as Bayard and Narcissa Sartoris approach it, accompanied by a shift in the narrator's voice toward the pastoral: "and of late afternoons, with Indian summer upon the land and an ancient sadness sharp as woodsmoke on the still air, Bayard and Narcissa would drive out to where, beside a dilapidated cotton house on the edge of a wooden ravine above a spring, the tenants brought their cane" (*FD*, 313). Yet the very language of the dominant class of landowners contains within it the incoherence of the scene's economic (dis)order—in the awkward use of a possessive pronoun (*their* cane) whose antecedent is ambiguous; and in the grudging and derisive acknowledgment of "one of the negroes, *a sort of patriarch*" who owns both the mill and the mule (*FD*, 313; emphasis added). Because the language of this scene is dialogized, it must represent the fact of black property ownership; but it also represents the efforts of the dominant classes to elide this fact and to represent the black Other as an object of ritual scorn. In this sense, even the long apostrophe to the mule—rather than to the black workers who populate this scene—can be interpreted as a further attempt to obscure the disturbing fact of black independence, which the mill owner's ownership of the mule makes irrefutable.

Dialogization ensures the representation of suppressed voices of dissent and confrontation, although these voices will often be distorted, muffled, or disguised in ways that require, and sometimes defy, interpretation. But even when these are represented under the trope of laughter, the result is not always funny. Whereas poem V from "Mississippi Poems" idealizes labor as unalienated and rewarding (the earth traversed by the laborer is "his own"), *Flags in the Dust* represents black agricultural work under the modern share system as a pointless "plodding in a monotonous circle . . . round and round" (*FD*, 313). Indeed, throughout *Flags in the Dust* black farmers work while white farmers hunt. And it should be understood that a narrator who speaks of winning "the prone South from beneath the iron heel of Reconstruction" is voicing a trope of proslavery historiography which is clearly allied with the dominant white classes of the modern South, because any voice that considers Reconstruction to have been an "iron heel" at the throat of the entire South would not speak for African Americans, whose political enfranchisement was greatly furthered by the Reconstruction governments of 1865–78. This same voice argues, a little further into the passage, that the mule is "misunderstood even by the creature (the nigger who drives him) whose impulses and mental processes most closely resemble his" (FD, 314).

Racial scorn can be found throughout Faulkner's novels, but this does not mean that it comes directly from Faulkner. Rather, it was part of the discourse of race that was available to this white southern writer as he sought to represent the lived experiences of the people who inhabit his imagined Yoknapatawpha County. While Cowley and his generation of American critics could consider Yoknapatawpha the product of Faulkner's individual genius ("a cosmos of my own," Faulkner would claim, where he was "sole owner and proprietor"), Bakhtin's insistence upon the social origin of novelistic language requires a decentering of the author in literary criticism, and an effort to understand the implications of the idea that "in the everyday speech of any person living in society, no less than half (on the average) of all the words uttered by him will be someone else's words" (DI, 339). In terms of the discursive architecture of Faulkner's novels, this means that more than half of the ideological phrases—what Bakhtin calls "ideologemes"—more than half of the rhetorical strategies and inflections of race, class, and gender in Faulkner's texts, are not his "own" but rather the textualization and "novelistic" representation of preexisting languages of the social formation. Richard Gray makes this point in his critical biography of the writer: "If we are ever to understand Faulkner properly, we need to situate him among the voices that circled and inhabited him. We need, in effect, to perceive his private life as part of the public life of a particular locality and moment in history. The aim of this should not be to deny his individuality, but to acknowledge that this individuality was the product of a series of intersecting, social and cultural, forces—and of Faulkner's active engagement, his entry into dialogue, with those forces."[5] As Gray's argument suggests, Faulkner's most notorious, sometimes racist statements as an individual cannot be brushed aside with a few allusions to literary theory. But when racist propaganda surfaces in his novels, we should consider it the expression of one of the languages of the modern South and explore the ways in which it is confronted and contradicted by other languages of the social formation, which, because of their dialogized nature, also are represented in Faulkner's novels.

Racial scorn is present in Faulkner's earliest novel, *Soldier's Pay* (1926). In this novel, the representations of blacks are almost entirely determined by the stereotypes of white supremacist ideology, which held that blacks were unfit as managers of their own labor and therefore required the constant supervision of whites, and that blacks were naturally happiest when in the service of whites. We see these assumptions at work in the opening chapters, in the character of the black railway porter who, "with the instincts of his race," meticulously serves Donald Mahon and his military comrades, presumably out of loyalty to a white fellow-southerner (*SP*, 24). The porter takes no action without first consulting Mahon, and like all blacks in this novel, he is ever ready to serve. Another avatar of this figure of the loyal black servant appears toward the end of *Soldier's Pay,* in the black youth "reclining miraculously" at the train station as he waits to assist Joe Gilligan with Mrs. Powers's baggage. The youth springs into action only when his companion, Joe, tells him, "Git up dar, boy. Dat white man is talkin' to you" (*SP*, 298). Blacks in *Soldier's Pay* are also something less than human, evoking the ugliest proslavery claims of the eighteenth and nineteenth centuries. The railway youth watching Mrs. Powers's bags (as directed by Joe), slouches beside them, "going to sleep immediately, like a horse" (*SP*, 298). And earlier (in an effort that is rare in this novel), the narrator attempts to represent the inner speech of a black driver, yet can do so only in terms that dehumanize him: "Ketch me asleep, he kill me. But I got mule blood in me: when he sleep, I sleep; when he wake, I wake" (*SP*, 147). Clearly, Faulkner's early representations of blacks are dominated by the proslavery voices he heard as a youth (according to biographer Joseph Blotner, Faulkner's first-grade teacher gave him a copy of Thomas Dixon's *The Clansman: An Historical Romance of the Ku Klux Klan*) and as a young man writing this novel in New Orleans in the 1920s.[6] But as his novelistic style developed, and particularly as he made his "great discovery" of Yoknapatawpha, such representations became more dialogized and less ruled by the fictions of white fantasy. His novels still would be replete with the dominant languages of his time, but increasingly these intersect with the languages of resistance and opposition, making the novels more fully representative of the discursive atmosphere of the modern South.

A brief discussion of two moments of black resistance, one from *Flags in the Dust* and one from *The Unvanquished* (1938), will illustrate this point. *Flags in the Dust* is set in the aftermath of World War I, when returning black veterans were demanding that the promises of democracy for which they had fought in Europe be made available to them in America. As Caspey reasons in *Flags in the Dust,* "War showed de white folks dey cant git along widout de colored man. Tromple him in de dust, but when de trouble bust loose, hit's 'Please, suh, Mr Colored Man; right dis way whar de bugle blowin,' Mr Colored Man; you is de savior of de country.' And now de colored race gwine reap de benefits of de war, and dat soon" (*FD,* 67). Caspey's emergence in Faulkner's fiction begins a revolution in the writer's representation of race. Caspey rejects the role of "negro"—first, by ignoring the summons of the white matriarch, Aunt Jenny Du Pre, as he leaves the Sartoris household for town; and later, by refusing Old Bayard's demand that he saddle his horse: "I aint workin' here," Caspey tells his mother; "Whyn't you go'n git his hoss fer him?" (*FD,* 86). Caspey's refusal to perform the role of loyal servant completely baffles Aunt Jenny and Old Bayard, for it interrupts a dialectic of racial role-playing upon which their own identities as privileged white southerners are founded. In this early novel, however, Faulkner is unable to sustain this tension; by the end of *Flags in the Dust,* Caspey is once again following young Bayard through a night's opossum hunting "with a streaked and blackened lantern and a cow's horn slung over his shoulder" and presumably exuding "that unmistakable odor of negroes" that all blacks seem to have in this novel (*FD,* 317, 389). But his initial refusal to perform the submissive role assigned to him by the white aristocracy sets a pattern that will be replayed to one degree or another in many of Faulkner's novels.

Caspey's later avatar, the Loosh of *The Unvanquished,* is not so easily transformed into an object of derision, or into the white-fantasy figure of the loyal servant. In this novel, the Old Bayard of *Flags in the Dust* is a youth during the closing battles of the Civil War. He and his playmate Ringo have constructed a model of Vicksburg, Mississippi, out of mud and wood chips, and are engaged in a drama that celebrates the southern war effort against the North. Loosh, Ringo's uncle, laughs at the two boys because he knows that Vicksburg has recently fallen to Union troops. He sweeps away their model and proclaims, "There's your Vicksburg" (*TU*, 5). Jubilant, he then announces that Corinth has fallen also, and that John Sartoris, Bayard's father, has had to return to Mississippi from Tennessee because of successive Confederate defeats. As I will detail more fully in chapter 1, this opening scene of *The Unvanquished* reflects a general crisis in the process of southern white identity formation, one that is rooted historically in the agency of blacks at the time of the Civil War. This crisis was repeated in the modern era by the refusal of returning black World War I soldiers to tolerate America's racial status quo, and it is observable in Faulkner's Yoknapatawpha fiction for the first time in Caspey's refusal to perform the role of "negro," which is necessary for the ratification of Old Bayard's and Aunt Jenny's understanding of themselves as privileged white southerners. Bayard's first-person narration of *The Unvanquished* can thus be read as a kind of lamentation upon his own lost identity, one that naturally returns to the Civil War as the historical and political moment, the "primal scene," of this loss.[7] Significantly, his lamentation also returns to the specific event of Loosh's laughter, which is a kind of repetition of Caspey's laughter at Old Bayard's demand for service out of loyalty to the Sartoris family.

What is significant about Faulkner's representation of this crisis in *The Unvanquished* and *Flags in the Dust* is that, while in the earlier novel the crisis initiated by Caspey's resistance is resolved through the transformation of Caspey again into the figure of the loyal servant, in *The Unvanquished* this transformation is impossible. Bayard perceives Loosh through the lens of racial scorn: when Loosh destroys what amounts to Bayard's fantasy construction of the South, all Bayard can see is his "cannonball" head and "his eyes a little red at the inner corners as negroes' eyes get when they have been drinking" (*TU*, 4). But these proslavery tropes do not ultimately reduce Loosh to a comic figure. Rather, Bayard must acknowledge that Loosh has run away from the Sartoris plantation to join the Union army. As Loosh's action exposes the falsehood of white claims about loyal wartime slaves, Bayard, narrating this scene from a moment in time much closer to that of *Flags in the Dust* than to the Civil War, faces a crisis of identity formation as he realizes that he can no longer take for granted the dialectic that has ratified his own (and his family's) sense of racial and class superiority.

Faulkner's thinking about race and racial difference changed over the course of his career, and this is reflected in the novels he wrote. Some readers claim he became more "political." In the words of Faulkner editor Noel Polk, "one of the loveliest minor effects of his political engagement can be traced in the fiction: in the early works he nearly always wrote *negro*, with a lower case *n*; in *The Town*, his first novel after the years of political turmoil, he invariably capitalized it. *Go Down, Moses* contains a mixture of *N* and *n*, especially in the final chapter; it is perhaps a conscious, perhaps an unconscious, distinction Faulkner was beginning to make, even in 1942."[8] The gradual change from lower- to upper-case *N* signifies a transformation in the thinking of the private individual William Faulkner, but it also reflects changes in the discourse of race that occurred during his career as a novelist. There is always this tense reciprocity between the individual subjects who are the "authors" of discourse and the discourses themselves, which, to the degree that they are a function of the entire social formation, actually produce the subjects who "speak" them. According to David Minter, Faulkner ruminates upon this possibility in a manuscript fragment, wondering if he "had invented the world" he wrote about, "or if it had invented me" (*LW*, 103).

The uneasy relation between discourse and the individual subject is a major theme of this study. If it is true that Faulkner's writing about race is the product of both his own individual thinking and of developments in the discourse of race which in many ways are out of his control, we must acknowledge the same for other discourses of culture reflected in his novels, such as the discourses of historiography (chapter 1), law (chapter 2), labor (chapter 3), ethnography (chapter 4), and film (chapter 5). To resolve this tension in the following chapters, I consciously seek a middle ground between Bakhtin's stylistics of the novel (and his reliance upon the author as the ultimate source of novelistic style) and Michel Foucault's model of discourse as an autonomous, self-regulating domain in which the production of subject positions is all but incidental. In Foucault, one immediately confronts the dilemma of individual agency, because in *The Archaeology of Knowledge,* he insists that the historical subject is little more than a discursive effect, devoid of any "real" subjectivity and hence without agency to effect historical or political change. As David Shumway suggests, Foucault is not interested in "actual subjects" so much as the "subject positions that are more or less defined by the discourse itself."[9] After *The Archaeology,* however, and particularly in his statements on genealogy as an analytical method, Foucault appears to have opened the study of discourse to the possibility of a subject that is not only subjected to, but also the subject of, particular instances of discursive power.

In "The Discourse on Language," a speech delivered on the occasion of Foucault's appointment to the Collège de France, Foucault added a social and institutional dimension to the study of discourse, in the form of disciplines. Disciplines "are defined by groups of objects, methods, their corpus of propositions considered to be true, the interplay of rules and definitions, of techniques and tools; all these constitute a sort of anonymous system, freely available to anyone who wishes." Despite this free availability of the formative elements of discourse, disciplines determine what may be considered true within a particular discourse, "imposing a certain number of rules upon those individuals who employ it, thus denying access to everyone else."[10] Foucault's "genealogist" of history therefore seeks past moments of struggle between groups and institutions over the rules of discursive formation and exclusion, identifying the "subjugated knowledges" of disciplines, by which Foucault means two things: "historical contents that have been buried and disguised in a functionalist coherence or formal systematization"; and "a whole set of knowledges that have been disqualified as inadequate to their task or insufficiently elaborated." Foucault's shift from treating discourse as a "self-contained and self-generating machine" to the placing of discourse "in the context of rules of exclusion and restrictions deriving from social interests and practices" thus creates a window in the study of discourse in which change can occur according to the will of individuals, as long as we (paradoxically) understand these individuals to be operating in the service of larger group or institutional interest.[11]

In another widely discussed essay, "Nietzsche, Genealogy, and History," Foucault offers the terms *Herkunft* ("descent") and *Entstehung* ("emergence") as the tools of genealogy, but again the objects of historical analysis are groups, disciplines, and institutions, rather than individuals. For instance, the analysis of *Herkunft* "often involves a consideration of race or social type." Genealogical history seeks "discrete and apparently insignificant truths" of the past in order to discover the historical descent of alterations that have occurred in the rules of discursive formation in the interest of particular groups or political entities. As the analysis of *Entstehung*, genealogy likewise views historical change as "the violent or surreptitious appropriation of a system of rules" by one group or another. Foucault qualifies his use of these terms, emphasizing that the analysis of discursive "descent" should not be confused with the search for origins; nor should the "emergence" of different rules within a discourse be considered "the final term of an historical development." Both these errors result from thinking of history as gradual evolution, whereas Foucault would understand it as a series of violent eruptions. Rather than "erecting foundations," the genealogical search for discursive descent "disturbs what was previously considered immobile, it fragments what was thought unified." Moreover, Foucault is quick to detach the individual agent from history's disruptive moments: "No one is responsible for an emergence; no one can glory in it, since it always occurs in the interstice." Readers seeking a "founding subject" at the center of historical or political change would therefore still be disappointed by the Foucault of these two essays, who believes that this "theme [of the founding subject] . . . permits us to elide the reality of discourse." Yet for the analysis of discursive change within and between groups, disciplines, and institutions, Foucault's elaboration in these essays of a consistent terminology and a specific object of investigation is a welcome development from *The Archaeology of Knowledge*.[12]

A brief reflection upon specific "eruptions" in the discourse of American historiography of the Civil War and Reconstruction, and their effect upon Faulkner's own writing of southern history, will illustrate how Foucault's genealogical method and the concepts of *Herkunft* and *Entstehung* might help to navigate a discursive approach to Faulkner. Focusing on the particular discipline of American historiography allows us to follow the shift in Foucault's work after *The Archaeology*

from the view that discursive domains should be considered autonomous (independent of social determinations), to one that understands
their changing rules of formation as a consequence of institutional and
group practices. John David Smith has detailed the extent to which late-
nineteenth- and early-twentieth-century American historiography of
the Civil War and Reconstruction operated according to a system of
rules that guaranteed the continuous recirculation of proslavery stereotypes of African Americans.[13] That this proslavery discourse was then
made "freely available to anyone who wishes" by the discipline of
American historiography is evident when we recognize the pervasive-
ness of proslavery assumptions about race and history in other discursive domains, such as the early films of Thomas Edison and D. W.
Griffith, and the literary productions of writers such as Thomas Nelson
Page, Clarence Dixon, and even Faulkner. Clearly, American historiographers who participated in what W. E. B. Du Bois, emerging in the
mid-1930s, was to label the "propaganda of history" were observing disciplinary rules of formation and exclusion as they participated in
a discourse on the American past that solidified their own race and
class interests. When it recognized as "within the true" the story of loyal
slaves, munificent planters, and scurrilous Yankees and carpetbaggers—as well as historical premises such as that represented in W. E.
Woodward's statement that American slaves are "the only people in the
history of the world, so far as I know, that ever became free without
any effort of their own"[14]—the profession of American historiography
simply maintained its practice of recognizing the qualifications of a particular kind of historian, of particular kinds of historical documents,
evidence, and conclusions, and of a particular, prejudicial morality
of history that privileged white accomplishment and presumed black
passivity.

What sense, then, can we make of the remarkable effort at revisionist
historiography by W. E. B. Du Bois in *Black Reconstruction in America,*
in which he seemingly dismissed the rules of American historiography
and demonstrated the extent to which previous histories of the Civil
War and Reconstruction were little more than race propaganda? Not
only did Du Bois's opus correct the misrepresentations of past historians, it transformed the categories of what does and does not count as
historical evidence, since Du Bois did not utilize the standard historio-

graphical resources—state, university, and courthouse archives—but instead "confined himself to government reports, proceedings of state constitutional conventions, unpublished dissertations, and virtually every relevant published monograph." As a black historian working in the Jim Crow South, Du Bois was precluded from utilizing the archives of "standard" white historiography; as David Lewis writes, "it is hard to imagine Du Bois motoring from 'white' court house to campus entreating entry of redfaced custodians." Yet the very practice of excluding Du Bois from these sources and from the inner circle of respected historiographers determined the revisionist character of his work. Du Bois's position vis-à-vis the discipline of American historiography thus derived from the discipline's rules of formation and exclusion, but it was also impossible according to these rules, which is why his historiography was largely dismissed by the profession. As with Foucault's example of Mendel, whose early statements on plant genetics were not recognized as "within the true" by nineteenth-century botanists, Du Bois "spoke of objects, employed methods and placed himself within a theoretical perspective totally alien to the [historiography] of his time."[15]

Black Reconstruction thus represented a discursive "eruption" within the discipline of American historiography. In chapter 1, on *The Unvanquished,* I argue that this eruption affected the shape of Faulkner's writing about the Civil War and Reconstruction. When Faulkner returned in 1938 to stories first published in the early 1930s in the *Saturday Evening Post,* the discursive domain regarding Civil War and Reconstruction historiography had altered significantly, because the proslavery assumptions that previously had determined the practice of historiography had come under assault by Du Bois and other revisionists. Because of the dialogic nature of his novels, Faulkner's own practice of representing southern history had to change as well. This reading of Faulkner's revisions does not require material evidence of his having read Du Bois's work. Faulkner was an attentive listener; the works of Joyce and Freud heavily influenced his novels, for instance, even though he often claimed not to have read them. Faulkner once told Henry Nash Smith the following: " 'You know,' he smiled, 'sometimes I think there must be a sort of pollen of ideas floating in the air, which fertilizes similarly minds here and there which have not had direct contact. I had heard of

Joyce, of course,' he went on. 'Someone told me about what he was doing, and it is possible that I was influenced by what I heard.'"[16] As a southerner raised on stories that cast the Civil War as a battle waged between white "brothers," Faulkner would have retained and used (consciously or not) any startling information he heard about the agency of slaves and free blacks during the war, whether as Union soldiers or spies, or as willful saboteurs of the South's wartime economy. These facts about the wartime roles of African Americans were part of the "pollen of ideas" in the 1930s, and (as I argue in chapter 1) they are reflected in Faulkner's late-1930s revisions of *The Unvanquished.* The novel continues to voice proslavery stereotypes, but the late-1930s additions and revisions also revise these stereotypes in a manner that is suggestive of Du Bois's revisionist historiography in *Black Reconstruction.*

My approach to the Faulknerian subject is "discursive" to the extent that I begin each of the following chapters with a discussion of historical discontinuities within particular discourses of culture, what Foucault calls "caesurae breaking the instant and dispersing the subject in a multiplicity of possible positions and functions."[17] My claim is that the discourses of historiography, law, labor, anthropology, and film experienced certain "eruptions" whose radical effects on subjectivity and the process of subject-formation determined the formation of Faulkner's literary texts and the subject positions they make available to their readers. While each of the following chapters thus departs from Foucault in order to examine the effects of discursive change upon individual subjectivity in Faulkner, I purposely retain the tension between the individual and the group that derives from my use of Foucauldian concepts of history and discourse. Following Bakhtin, I view the Faulknerian text "as a rejoinder in a given dialogue, whose style is determined by its interrelationship with other rejoinders in the same dialogue" (*DI,* 274). Unlike Stephen Ross's Bakhtinian reading of voice in Faulkner, however, I am keen to adhere to Bakhtin's stricture that "any stylistics capable of dealing with the distinctiveness of the novel as a genre must be a *sociological stylistics*" (*DI,* 300).[18] While studies such as Ross's, and Philip Weinstein's *Faulkner's Subject: A Cosmos No One Owns,* attend to the internal dialogism of Faulkner's language within the oeuvre of his texts, I adhere to the precept that the "internal social dialogism of novelistic discourse requires the concrete social context of discourse to be exposed" (*DI*, 300).[19]

This means that the following chapters stake out a territory between authorial intention and cultural analysis that some readers might find uncomfortable. Rarely do I demonstrate a direct, traceable influence between a discursive shift and its textualization in Faulkner's novels and stories. I do not hold the journal entry in which Faulkner ruminates upon Du Bois's revisionist stance in *Black Reconstruction,* for instance. And although Faulkner's lifelong interest in the law, nurtured through both family tradition and his friendship with Phil Stone, adds to the plausibility of my argument in chapter 2, I do not detail that interest any further than it has already been addressed by other capable scholars and biographers.[20] Clearly, my reluctance to seek material evidence of the connections I observe between the various cultural discourses and the voices of Faulkner's novels results from my unorthodox pairing of Foucault and Bakhtin. For his part, Bakhtin contradicts himself on the point of authorial intention; while he recognizes that "language is not a neutral medium that passes freely into the private property of the speaker's intentions," he nevertheless champions the concept of the author, seeing his intentions "refracted" in the artistic composition of the novel's languages (*DI*, 294). Indeed, this contradictory stance leads to some rather clumsy passages in Bakhtin: "It is as if the author has no language of his own, but does possess his own style, his own organic and unitary law governing the way he plays with languages and the way his own real semantic and expressive intentions are refracted within them" (*DI*, 311). Such logical binds would present no dilemma to Foucault, for whom the author is merely a function of literary discourse, an effect of history just like the concept of the individual subject.

In the following pages, I consciously resist the urge to choose between Foucault's and Bakhtin's positions regarding the "unitary" designs of the author, for I want to draw upon both theorists to conceptualize the connection between discourse, language, and the production of subjectivity and subject positions within the discourses of culture (including Faulkner's literary discourse), and it is precisely where Foucault and Bakhtin diverge on the concreteness of the author (or the individual subject itself) that I make my own diversions into the "concrete social context" of discourses in dialogue with Faulkner's texts.

Admittedly, my refusal to pursue Foucault's argument regarding the ineffectualness of the individual subject stems from my own uneasiness about the implications of such a theory. Like Paul Smith, I am reluctant to abdicate my sense of myself as a thinking individual who can effect change within my own sphere of action, despite my understanding that this might be an ideological illusion which is only maintained by the practice of reading and writing about "authors" like William Faulkner.[21]

One consequence of a discursive approach to Faulkner is that issues of race, class, and gender are subordinated to an analysis of the discourses of culture—indeed, are considered "effects" of the latter. Without question, race (to take one example) is a central concern of Faulkner's major novels, but the tendency in Faulkner studies to treat racial discourse as an abstraction separate from the determinations of other cultural domains dehistoricizes it beyond usefulness as a category of ideological conditioning.[22] Although my use of Foucault in approaching the Faulknerian subject requires me to treat race, class, and gender in terms of group politics and therefore may seem at times to fall into generalization, I hope that my placing of these politics in relation to specific discursive and historical contexts enables me to escape the sort of teleology that weakens other discussions of this topic. I also hope to avoid reducing the immense variety of discourse found in Faulkner's literary productions to a single thesis or grand, explanatory argument. My intention is to describe the possibilities of a discursive reading of Faulkner, rather than to claim privileged access to the entire oeuvre of Faulkner's work.[23] Moreover, my aim is to demonstrate the possibilities of a historically discursive approach to Faulkner, rather than to provide an exhaustive reading of all of Faulkner's most "canonical" texts. In fact, I specifically chose to address the issue of racial identity-formation in *Intruder in the Dust* rather than in *The Sound and the Fury, Light in August,* or *Go Down, Moses,* precisely because the number of excellent readings of race in these novels puts them at risk of being formulated in the canon as Faulkner's "best" examinations of southern racial history.

By placing Faulkner's texts generally, and his representation of race, class, and gender specifically, in relation to discourses of culture contemporary with them, I hope to reveal some of the ideological pressures that produced the categories of "author" and "subject"—as well as the identity "Faulkner"—that we know today. I begin with historiography—the practice of writing about the past, and therefore of constructing one's own sense of a self in relation to the past—because Faulkner achieved his "voices" as a novelist only when he abandoned his identity as a decadent, modernist poet and began to revisit the legends of his family and his region. Every biographer of Faulkner has noted the significance for his novels of the legends he was told about the South, about Mississippi, and about his family's role in the creation of both. When Faulkner decided to return to these legends in *Flags in the Dust,* and especially in *The Unvanquished,* however, he would not simply reproduce them and the monological worldview they espoused. Instead, his novels also would echo the contemporary voices of revolution and resistance that contested the worldview of the South's dominant families.

CHAPTER 1

Revisionist Historiography, Agrarian Reform, and *The Unvanquished*

Faulkner's first Yoknapatawpha novel, *Flags in the Dust* (1926), was both a stunning accomplishment and a demoralizing experience for the writer. The accomplishment was Faulkner's discovery of two great themes to which he would return throughout his career: family, and regional history. But his publisher, Horace Liveright, was unable to see the unity in these themes, each a metaphor for the other. As a result, the novel that Faulkner believed would make his reputation Liveright rejected out of hand, advising him not to seek its publication. Liveright's rejection devastated Faulkner, but it was also a kind of inspiration, as David Minter observes: "Had *Flags in the Dust* been accepted and published immediately, Faulkner probably would have returned to 'Father Abraham,' and almost certainly would not have done what he did, which was to write *The Sound and the Fury*" (*LW*, 81). In *The Sound and the Fury* (1929), Faulkner continued to work with the family structure as a central metaphor signifying the diminished quality of modern existence. But whereas the story of modern-day Sartorises in *Flags in the Dust* is set against the "heroic" adventures of Colonel John Sartoris during the Civil War and Reconstruction, in *The Sound and the Fury* the metaphor of family subsumes any parallel figures representing southern regional history.

Faulkner's use of the family structure as a metaphor for modern degeneration in *The Sound and the Fury* derives not so much from *Flags in the Dust*'s depiction of four generations of Sartorises, as from that novel's portrayal of one generation of Benbows, and particularly from Horace Benbow's incestuous desire for his sister Narcissa. True, young Bayard Sartoris's modern cynicism does inflect Jason Compson's bitterness over his dispossession of his inheritance, but it is Horace's forbidden desire for his sister which, in Quentin Compson, becomes the metaphor for an impossible desire to reclaim lost innocence as well as lost racial, economic, and class privilege. Similarly, while there is a parallel between the declining generations of the Compson family in *The Sound and the Fury* and those of the Sartorises in *Flags in the Dust,* in the latter the Sartorises' genealogy is handed down to both Old and Young Bayard in the form of legends and myths about the founding of the county and the morality of the Civil War, whereas family history in *The Sound and the Fury* is surprisingly detached from regional history and from legends about the role played by Compson ancestors in that history. However much the Compson brothers' desire to regain their lost sister might also symbolize the white South's desire to recuperate a mythologized sense of regional wholeness that it imagined it lost in the Civil War, this theme is not developed overtly in *The Sound and the Fury* (as it would be in *Absalom, Absalom!* [1936]): "At a few points in Quentin's section," John Matthews writes, "the prose crinkles on the verge of making a connection between the private obsession with Caddy's purity and the larger questions of the South." Matthews's strained language reflects his recognition that the reciprocal metaphorical significance that critics often observe between the fate of the Compson family and the fate of the South is more a product of Faulkner's writing *after* 1929, especially his elaboration of the Compson story in *Absalom, Absalom!* and in the "Compson Appendix" (1946), than of the text of the novel itself. Echoing Jean-Paul Sartre's influential reading of the novel, Matthews writes that "in *The Sound and the Fury* history makes itself felt by being forgotten, by making itself into a background blur."[1] It is as though Faulkner's disappointment over Liveright's and other publishers' rejection of *Flags in the Dust* caused him to disentangle, to the extent that it is possible, the narrative of the family from the narrative of its relation to southern history, and then to focus on the one that was closest to him as a young man and as a developing writer: the story of a once-great family that has deteriorated as it has followed the rest of the world into the modern era.

It would be a mistake to press this interpretation further, because at one level Faulkner's novels are all deeply saturated with the contingencies of southern history. But the priority given to family over southern regional history in *The Sound and the Fury* does indicate the significance of the *Flags in the Dust* debacle for Faulkner's thinking about his Yokna-patawpha saga, as well as the importance of Faulkner's efforts once again to unify these themes in two novels of the 1930s, *Absalom, Absalom!* and *The Unvanquished* (1938). Ever since Malcolm Cowley introduced Faulkner's work as a grand effort "to make his story of Yoknapatawpha County stand as a parable or legend of all the Deep South," critics have argued, one way or another, that the elaboration of Thomas Sutpen's story in *Absalom, Absalom!* parallels the myths and legends that post-Reconstruction whites told about themselves and about their region's origins. It should be no surprise that a similar parallel exists between these myths and legends and young Bayard's narrativization of his father's "heroic" adventures in *The Unvanquished*, because Faulkner's writing and revising of *The Unvanquished*'s individual stories framed his work on *Absalom, Absalom!* At about the same time in early spring 1934 that Faulkner summarized for his editor, Hal Smith, the basic outline of "Dark House" (later *Absalom, Absalom!*), he put this work aside to earn money by writing "potboiler" stories about John Sartoris which were narrated by Sartoris's son, Bayard.[2] He wrote "Ambuscade," "Retreat," and "Raid" in a few months, selling them as part of a series to the *Saturday Evening Post*. He resumed work on *Absalom, Absalom!* in Hollywood in July of that year but by August was back in Oxford, where he completed the Sartoris series with "The Unvanquished" (later retitled "Riposte in Tertio") and "Vendee."[3] He began *Pylon* in October 1934, but was able to return to *Absalom, Absalom!* again in March and, working sporadically, was close enough to completion in late December 1935 to hand the manuscript to his Hollywood friend Dave Hempstead, declaring it "the best novel yet written by an American."[4] A year later, Faulkner was again in Hollywood, this time with Estelle, Jill, and two servants, and again concerned about money. Having interested Random House in his plan to revise the earlier Sartoris stories into a novel, he began work on *The Unvanquished* in the spring of 1937, completing his revisions by mid-July.

Although written in more accessible prose than *Absalom, Absalom!* the text of *The Unvanquished*, as well as its tangled history of publication and revision, demonstrate Faulkner's most complicated themes: the relativity of historical knowledge and experience; the instability of the subject when confronted with upheavals in the discourses of culture that surround (and, in many ways, produce) it; and the production, through culture, of an ideological matrix that (re)produces the individual subject's sense of a coherent self, yet is itself subject to historical change and internal contradiction. In this chapter, each of these elements of Faulkner's most powerful fiction will be explored under the sign of revision. On one level, the final version of *The Unvanquished* demonstrates Faulkner's revised and somewhat more complicated understanding of the agency of African Americans during the Civil War and Reconstruction, compared to his relatively uncritical use, in *Soldier's Pay* and *Flags in the Dust* and in the early *Saturday Evening Post* stories, of proslavery stereotypes such as the benevolent planter, the almost invisible poor white, and the loyal slave. These staples of Reconstruction historiography were under scrutiny in the 1920s and 1930s by revisionist historians such as W. E. B. Du Bois, whose *Black Reconstruction in America* condemned the bulk of American historians as disseminators of race propaganda; and James S. Allen, whose Marxist critique in *Reconstruction: The Battle for Democracy* exposed the class biases of conventional Civil War and Reconstruction historiography.[5]

I do not claim that Faulkner's revisions of his historical narrative are directly motivated by a desire to reproduce the revisionist historiography of Du Bois, Allen, and others. Indeed, the one explicitly Reconstruction-era story in the collection, "Skirmish at Sartoris," romanticizes the history of violent white voter fraud every bit as much as the proslavery historiography that the revisionists sought to correct. But as David Minter notes, Faulkner "was of at least two minds about his tendency to romanticize southern resistance, just as he was about the *Post*'s conception of fiction" (*LW*, 146). Especially after he had labored so hard to represent the complexity of historical experience in *Absalom, Absalom!* Faulkner hoped to redeem his "potboilers" by revising their two-dimensional representation of history, and this meant adding a dimension of African American agency which was unavailable to him as a younger writer (in *Soldier's Pay* and *Flags in the Dust*) and which would have complicated the *Saturday Evening Post* stories beyond an acceptable level for the magazine's readers. The early *Saturday Evening Post* version of "Ambuscade," the novel's first story, contains the first traces of this agency in Loosh's destruction of the model of Vicksburg that young Bayard Sartoris and Marengo (Ringo), Loosh's nephew, have constructed. But Faulkner's revision of this story emphasizes Loosh's rebelliousness, and his additional revisions highlight, in ways that the original *Saturday Evening Post* stories do not, the strategies of resistance of other Sartoris slaves as they refuse to collaborate in their own oppression.

A second goal is to determine the effect of 1930s revisionist historiography upon the stability of southern white male identity, as this is represented in Faulkner's texts and in the writing of other prominent southerners who responded more directly to the revisionist historians' claims. This will require a comparison of Bayard Sartoris—whose coherent sense of himself as Old Bayard, the southern patriarch of *Flags in the Dust,* becomes highly unstable as Faulkner transforms him into the narrator of *The Unvanquished*—with the Nashville Agrarians, the self-styled spokesmen for the modern South who aggressively challenged the revisionist historiography of Du Bois and others. We must ask why the Agrarians were so hostile toward historians who sought to produce a version of southern history that included African Americans as thinking, motivated agents. One answer is that their own identities as southern white males relied upon a number of strategies of evasion and denial that were comfortably available in traditional, "southernist" historiography. Acknowledging the propagandistic nature of the histories condemned by Du Bois would have forced the Agrarians to admit that the concepts of race, class, gender, and ethnicity that confirmed their self-image were little more than historical fictions. Bayard Sartoris is nostalgic for a version of southern history that produced the Sartorises as a first family of the South in their own minds and in the minds of other Yoknapatawphans. By the mid-1870s, the approximate time frame of "An Odor of Verbena," the fictions of history that supported this privileged positioning had dissolved, causing Bayard to "stick out" in the New South as a second-generation Bourbon. While the Bourbons never attained any real political power in Mississippi following its "redemption" in 1876, Bourbon nostalgia over an idyllic antebellum South did monopolize American historiography of the postbellum period. This nostalgic view of southern history—replete with proslavery stereotypes about southern blacks—sustained southern white identity through the turn of the century. But it was fractured by the revisionist historiographers of the 1930s with catastrophic consequences for fictional characters like Bayard Sartoris, as well as for would-be southern spokespersons among the Agrarians.

The stakes of this contest over the fictions historically used to prop up what the narrator of *Intruder in the Dust* calls the "white man's high estate" were economic as well as academic (*ID,* 134). Since the Agrarians' proposals for land reform were based upon the ideal of individual liberty through property ownership, if land was to be redistributed—according to their proposals or through some New Deal alternative—the question of exactly who "counts" as a politically enfranchised southern "individual" in the official narrative of the South would have specific economic consequences. Proposals for economic reform emanating from Agrarian historians such as Frank Lawrence Owsley did not include black farmers precisely because independent black subjectivity had never been a component of the history of the South that informed Agrarian economic theory. Within the context of Depression-era critiques of monopoly capitalism and the threat it posed to the principles of American democracy, the suggestion by Du Bois and other Marxist historians that white workers reject their racial alliance with the descendants of antebellum planters and ally themselves instead with black labor was a source of real anxiety to the Agrarians and other empowered whites. The Agrarians specifically allied themselves with white Democratic politics in the 1930s, disavowing the fact that many of their own proposals for land reform originated in post-Reconstruction alliances between black Republicans and poor white farmers against the monolithic Democratic Party in the South.

The 1930s revision (in *The Unvanquished,* in *Black Reconstruction,* and in the Agrarians' essays) of the post-Reconstruction debate over the future of democratic capitalism—capitalism with a truly free and empowered labor market—thus forms a third discursive register of Faulkner's text. By juxtaposing the defensive postures and strategic responses of the Old South at the moment of its ostensible demise (the Civil War) with those of contemporary Agrarian historians and economic theorists experiencing their own moment of epistemological crisis, Faulkner's text allows us to hear many of the voices of the 1930s that sought to assert a measure of control over the present by revising contemporary attitudes about the past.

Revising the Past in "Ambuscade"

Faulkner's revisions of "Ambuscade," the story that opens *The Unvanquished*, begin with the first paragraph. In the version that appeared in the September 29, 1934, issue of the *Saturday Evening Post*, the first paragraph contains a straightforward description of Bayard and Ringo's mud-and-woodchips model of Vicksburg and of Loosh's sudden approach. In his revisions for the novel, however, Faulkner expanded his description of the model of Vicksburg, making it a symbol of the lost cause of the Confederacy—of both its inevitable destruction and the willful refusal of the white ruling class to accept its passing. In the revised story, Bayard, the narrator, remembers that

> it (river, city, and terrain) lived, possessing even in miniature that ponderable though passive recalcitrance of topography which outweighs artillery, against which the most brilliant of victories and the most tragic of defeats are but the loud noises of a moment. To Ringo and me it lived, if only because of the fact that the sunimpacted ground drank water faster than we could fetch it from the well, the very setting of the stage for conflict a prolonged and wellnigh hopeless ordeal in which we ran, panting and interminable, with the leaking bucket between wellhouse and battlefield, the two of us needing first to join forces and spend ourselves against a common enemy, time, before we could engender between us and hold intact the pattern of recapitulant mimic furious victory like a cloth, a shield between ourselves and reality, between us and fact and doom. (*TU*, 3–4)

In this new language, the model of Vicksburg represents the recalcitrance of land- and slave-owning southerners in the face of northern military advances. In addition to expanding the model and making it "live" as a projection of the white South's image of itself as a beleaguered population, Faulkner's revisions situate the moment of Bayard's narration more carefully than it had been in the *Post* stories. His revisions introduce tension between an older Bayard who is narrating these events—who knows the extent of his and his family's attenuation as a result of the war—and the Bayard of the revised stories—who is still an innocent, but who, over the course of the stories, becomes implicated in the postwar worldview of the Sartorises and other erstwhile slaveholders. From the vantage point of the future moment of narration, Bayard can describe his and Ringo's effort to keep the trench around their city (representative of the Mississippi River around Vicksburg) filled with well water as "a prolonged and wellnigh hopeless ordeal." This revised Bayard even knows that the fantasies of Confederate victory that he and Ringo enacted in the course of their play were a chimera, "a shield between ourselves and reality." A passage Faulkner inserted a few pages later further underscores Bayard's heightened sense, as narrator, of the South's vulnerability, and of the self-delusions of those southerners who denied it. Bayard comments upon his father's queer smell, "which I believed was the smell of powder and glory, the elected victorious but know better now: know now to have been only the will to endure, a sardonic and even humorous declining of self-delusion" (*TU*, 10). These initial revisions indicate that the Bayard who narrates *The Unvanquished* is less sure of himself as a member of the ruling class than he was in the *Saturday Evening Post* version of the story, less certain of the legitimacy of his and his family's claims to white privilege.

We can explain this change in Bayard's character in at least two ways. First, we might recall that in *Flags in the Dust*, Bayard explodes in violence against Caspey when Caspey, a returned soldier, refuses to resume the role of loyal servant and thereby confirm for Bayard his identity as southern patrician and landowner. Bayard crashes a piece of stovewood into Caspey's skull in response to Caspey's mocking him (*FD*, 86–87). Bayard's return to a moment of laughter, this time Loosh's as narrator of the opening scene of *The Unvanquished*, thus marks a repetition of a scene of rebellion against the ruling class that is utterly disarming to Bayard. While the relations of production that empowered John Sartoris before the Civil War are under assault in the events of the Civil War that Bayard narrates in *The Unvanquished*, we must remember that those that empower Bayard himself in the early twentieth century, closer to the moment of his narration of these stories, are also under assault by the civil rights demands of returning black war veterans. The mocking laughter of the oppressed is thus the "originary moment" of "Ambuscade" in a double sense: it is a reiteration for Old Bayard of Caspey's ridicule in *Flags in the Dust;* and it initiates a series of assaults upon the legitimacy of Bayard's inherited economic and racial privilege in "Ambuscade" and in the other stories of *The Unvanquished.*

Bayard's sense of himself is further fractured by the conjunction in "Ambuscade" of black agency with the moment of the South's (and his family's) military defeat, a conjunction that was not fully developed in the early version. In both the original and revised versions of the story, Loosh's rebellion against the Sartorises is signified by his destruction of Bayard and Ringo's map of Vicksburg. Whereas Caspey's refusal to perform the role of loyal servant in *Flags in the Dust* is momentary, Loosh's disloyalty continues through the end of the war in both versions of "Ambuscade." In both versions, too, Loosh is suspected (correctly) of collaborating with the enemy by John Sartoris, who has returned to protect his farm and family from advancing Union troops as well as from the threat of sabotage posed by rebellious slaves. But in his revisions for the novel, Faulkner inserted passages that detail the facts of black agency in the Confederacy's defeat, and these heighten Bayard's sense of crisis. For example, Bayard now sees that the prospect of emancipation carries religious significance for Loosh; when Loosh tells him that Union troops are in nearby Corinth, Bayard notes, in language added in 1937, that "he sounded as if he were about to chant, to sing" (*TU*, 5). At another point, Bayard recalls literally fainting on the steps to his room while listening to his father and grandmother talk; partly due to physical exhaustion, Bayard's fainting also results from his shock at hearing that Loosh was correct about the fall of Vicksburg and Corinth. Trying to understand his loss of consciousness at just that moment, Bayard says (in a line Faulkner added in 1937), "perhaps there is a point at which credulity firmly and calmly and irrevocably declines, because suddenly Louvinia was standing over us, shaking us awake" (*TU*, 18). Loosh's symbolic destruction of Bayard's model has proven true for the real city of Vicksburg, and Bayard's resulting loss of "credulity" in Confederate war propaganda is accompanied by his loss of consciousness on the stairs. Finally, in another line Faulkner inserted while revising the story, Bayard says that he must keep an eye on Loosh, "because if we watched him, we could tell by what he did when it was getting ready to happen" (*TU*, 21). Bayard thus articulates the planters' wartime fear of slave insurrection, a fear that was not so overt in the *Saturday Evening Post* version of the story. Loosh is hardly the stereotype of the loyal servant in the earlier version of "Ambuscade," but the expansion of the wartime threat of slave insurrection as a theme of *The Unvanquished* indicates Faulkner's heightened awareness of the wartime (both Civil War and World War I) agency of blacks as he revised the stories for this novel.

Loosh's wartime agency, restrained in the early version but forcefully asserted in *The Unvanquished,* is a good example of the homology that exists between Faulkner's revisions and the work of revisionist historiographers of the Civil War and Reconstruction. One staple of the pro-slavery historiography that dominated the late nineteenth and early twentieth centuries is the stereotype of the passive Negro, the only slave population in history "that ever became free without any effort of their own" (*BR,* 716).[6] To correct this false perception, Du Bois writes in *Black Reconstruction* about the various tactics of a semiofficial general strike called by black labor after the North's military successes became apparent. One tactic in this strike involved the transferral of black labor onto the North. In Du Bois's interpretation, the South had relied upon slave labor to win the war, because, while the North had to leave a substantial number of its fighting population behind to feed and equip its army, the South had no such limitation. Southern landowners assumed that the slaves they left behind would maintain the wartime economy. In choosing finally to bestow their labor upon the North in large numbers, blacks hastened the war's end, because the fighting force of the Confederate army was depleted by those numbers that had to return home to manage their farms, while the Union army was strengthened by escaped slaves (*BR,* 57). These pieces of revisionist historiography are reflected in "Ambuscade" when Vicksburg falls. It was at just this time that many slaves abandoned their plantations and joined the federal army. As Du Bois writes, "When Vicksburg fell, the center of perhaps the vastest Negro population in North America was tapped. They rushed into the Union lines" (*BR,* 82). In Faulkner's text, it is just when Vicksburg falls that Loosh begins to encourage the Sartoris slaves to leave the plantation in search of freedom, or in aid of the northern war effort. And it is just at this time that John Sartoris is compelled to return home in anticipation of what amounts to a crisis in the relations of production on his farm.

Sartoris's unexpected return reflects Du Bois's thesis about the general strike causing a depletion of the Confederate fighting force. A second tactic of the general strike against the conditions of black labor in the South is signified by a specific revision Faulkner made to this section of "Ambuscade" for the 1938 novel. This tactic involved a general "slow down" among slave laborers—another method by which they could "stop the economy of the plantation system" (*BR, 67*)—and it can be observed in a humorous revision which sees John Sartoris planning to hide his livestock in a new stock pen in a well-concealed creek bottom to protect it from confiscation by advancing federal troops. Sartoris orders two of his slaves, Loosh and Joby, to construct the pen, but in the end he must perform most of the labor, because Loosh and Joby are intentionally inefficient at their task. As Bayard recalls:"Father was everywhere, with a sapling under each arm going through the brush and briers almost faster than the mules; racking the rails into place while Joby and Loosh were still arguing about which end of the rail went where" (*TU,* 12). Later, Sartoris, Bayard, and Ringo leave Loosh and Joby "with the last three panels to put up," but when Bayard and Ringo return to the new pen with the livestock, they find that the two slaves have erected only two, and they must complete the third in the dark (*TU,* 13). The South has a long history of interpreting such strategies of resistance as evidence of the proslavery argument that blacks were fit by nature for heavy work but unfit to rule or to control their labor. It would be a mistake, however, to conclude that Faulkner added this scene depicting Joby and Loosh's inefficient labor simply to comply with a staple of proslavery ideology. There is enough humor and sardonic irony in Bayard's reminiscence to suggest that it is the product of white anxiety over recently discovered evidence of black agency in the South's defeat. Such examples of black resistance would not have been available to Faulkner when, as a youth, he listened to his family's stories of Confederate heroism. But they were available to him in the late 1930s as a result of the work of Du Bois and other revisionist historiographers.

As narrator of "Ambuscade," Bayard knows that his family's survival depends in part upon the participation of subjected classes of black slaves in the ratification of the ruling class's political status. Clearly, his father's status as a planter is economically dependent upon the labor of his servants, but John Sartoris's identity as southern planter is also psychologically dependent upon the presence of disempowered blacks, whose obedience to his rule confirms the "structures of feeling" that organize everyday experience for him. In "Ambuscade," this dialectic of white male identity formation is under assault by the approaching Union army, whose victory will emancipate the slaves and thus remove the object of ritual scorn upon which the dialectic relies. This is a matter of concern for John Sartoris and also for his son Bayard, who would be faced with a similar assault in the form of post–World War I veterans' demands for civil rights. This concern is articulated in Bayard's awareness, especially in the revised version of the story, of the effect of Loosh's rebellion upon Ringo.

This is evident in the paralysis Ringo experiences in response to his uncle's destruction of the model of Vicksburg. "Ringo didn't move, he just looked at me," Faulkner writes in lines added during his revisions (*TU*, 6). While in the earlier version of the story Bayard simply reassembles the model and verbally denies Loosh's claims about southern military defeats, in the revised version Faulkner has added a long passage in which Bayard contemplates how best to regain Ringo's allegiance:

> But I was just talking too, I knew that, because niggers know, they know things; it would have to be something louder, much louder, than words to do any good. So I stooped and caught both hands full of dust and rose: and Ringo still standing there, not moving, just looking at me even as I flung the dust. "I'm General Pemberton!" I cried. "Yaaay! Yaay!" stooping and catching up more dust and flinging that too. Still Ringo didn't move. "All right!" I cried. "I'll be Grant this time, then. You can be General Pemberton." Because it was that urgent, since negroes knew.
> (*TU*, 6–7)

Whereas Ringo quickly accepts Bayard's reconstitution of their symbol of the Confederacy in the *Post* version of the story, in the revised version Ringo resists Bayard's efforts to recast him as the stereotype of the loyal slave and companion, deferring the moment of his conscription by blankly and silently contemplating Bayard's actions.

Moreover, two seemingly minor linguistic elements of this passage suggest turmoil in Bayard's thinking about his position vis-à-vis his family's servants. First, the shift in tense from "niggers know" to "negroes knew" signifies the impact of this childhood memory upon Bayard's consciousness. As a youth, Bayard may have suspected Ringo's newfound doubts about the claims of Confederate invulnerability implicit in their model of Vicksburg, but as the older narrator of the story, Bayard is now certain that his friend was approaching the point of no return with respect to his allegiance to the white South and to the Sartorises. Second, the shift from the epithet "niggers" to the more respectful (for 1937) "negroes" signifies the consequences of this moment of narration for Bayard. Bayard can no longer treat Ringo as a "nigger" and therefore can no longer rely upon the dialectic according to which white southerners used "niggers" to produce themselves as the South's ruling class.

One other example from Faulkner's revisions will bear out the thesis that they indicate Bayard's anxieties over his and his class's loss of racial control at the moment of the South's defeat, as well as at the moment of his narration of these stories. In both versions of "Ambuscade," Bayard and Ringo abandon their ruined model to greet John Sartoris, who has returned unexpectedly to prepare his family for the approach of Union troops. The two versions are similar in contrasting this homecoming to one the previous spring. As Bayard remembers in the revised version in *The Unvanquished,* upon seeing Sartoris's arrival "Ringo and I ran down the drive to meet him and return, I standing in one stirrup with father's arm around me, and Ringo holding to the other stirrup and running beside the horse" (*TU,* 8). Following this line, however, Faulkner has made small but significant revisions. The *Saturday Evening Post* version reads as follows:

> But this time we didn't, and then I went up the steps and stood by Granny while father came up and stopped . . .[7]

In revising for the later novel, Faulkner substituted the following language:

> But this time we didn't. I mounted the steps and stood beside Granny, and with Ringo and Loosh on the ground below the gallery we watched the claybank stallion enter the gate. (*TU,* 8)

In the earlier version, Ringo's "standing" at the time of Sartoris's return is ambiguous. He may have followed Bayard onto the porch or remained behind. But the revised version very carefully positions Ringo on the ground with Loosh, below the level of Bayard and his grand-mother. As if to emphasize Ringo's allegiance to Loosh at the moment of Sartoris's return, the revised passage concludes by reasserting the divide between slaveowner and slave, this time from John Sartoris's perspective atop his horse: "He stopped; he looked at Granny and me on the porch and at Ringo and Loosh on the ground" (*TU*, 9).

Certainly, Bayard's loss of control over Ringo in this scene is momentary; Ringo is soon teaming up with Bayard again to shoot Union soldiers for coming to emancipate him and the other slaves. Faulkner was not looking to revise each of the stories so significantly as to make a rebellious slave out of Ringo in addition to Loosh. Yet, at these moments of revision Faulkner's text "voices" the work of revisionist historians who sought to free the standard historiography of the Civil War and Reconstruction from the assumptions of proslavery historiography. His revisions thus signify an "emergence" in the discipline of historiography, the stated purpose of which was to retrieve the suppressed facts of black agency and political subjectivity in the years during and just after the Civil War. If revisionist historiography of the 1920s and 1930s made the facts of black agency irrepressible for Bayard Sartoris, leading him to a crisis in the dialectic of identity formation upon which the members of his race and class had relied for generations, we might look for evidence of similar crises among Bayard's historical analogues, second- and third-generation Bourbons of the modern South who found their positions as spokesmen for their class and for their region increasingly untenable as the facts of class and race exploitation at the root of Depression-era conditions in the South became undeniable.

The Nashville Agrarians viewed the crises of the 1920s and 1930s from an economic and racial position similar to that of Bayard Sartoris in the moment of his narration of stories in *The Unvanquished,* and by comparing their respective positions, we can observe the further consequences for members of the South's ruling class of "eruptions" in the discourse of historiography. By constantly looking back to the moment of black political emergence in the South (the "moment" of the Civil War) through the narrative perspective of an aged and somewhat powerless Bayard, Faulkner's novel conducts a kind of genealogy of the white South's discursive response to black demands for equal protection under the Constitution. Continuing my discursive reading of his revisions of this novel will allow me to chart in some detail the historical "descent" of these responses, from the first black codes following the "redemption" of southern states in 1876–78 to the voting requirements that continued black disfranchisement through the first half of the twentieth century. The aim of such a reading is not to show that "the past actively exists in the present" for Faulkner or for us, nor "to go back in time to restore an unbroken continuity that operates beyond the dispersion of forgotten things."[8] Rather, by retrieving the accidents of the past, the contingent effects produced by a legal apparatus that developed after the Civil War to deny African Americans political protection from vindictive white governments, we can observe how this apparatus was being reformulated in new ways in the Agrarians' proposals of the 1930s, particularly in their advocacy of "yeomanry" as both a theoretical and a practical solution to the problems of the Depression in the rural South.

A Genealogy of Discursive Strategies

The fundamental assumptions of proslavery ideology held that the African "race" was of a lower order of humanity than whites. Whether they arrived at this conclusion by identifying Africans as the descendants of Ham and then misreading the curse placed upon Canaan in Genesis 9:20–27, or by asserting divine authority over African "pagans" and then justifying slavery as a means of Christianizing the populations of the Dark Continent, or by latching onto the newer uses of science that "proved" the smaller cranial capacity of nonwhite races, those who drew upon proslavery ideology to justify their own privilege availed themselves of a centuries-old dialectic in which their own superiority was ratified through the assertion of the inferiority of the Other. This dialectic is part of the discourse of race in the New World, its tropes dating back to European explorers' first descriptions of New World monsters and then made freely available to all who would buttress their own economic and psychological standing by degrading that of others. The Agrarian historian Frank Lawrence Owsley participated in this dialectic when he opened his contribution to *I'll Take My Stand* by looking back to the period of Reconstruction and describing it as an era when southern governments were "turned over to the three millions of former slaves, some of whom could still remember the taste of human flesh."[9] Owsley's statement aptly illustrates the dialectic of dependency and disavowal at the heart of white racial identity-formation: psychologically, whites depended upon a ritual scorning of the black Other to construct the social and legal fictions that supported white privilege and disavowed black equality, just as, economically, southern whites have always depended upon black labor but have disavowed this dependence through racist propaganda about black laziness and inefficiency.

In this section, I will focus on two of Faulkner's 1937 revisions—one to "Ambuscade," the other to "Raid"— which register this dialectic of white male subject-formation in both the Reconstruction and 1930s Agrarian contexts. In both cases, the construction of a privileged center is based upon the political, economic, and psychological denial of an Other that is nevertheless fundamental to the very existence of the binarism that privileges one race, class, or gender over another. My purpose in discussing these examples is to detail the post–Civil War construction of a category of the "experienced" as a domain of white privilege, which was then deployed in white supremacist rhetoric as the "natural" prerequisite for full political enfranchisement. We will see that the category of the "experienced" that is represented in Faulkner's revisions is homologous with that which developed historically in the black codes that followed Reconstruction. In the 1930s, while Faulkner was writing and revising the stories of *The Unvanquished,* this category was again reformulated in the Agrarians' proposals for economic reform, as part of their effort to consolidate control over the intellectual centers of the South. Triangulating my reading of *The Unvanquished* in this manner will demonstrate once more the discursive effect of revisionist historiographers upon 1930s representations of southern history—in this case, because of the reaction that revisionist historiography elicited from the contributors to *Who Owns America?* (1936), the Agrarians' answer to Depression-era conditions in the South.

We have already observed one manner in which the antebellum plantocracy reproduced its system of privileges in the play between Bayard and Ringo that opens "Ambuscade." In that example, a privileged center is represented by the city of Vicksburg and supported through a ritual of assault and defense. The scene climaxes with a moment of crisis initiated by Loosh's destruction of the boys' map, which is resolved (albeit tentatively) when Bayard invites Ringo to perform the high-status role of Confederate General Pemberton, an invitation Bayard deems necessary "because it was that urgent, since negroes knew" (*TU*, 6–7). In two other scenes, both added during Faulkner's late-1930s revisions, Bayard is similarly concerned with the privileges that empower him over his companion, Ringo; in each instance, we will see, these privileges devolve as a matter of "experience."

In "Ambuscade," Ringo asks Granny Millard to read about "Cokynut cake" because, as Bayard explains,

> we had never been able to decide whether Ringo had ever tasted coco-
> nut cake or not. We had had some that Christmas before it started and
> Ringo had tried to remember whether they had had any of it in the
> kitchen or not, but he couldn't remember. Now and then I used to try
> to help him decide, get him to tell me how it tasted and what it looked
> like and sometimes he would almost decide to risk it before he would
> change his mind. Because he said that he would rather just maybe have
> tasted coconut cake without remembering it than to know for certain
> he had not; that if he were to describe the wrong kind of cake, he would
> never taste coconut cake as long as he lived. (*TU*, 19–20)

Far more is at stake in this passage than the eating of cake. Although the moment of representation (Granny reading to Bayard and Ringo) implies an equality of experience between two childhood companions, the scene becomes an occasion to redraw the color lines that in fact determined experience in the plantation South. We might recall that the moment of narration for these stories is much later than their moment of representation—the Bayard who narrates "Ambuscade" is much closer in age and experience to the Bayard of *Flags in the Dust*, whose privileges as a landowning patriarch are under assault by the civil rights movement that followed the return of black soldiers from World War I. This is in part why a scene depicting an equality of experience (Granny reading to Bayard and Ringo) is immediately displaced by a scene that insists upon basic inequalities, with Bayard and his family seated at their Christmas table and Ringo and his family of servants eating leftovers in the kitchen. For Bayard, the iteration of the Christmas memory each time Granny entertains the children is also an occasion for the iteration of the racial privilege Bayard enjoys as a Sartoris. Moreover, Bayard's narration of this moment of reminiscence enucleates a puzzle of racial experience that he has sought, without success, to solve since his own childhood. "Now and then I used to try to help him decide": if only Ringo could decide that he had not had Bayard's cake then Bayard could continue to eat it too, secure in the knowledge that this separated his experiences as a Sartoris from those of the servant class. For his part, Ringo has learned the strategy of the subaltern—has learned (from his uncle?) endlessly to defer the moment of Bayard's self-ratification and thus to defer also the addition of one more category of experience that, on grounds of race, would be denied him "as long as he lived."

Bayard's narration of the stories in *The Unvanquished* is replete with these instances of anxiety over his class and racial privilege, but they have been obscured in Faulkner criticism because so many of Faulkner's readers want to find in Bayard and Ringo's friendship a bond that transcends the politics of race in much the way that, for some, Mark Twain's Huck and Jim overcome their culture's prejudices as they travel the Mississippi. But Bayard's narration (like Huck's) is *polyphonic,* its individual words the site of contestation between the social classes of the modern South, and therefore we must break the habit of listening only to those voices that are most familiar to us as late-twentieth-century readers of modern literature. In the following passage from "Raid," for instance—also added during Faulkner's late-1930s revisions—we can hear the voices of Faulkner's time (as well as our own) that might have called for racial harmony, but we can also detect the sort of rhetorical and legal manipulations of language that served to segregate racial experience in the post-Reconstruction South. Here Bayard is recounting how, on the way to Hawkhurst, Ringo kept him and Rosa Millard awake "by talking of the railroad which he had never seen though which I had seen that Christmas we spent at Hawkhurst. That's how Ringo and I were. We were almost the same age, and Father always said that Ringo was a little smarter than I was, but that didn't count with us, anymore than the difference in the color of our skins counted. What counted was, what one of us had done or seen that the other had not, and ever since that Christmas I had been ahead of Ringo because I had seen a railroad, a locomotive" (*TU,* 80–81). Again, the language of companionship in this passage obscures the issue of access to "experience," access which maintains Bayard's sense of privilege, as well as Ringo's exclusion from the Sartorises' experience of southern life. The theme of many of Faulkner's revisions is thus the construction of "experience" as a domain of white privilege, which is reproduced rhetorically each time Bayard recalls a moment in which his and Ringo's experiences *seem* to be equal: when he and Ringo are about to listen to Granny read about cake, in one instance; when the three of them are riding to Hawkhurst together, in another. The internal dialogism of these passages allows "experience" to be posited as a racial equalizer on one level but as the exclusive domain of the privileged on another.

The tension that allows both of these readings is a consequence of white southerners' use of "experience" as what Foucault calls an "origin of morality," a prerequisite for political and civil rights in the earliest days of Reconstruction as well as at the time of Faulkner's revisions.[10] During the Reconstruction period, political power became concentrated in the South's courts and legislative houses, which produced the legal decisions that led to each state's "redemption" by 1878. One example of this process involved a controversial decision handed down by the Mississippi Supreme Court on September 17, 1866, which embodied the ambivalent attitude toward "experience" reflected in Faulkner's revisions of "Ambuscade" and "Raid." Against the argument of James Lewis, a freedman and former Union soldier convicted of carrying a firearm in public, that the Thirteenth Amendment "made him free, and *ipso facto* vested him with all the rights of a citizen under the Constitution of the United States, one of which was the right to bear arms," Mississippi Chief Justice A. H. Handy found the federal government's recent civil rights act "in contravention of the Constitution" and used the then-popular argument that freedom from slavery has never simultaneously conferred full civil rights. He then concluded that the freedmen's "*status* should be left to the development of time and experience."[11] The judge was deliberately ambiguous in his use of the word "experience"; like other figures of the time charged with reconstituting white authority during Reconstruction, he found it useful in his decision to circulate terms with shifting social meaning.[12] Both Bayard and Judge Handy construct from their respective positions of authority a privileged space for "the experienced," using this as a category of evidence to support or deny a claim to citizen-status and, therefore, political empowerment. One consequence of this rhetorical and political use of the category of the "experienced" is the predication of civil rights on prior experience, on what one person (or one's ancestors), in the words of Bayard's reminiscence, "had done or seen that the other had not."

The logic of Judge Handy's decision, as well as that of the later grandfather clauses, is observable also in the Agrarians' proposals of the late 1930s, based as they are on the redefinition of liberty as the consequence of "effective" property ownership. In "Notes on Liberty and Property," Allen Tate distinguishes between legal and effective ownership: the external ownership of property in the form of stocks is legal but not effective, because the stockholder is responsible only for the stocks and not the material property. For Tate, this divorces the stockholder from the source of liberty: "it cannot be said," Tate writes, "that he in any sense controls the means of production. Control, the power to direct production and to command markets, is freedom" (*WOA*, 82). Since the Agrarians saw economic collapse and the loss of freedom as the consequence of dispersed ownership with concentrated control, their solution was to propose policies that would encourage individual ownership and profitable private business. When they described the indigenous southern farmer and small businessman who would benefit from their proposals, however, the Agrarians relied upon the proslavery version of southern history, which elided the facts of black agency and "effective" black property ownership. The Agrarians, in other words, relied upon the category of the "experienced" to formulate their vision of the South's future, a vision which, for this reason, would have reproduced the inequalities of experience that had defined racial identity in the South since before the Civil War.

George Marion O'Donnell, for instance, advocated specific proposals—land distribution and lower land taxes, cheap rural electricity, and increased public funding for agricultural research—which would rehabilitate the southern tradition of subsistence farming. This tradition is not racially neutral, however: "Yeoman is a good, healthy, Anglo-Saxon word for the sort of farmer who lives within this tradition," O'Donnell writes (*WOA*, 167–68). His proposals aimed to raise the tenant farmer to the yeoman class, but his qualification of the proposal is obviously coded to allow for the exclusion of politically powerless black sharecroppers: "In any such program, of course, one must remember that not all tenants are capable of operating farms for themselves, not all tenants are capable of working without careful supervision; the less able and responsible tenants will be left to work on the agrarian plantations" (*WOA*, 173). One reason I think O'Donnell specifically excludes black farmers from his Agrarian reform is that his language in this passage reiterates the proslavery assumptions about black labor that we saw ironized in Faulkner's revision of the scene in "Ambuscade" in which Joby and Loosh, by being intentionally inefficient in building the pen for Sartoris's livestock, participate in a slave-initiated protest against the conditions of labor in the slave South. But Agrarian proposals all but insisted upon the exclusion of black workers, because all of their reforms were predicated upon an initial modification, if not the outright repeal, of the Fourteenth Amendment, which granted freed slaves the rights of full citizenship under the Constitution—in particular, the right to equal protection under the law.

The Agrarians condemned the Fourteenth Amendment because it protected the foreign (i.e., northern) owners of land monopolies from legislation that southern governments might pass to curtail corporate development. At the heart of the issue was the legal precedent for treating corporations as "persons" guaranteed equal protection under the Constitution. In 1882 Roscoe Conkling, a member of the 1866 committee that drafted the Fourteenth Amendment, argued that "he and his colleagues in drafting the due process and equal protection clauses intentionally used the word 'person' in order to include corporations."[13] The Supreme Court was persuaded by Conkling's argument, confirming in 1886 that corporations should be viewed as artificial persons. Richard B. Ransom, in his contribution to *Who Owns America?* articulated the Agrarian protest of this interpretation: "By legal courtesy corporations are persons; by legislative sanction they may possess the control of property or services without specific accounting and independent of any personal responsibility; by business custom their managements may collectively accomplish corporate acts and corporate policies which any decent personal morality would reject as illegal or unfair" (*WOA*, 69). Understandably, the Agrarians wanted to weaken the rights of corporate "persons" as part of their land redistribution schemes. But in advocating the repeal of the Fourteenth Amendment, they found themselves predicating their proposals upon the repeal of the very constitutional amendment that conferred upon blacks the rights of full citizenship. This would have to mean that black southerners' claims to be included in any political or economic reformulation of the South would also be weakened.

It is unlikely that this weakening of the political status of blacks would have disturbed a historian like Owsley, who had blasted the "three Negro writers and one carpetbag ex-governor" who he alleges were the lone dissenters from the Agrarian reading of the Fourteenth and Fifteenth Amendments. "These two amendments," Owsley writes, "were incorporated into the Federal Constitution by open fraud and violence supported by Federal troops in the South, and congressional legislation which even the Federalist Supreme Court would have thrown out had they not been intimidated by the Radical leaders" (*WOA*, 54–55). Most important for Owsley and other Agrarians was that northern property owners cease exploiting the natural and human resources of an impoverished region. But because of their reliance upon an exclusionary vision of southern history (as well as southern identity), the Agrarians' proposals reproduced the prejudices of Democratic Party politics that maintained black disfranchisement through the Depression and beyond.

Like Bayard's revised memories in "Ambuscade" and "Raid," the Agrarians' proposals deployed a rhetoric of equality for all "southerners"; but these instances of rhetorical democracy were (also like Bayard's) the occasion for racial differentiation. Bayard recalls segregated dinners and privileged encounters with railroads, just as O'Donnell is quick to "remember that not all tenants are capable of operating farms for themselves." And finally, just as we can imagine that Bayard's anxieties regarding his control over Ringo in *The Unvanquished* are triggered by the civil rights demands of Caspey (in *Flags in the Dust*) and other returned World War I veterans, the Agrarians' anxieties over the direction of economic reform in the South are triggered, at least in part, by the rhetorical power of the "three Negro writers and one carpetbag ex-governor" who supported both the letter and the spirit of the Fourteenth Amendment. Like the revisionist historiography that recognized black agency at the moment of the slaveholding South's demise, the Fourteenth Amendment was an affront to the segregationist/Agrarian white South, because it revealed inconsistencies in (and thus was a threat to) the supremacist ideologies that for generations had privileged one experience of the South over all others.

Poor Whites, Yeoman Farmers, and "An Odor of Verbena"

The Fourteenth Amendment threatened the Agrarians for exactly the same reason that Loosh's destruction of the model of Vicksburg created anxieties in Bayard and his father John Sartoris. Each "act" signified blacks' demands for political equality. Each also led to what the narrator of Faulkner's first novel, *Soldier's Pay* (1926), calls "the lying-in period of the K. K. K." (*SP*, 277). We see the birth of Klan mentality represented in "Skirmish at Sartoris," in which John Sartoris murders Reconstruction election officials, steals the town's ballot box, and is celebrated as a hero by the men who once served him as soldiers. Having lost much of its power by the end of the nineteenth century, the Klan experienced a rebirth by the end of World War I, when southern whites once again cloaked themselves to put down black claims for equality. These instances of white consolidation depended upon the ritual of racial scorn, in which the superiority of whites—even dirt-poor whites—is "ratified" through the degradation of the racial Other. Throughout the election scene in "Skirmish at Sartoris," for instance, Cash Benbow, the black Republican candidate for marshal of Jefferson, is mocked as an incompetent puppet of unscrupulous carpetbaggers. In the context of post-emancipation labor relations in the South, this ritual scorn served a second purpose—the separation of black and white workers, whose resulting racial animosities would prevent them from uniting around their common interests as laborers. When Du Bois, James Allen, and other Marxist historians set out to revise accepted historiography of the period, they had the conscious goal of shifting what had been a racial alliance among southern white men—from which issues of class consciousness were bracketed in the interests of white supremacy—toward an alliance of labor built upon common concerns among black and white workers.[14]

Du Bois sought to unify black and white labor, first, by recognizing the neglect the white proletariat had suffered since the Civil War: "In all this consideration, we have so far ignored the white workers of the

South and we have done this because the labor movement ignored them and the abolitionists ignored them; and above all, they were ignored by Northern capitalists and Southern planters. They were in many respects almost a forgotten mass of men" (*BR*, 26). Having recognized the historical economic deprivation of the white worker in the South, Du Bois ties this deprivation to the white workers' unnatural alliance with the slaveholding southern oligarchy in the war. In Du Bois's interpretation, the southern oligarchy, representing planter interests, championed the doctrine of "popular sovereignty" (which would allow the inhabitants of territories gained in the Mexican War to determine for themselves whether to enter the Union as free or slave states) because they were confident that proslavery Constitutions could be compelled in most elections, by violence if by no other means. Free Soilers in both the North and the West wanted to contain slavery in the southern states, to preserve the value of free labor elsewhere. All sides, in other words, were concerned with the relation between slavery and Union but were motivated most of all either by fear of, or by faith in, free labor. Du Bois quotes Frederick Douglass's paradoxical phrasing of these respective positions: "The South was fighting to take slavery out of the Union, and the North fighting to keep it in the Union; the South fighting to get it beyond the limits of the United States Constitution, the North fighting for the old guarantees;—both despising the Negro" (*BR*, 61). By equating the country's neglect of poor white labor with its hatred of blacks, Du Bois argued that free labor was the real threat to the South's slave-based planter society, and therefore the primary cause of southern secession. In addition to revising the nation's "southernist" narrative of Reconstruction, then, Du Bois sought to form an alliance between black and white labor in the South, based upon common interests that had been occluded, first, by the racial politics of the slaveholding oligarchy, and second, by the tradition of proslavery historiography, which had cemented anti-black prejudices in the historical imagination of white Americans. For this reason, Du Bois's revisions were also a threat to 1930s Agrarian Democratic ideology, because they proposed not only a racially inclusive southern historiography but also a truly democratic and organized American labor movement, one undivided by racial hatred.

The revisionist historiographers of the 1920s and 1930s were not the first to propose such an alliance. Many nineteenth-century Americans who opposed slavery did so less out of abolitionist zeal than out of the realization that free labor, black or white, was more profitable (for both workers and owners) than slave labor. Southern planters, however, and the owners of railroads, mills, and small businesses that supplanted them as political powers after the war, continued to believe that their profits were dependent upon a divided labor force and committed themselves to a race-based politics that would prevent black and white workers from organizing. Immediately following the "redemption" of Mississippi governments by white-supremacy Democrats in 1875–76, factions began to develop within the Democratic Party over monetary and agricultural policy, especially over the influence that corporations, banks, and railroads exerted upon Democratic legislators. Although Democrats repeatedly managed to entice enough support from black Republicans to win substantial majorities, the threat that black Republicans and disgruntled poor white Democrats would organize themselves as Independents was ever-present. To discredit such alliances, Democratic politicians and newspapers demonized Independent leaders as carpetbaggers, profiteers, and traitors to both their country and their race. Often these papers cast the Independents as the remnant of despised Radical Republicans of the Reconstruction years.[15] For their part, however, the Independent leaders represented themselves as opponents of the Democrats' petty politics, as men who "had merely grown tired of selfish politicians who kept urging the color line in politics in order to perpetuate their control of the partisan organization" (*Rev,* 22).

Given the degree of animosity that white Democrats felt toward those who proposed such alliances between black and white interests in the South, it is not surprising to find John Sartoris murderously breaking up the Republican election at the end of "Skirmish at Sartoris." It is surprising, however, to read what is arguably the most significant revision Faulkner made to any story in *The Unvanquished,* the section on Buck and Buddy McCaslin's "ideas about social relationship," which Faulkner added to "Retreat" during his 1937 revisions. These involve, first, the freeing of all labor in the South, and second, the organizing of labor according to its own interests rather than those of the planter class. "They had some kind of a system of book-keeping," Bayard tells us, "by which all their niggers were to be freed, not given freedom, but earning, buying it . . . in work from the plantation" (*TU*, 48). More than simply recognizing their slaves' right to the profits of their labor, the McCaslins' scheme places their slaves on the same level of indenture occupied by many poor whites upon immigrating to America. Further, Buck and Buddy propose an economic order based upon common worker interests regardless of racial identity: they "had persuaded the white men to pool their little patches of poor hill land along with the niggers and the McCaslin plantation, promising them in return nobody knew exactly what, except that their women and children did have shoes, which not all of them had had before, and a lot of them even went to school" (*TU*, 49). Like those of Allen, Du Bois, and other revisionists in the mid-1930s, Faulkner's late-1930s revisions acknowledge the material conditions of labor that could produce a natural alliance among black and white workers. Even Faulkner's brief reference to the schooling of poor whites as a consequence of their alliance with blacks signifies the fact that in the South, public-funded education for whites first developed in response to the Reconstruction-era demands of freed blacks and of the agents of the Freedmen's Bureau.[16] Implicitly, Faulkner's acknowledgment of the benefits of this alliance rejects—just as the revisionists rejected—the artificial division of southern labor according to the racial identity of individual workers, which had prevented labor from organizing successfully throughout the 1800s, and which continued to vex organizers in the 1930s.

Faulkner's revision of this and other stories suggests that independent black labor is the repressed fact of southern history that prevented the Agrarians of *Who Owns America?* from acknowledging the revisionist work of historiographers of the 1920s and 1930s, as well as their own intellectual debt to the Independent Alliances of the late 1800s. For although they set themselves up as the intellectual heirs of the planter class and espoused a retrograde racial philosophy to secure this claim, many of the Agrarians' economic reform proposals had their roots in the demands of the Independent Alliances. Just as the Greenbacks in 1878 called for "the reservation of public lands for actual settlers" (*Rev*, 21), for instance, O'Donnell and others called for local control of local land to correct what they perceived to be the problems of northern monopolies in the South. What the Agrarians were unwilling to consider was the role that would have to be played in their proposals by fully enfranchised black labor. By adding Buck and Buddy McCaslin's ideas about unified labor to "Retreat," and thereby signifying the biracial interests of the Independent Alliances as well as of the revisionist (Marxist) historians, Faulkner's revisions reveal the inherent inconsistency of the Agrarians' vision of a "return" to (white) Anglo-Saxon yeomanry in the South. They also strengthen the argument of critics of the Agrarians in the 1930s who pointed to sixty years of tenant and sharecropper hardship as evidence of the weakness of their proposals for an expanded system of Agrarian "yeomanry."

In "An Odor of Verbena," the one new story Faulkner wrote for *The Unvanquished* and thus his final "revision" of the overall shape of the novel, we can observe one other suppressed fact of southern history which the revisionists included in their historiography of the post-Reconstruction period, and which can explain why the Agrarians never did become the influential political force they aspired to.[17] This is the fact of the political demise of the planter class following Reconstruction and the rise of the populist Democratic Party, which saw its interests as separate from those of the erstwhile oligarchy. The Bourbons were not a significant post-Reconstruction power in the South; as Albert Kirwan writes, "the new leaders after the Democrats regained power in 1875 were, on the whole, men who had exerted little or no effect on state policy in ante-bellum days. Of the few who had been influential, none refused to accept the reality of Reconstruction, and they all set about adjusting the state to face the new conditions" (*Rev*, 8–9). What Kirwan wrote in 1951, Du Bois had recognized in 1935: "With the Civil War, the planters died as a class. We still talk as though the dominant social class in the South persisted after the war. But it did not. It disappeared. Just how quickly and in what manner the transformation was made, we do not know" (*BR*, 54). Du Bois does not examine the historical causes of this demise. But Faulkner's writing of "An Odor of Verbena" as his final revisionary gesture in 1938 suggests at least one cause that parallels Kirwan's analysis of the demise of the Bourbons as a political class.

Kirwan writes that those Bourbons who survived the transition to Democratic governments after Reconstruction did so because they were willing to make compromises with poor whites and with a growing middle class comprised of white men who had been shut out of politics before the war. This class of men is represented in Faulkner's text by the ex-soldiers of Sartoris's company, led by George Wyatt. For instance, it is George Wyatt who forges the ballots that are then substituted for those in favor of Cash Benbow in "Skirmish at Sartoris." It is also George Wyatt who encourages Bayard to form a new alliance with the white men of Jefferson after Bayard's nonviolent victory over his father's killer, Redmond, at the end of "An Odor of Verbena." But Bayard refuses to form this alliance. In deciding to return home instead of taking breakfast at the Holston House with his father's partisans, Bayard rejects the advice of a friend more schooled in the direction of southern politics since the war. George Wyatt understands that in the populist New South, positions of local authority are not won once and forever held (as in the plantocracy), but instead must be constantly won again in the opinion of the recently empowered townspeople. Wyatt's goal immediately after Bayard's defeat of Redmond, therefore, is to "publish" across Jefferson some signs of this victory:

> "Come on. We'll go to the Holston House."
> "No," I said. "No. Not there."
> "Why not? You ain't done anything to be ashamed of . . ."
> "Yes," I said. "I would do it again."
> "Be damned if I would.—You want to come home with me? We'll have time to eat and then ride out there in time for the—" But I couldn't do that either.
> "No," I said. "I'm not hungry after all. I think I'll go home."
> "Don't you want to ride out there with me?"
> "No. I'll go on." (*TU*, 250–51)

Wyatt wants to "retail" the moment of Bayard's victory over Redmond by retelling it to other white male citizens of Jefferson, perhaps thus ensuring his candidacy in the next round of local elections. Bayard's decision not to accompany Wyatt suggests his ignorance of the adjustments members of the planter class were required to make in order to maintain power in postwar southern society.

Bayard's refusal to follow Wyatt's counsel precipitates his political (and psychological) demise at the end of "An Odor of Verbena."[18] This demise is signified, first, by the overpowering presence of John Sartoris, which directly ties the Bayard at the end of *The Unvanquished* to the Bayard we see in the opening pages of Faulkner's first Yoknapatawpha novel, *Flags in the Dust*. In the final pages of *The Unvanquished*, Bayard recalls that he "didn't need to see him again because he was there": "he would always be there; maybe what Drusilla meant by his dream was not something which he possessed but something which he had bequeathed us which we could never forget, which would even assume the corporeal shape of him whenever any of us, black or white, closed our eyes" (*TU*, 252–53). Because the memory of his father will always be with him, Bayard is committed to a vicarious existence for the rest of his life. The only authority Bayard has over his family and community will be a diluted form of his father's legendary influence. In the first pages of *Flags in the Dust*, for instance, it is John Sartoris's fame that is signified when the townspeople call Bayard "Colonel"; and when Old Man Falls opens that novel with a tale of Sartoris's Civil War heroism, Sartoris becomes a palpable presence: "He seemed to stand above them, all around them, with his bearded, hawklike face and the bold glamor of his dream" (*FD*, 5). Despite the victory many readers have claimed for Bayard in "Verbena," it is obvious that Faulkner saw him as a failed son, unable to cope in the modernizing South in the way his father may have wanted him to. In fact, the final pages of *The Unvanquished* infantilize Bayard; he is reduced to his boyhood, kneeling at his Aunt Jenny's feet while he tells about his day. Finally, he becomes lost among the smell of verbena left behind by his stepmother, Drusilla.

Bayard's failures as a youth, events he clearly is mourning from his vantage as an older narrator in these stories, reflect the incapacity of his class to stabilize its strategies of self-ratification in response to alterations in southern politics following Reconstruction. For his part, George Wyatt is clearly attuned to the political benefits of populism, but the idea of distributing power and influence among the lower classes of whites, as James K. Vardaman and the other "rednecks" were ultimately successful in doing, is foreign to Bayard. The dialectic of self and Other which had empowered the Sartorises within the planter class was too deeply imprinted upon Bayard's unconscious for him to be able to modify it after Reconstruction, although, as narrator of these stories, he is clearly aware that these moments have been responsible for his impotence in later life. Bayard is momentarily successful on the Square, as George Wyatt makes clear: "Maybe you're right," Wyatt tells Bayard, "maybe there has been enough killing in your family without—Come on" (*TU*, 251). But his refusal to "come on," to distribute himself as a sign of popular democratic authority in the town, condemns Bayard to live out his life in attenuated relation to the political successes of his father. Similarly, the Agrarians' refusal to advocate truly democratic political and economic reforms for the South prevented their movement from ever obtaining the representative status they so eagerly sought for it.

CHAPTER 2

Figuring Legal Discourse in *The Hamlet* and *Knight's Gambit*

S hortly before his murder at the hand of his former business partner in "An Odor of Verbena," John Sartoris encourages his son to enter the legal profession. "The land and the time too are changing," he tells Bayard; "what will follow will be a matter of consolidation, of pettifogging and doubtless chicanery in which I would be a babe in arms but in which you, trained in the law, can hold your own—our own" (*TU*, 231). Sartoris's brief tenure as a politician has taught him an important lesson: the South's antebellum system of aristocratic privilege has been supplanted by a kind of industrial democracy, and the only hope for erstwhile planters to retain power and influence in the new system is to form political, legal, and business alliances with the new institutions of power—banks, agricultural corporations, and railroads. A man in Sartoris's position in the late 1800s would have placed his confidence in the law as a most effective vehicle of "chicanery," because such men benefited from the successful legal maneuvering of Ohio congressman John Bingham on behalf of railroad executives after the Civil War. Bingham was a railroad lawyer, and as a member of the Joint Committee of Congress that drafted the Fourteenth Amendment, he "had been responsible for the phraseology of Section One" of the amendment, which guarantees equal protection under the law to all "persons" born or naturalized in the United States.[1] What many historians call the "conspiracy theory" of the phrasing of this amendment holds that Bingham purposely used "persons" rather than "citizens" because, as the representative of his railroad employers, he wanted a term that would extend constitutional protection to corporate entities as well as to individuals. If a man like Sartoris could classify his railroad corporation as a "person," the profits he earned on that business would be protected, constitutionally, from anti-railroad factions that might develop in his state's legislature. Cast in these terms, Sartoris's plan for his son to maintain the Sartorises' political and economic fortunes by studying the law could be a result, however indirect, of the impressively strategic use of "person" by Bingham and others as an ambiguous signifier in federal legislation following the Civil War.

Sartoris's conception of the law as a tool that can be wrested by a determined individual and used for personal benefit is as much a product of the nineteenth century as are the epistemological allegiances of his son Bayard when he looks back, as the narrator of *The Unvanquished*, at the various "eruptions" of history that have affected his family's fortunes. Just as Faulkner's revisions of some of the stories that comprise *The Unvanquished* emphasize the anachronism of Bayard's residual, "plantocratic" epistemology, many of Faulkner's legal fictions written and published in the 1930s and 1940s demonstrate a historical inconsistency in John Sartoris's vision of his son's legal future. To be sure, there was no sudden end to legal chicanery in the early twentieth century at either the state or federal level. But by the early 1930s, in the years Faulkner wrote his first commercial detective fiction featuring Gavin Stevens, the legal profession in America had experienced a period of self-examination that radically altered the formalist legal paradigm that had dominated the nineteenth century.

By the early 1900s, the common understanding of the law of the United States as a body of legal principles handed down by tradition had been institutionalized through the adoption of the case method of legal education at Harvard Law School, under the direction of its dean, Christopher Langdell. Replacing a system dominated by lectures, Langdell's case method compelled the study of appellate court decisions and thus concretized the concept of precedent based upon "basic legal principles or rules."[2] This development in the method of American legal education adhered to the agenda of legal positivists who, more or less faithful to Hans Kelsen's "pure theory" of the law, sought to factor out the historical contradictions that accompanied the evolution of common law in the nineteenth century, by constructing a scientific model that could be analyzed mathematically and structurally. As Peter Goodrich has demonstrated, these developments toward a science of law parallel developments in linguistics, the science of language, which underwent a similar paradigm shift at around the same time, most notably with the work of Ferdinand de Saussure. In much the same way that Saussure sought to exclude historical contingencies from linguistics in order to examine language "scientifically," legal positivists sought to exclude the effects of individual instances of adjudication from what they believed to be their proper field of analysis: jurisprudence. What counted for them was the existence of a structure of normative legal ideas that could become the foundation of legal theory. In short, at around the turn of the century historical contingency was extracted from the common law in its transformation into jurisprudence, which was conceived as a body of first principles that could be applied objectively by impersonal judges and legislators.[3]

Shortly after the institutionalization of legal positivism at Harvard and other universities, however, legal "realists" emerged from within the profession to threaten the formalism of Kelsen and other positivists. Realists were skeptical of a rule of law that purported to exist outside the contingencies of historical events.[4] A brief history of legal realism as a movement would begin with Roscoe Pound's initial advocacy of "sociological jurisprudence" in 1907,[5] and end with its largely unaccounted-for demise shortly after World War II.[6] It reached the pinnacle of its influence in the 1930s, and its most complete definition in 1931, when Karl Llewellyn responded in the *Harvard Law Review* to some of Pound's criticisms of the movement's development, voiced earlier in that same journal.[7] Despite the heterogeneous interests of legal realists, they all expressed dissatisfaction with the practice of adjudicating syllogistically from first principles—as though these were available without mediation to lawyers and judges, rather than being sought out by them to apply to individual cases.[8]

The most complete discussion of the law in Faulkner is Jay Watson's *Forensic Fictions,* a very detailed analysis of Faulkner's lawyer characters and their use (and misuse) of southern traditions of rhetoric and oratory. However, neither Watson's work nor that of others interested in the law in Faulkner have treated the law as a discourse subject to the same historical contingencies as other discourses represented in Faulkner's texts.[9] Accordingly, I will focus on observable parallels between Faulkner's various representations of the law, and vicissitudes in American legal discourse from the 1920s through the 1940s. The discursive influence of legal realism is most evident in Faulkner's early detective stories, which were originally published in commercial magazines in the 1930s and 1940s and later collected in *Knight's Gambit* (1949). But I will begin my analysis by relating two legal spaces in Oxford, Mississippi, to Faulkner's representation of the law in *The Hamlet* (1940). This will allow me to demonstrate how legal formalism simulates the structures of other formalisms in southern culture, and how legal realism employed an alternative organization of space to assert its principles in the 1930s. After then reading the early *Knight's Gambit* stories in relation to legal realism's attempts to displace the authority of formalism, I will turn, in the final section of this chapter, to the title story of *Knight's Gambit* (written long after the commercial magazine stories), in which the emergent model of legal realism is itself transformed into a recuperated version of the prior formalism. In this final contrast, I hope to offer some insight into the waning of legal realism in America after World War II, and in Faulkner's representations of the law after *Knight's Gambit*. Throughout, however, my primary claim is the necessity of recognizing the historically determined differences between these two models of legal discourse, before we can fully understand differences in the various subjects of the law represented in Faulkner's texts.

As such, my claims in this chapter parallel those in chapter 1, because the legal realists' challenge to the foundational premises of legal formalism instantiates a revisionist paradigm similar to that which characterizes the challenge made by emergent, revisionist historiographers to the exclusionary narratives of proslavery historians and Agrarian academics. In writing *Black Reconstruction in America*, W. E. B. Du Bois was motivated by the sense that African Americans remained disfranchised long after the ratification of the Fourteenth and Fifteenth Amendments because the politicians (and historians) who defined "the South" as a political entity did not include African Americans in their vision of regional reform and progress. Bayard Sartoris's privileged white male subjectivity is under assault in *The Unvanquished* to the extent that his narration of the stories in that novel is inflected by the practices of revisionist historiographers (and their analogues in the post–World War I civil rights movement). Since Faulkner's representations of the two models of law that dominated the American legal profession from 1910 to 1950 are primarily articulated in his various representations of Gavin

Stevens, we should expect to find a similar measure of incoherence in Stevens's sense of himself as a concrete "individual," an incoherence caused by the tides of legal discourse he must navigate in the course of Faulkner's career-long experimentation with the figure of the lawyer and with the genre of detective fiction.

Two Models of the Law in Oxford and Yoknapatawpha

The city courtroom in Oxford, Mississippi, contains straight-backed wooden benches, a straight, wooden railing between the spectators and the legal participants, and an altarlike arrangement of authority in the front of the room. The authority to make a decision regarding a case appears shared among three to five magistrates, but there is no question that this domain is separate from that occupied by the litigants, lawyers, and spectators. This arrangement of the city courtroom "models" the principles of legal formalism, which posit a preexisting truth that it is the burden of the court to discover. Witnesses may testify and be questioned at the podium, but there is little suggestion that any new meaning can be produced in this room. Competing versions of events will be heard, a particular narrative will be determined "within the true," and this narrative will then be judged according to the letter of the law.

Many of the inhabitants of Yoknapatawpha County appear quite comfortable with this model of the law. Indeed, several assumptions made by characters in the "Spotted Horses" episode of *The Hamlet* parallel those of legal formalists. One of these is the formalists' investment in precedent, as evidenced by their use of the case method at Harvard University. The formalists' regard for precedent is matched by the importance the men on Varner's gallery attribute to the fact that "Anse McCallum brought two of them horses back from Texas once. . . . It was a good team" (*TH,* 306). According to this model, the setting of a precedent always implies the possibility of rule. Henry Armstid also reveals his faith in this logic when he first approaches Buck Hipps, who has just given Eck Snopes one horse for starting the bidding on another:

> "Is the fellow that bids in this next horse going to get that first one too?"
>
> "No," the Texan said.

"All right," the other said. "Are you going to give a horse to the man that makes the first bid on the next one?"

"No," the Texan said.

"Then if you were just starting the auction off by giving away a horse, why didn't you wait till we were all here?" (*TH*, 322)

Armstid's growing frustration with Buck Hipps is a result of his firm conviction that some rule must lie behind Hipps's otherwise irrational act of giving Eck the first horse. Working the puzzle every way he can, he finally appeals to a rule he feels all might agree upon, of equal opportunity in a democratic society. Armstid's implicit critique of Hipps's practice parallels the formalists' argument that a form of jurisprudence that is based upon legal precedent is the public's greatest guarantee of equal treatment before the law.

Armstid is taken advantage of because he assumes that horse trading, and this particular horse trader, operate from certain principles that will ensure a fair result. But this is not simply a case of being taken to the laundry and hung out to dry (as Faulkner's side-narration of Mrs. Littlejohn's domestic chores might suggest); successful horse traders like Buck Hipps capitalize upon rural beliefs in certain organizations of meaning that combine the formally religious with the formally legal. "What do you think that barn is," Hipps yells to the horses, "a lawcourt maybe? Or maybe a church and somebody is going to take up a collection on you?" (*TH*, 311). Hipps knows how to inflect the language of his profession with a combination of religious and legal discourse that the villagers of Frenchman's Bend will recognize, trust, and even succumb to. Hipps climbs a fence post as he auctions the horses, raising himself above the crowd as a minister would mount a pulpit before his congregation. And the crowd reacts as it has been conditioned to react under such circumstances—with humility and reverence: "Sitting on the post, he looked down at the faces along the fence which were attentive, grave, reserved and not looking at him" (*TH*, 316). Arranging himself and the crowd in this way, Buck Hipps is able to draw upon the respect for authority that characterizes formalist thinking about both law and religion among the villagers of Frenchman's Bend.

When these Yoknapatawphans think of law, they think of church, as when villagers are asked to construct a court in Whitfield's Grove to hear *Armstid v. Snopes* and *Tull v. Snopes:* "a wagon and four men were dispatched and returned presently from the church a mile away with four wooden pews for the litigants and their clansmen and witnesses" (*TH,* 356). The court in Whitfield's Grove deploys an arrangement of signifying objects similar to that in the city courtroom, because both borrow their sign-structures from a religious-formalist register recognizable to people likely to fall within their jurisdictions. In the grove, the authority of the city magistrate's bench is represented by "the single chair, the gnawed table bearing a thick bible which had the appearance of loving and constant use" (*TH,* 356). This mixture of the secular and the religious suggests that the residents of the county understand the law better when they approach it with a kind of reverence common to both religion and formalist jurisprudence.

By appearing to work from contractually agreed upon first principles, the justice of the peace who hears the two cases resulting from the "Spotted Horses" episode puts into practice another principle of legal formalism. In *Armstid v. Snopes,* Henry's wife seeks the return of the five dollars Henry took from her to buy one of the spotted horses. As the justice explains, the outcome in this case hinges upon who owned the horses at what time. Unless someone can prove that Flem owned the horses, Mrs. Armstid's complaint is against Buck Hipps: "The one you want to sue is that Texas man. And he's gone. If you got a judgment against him, you couldn't collect the money. Don't you see?" (*TH,* 359). Through a circular line of reasoning, the justice manages to avoid finding against Flem, almost as though this were his intention all along. In the second case the justice again presents ownership of the horse that injured Mr. Tull and destroyed his wagon as the crucial issue, thus appearing to begin from first principles: "The law says," he begins, and there follows a syllogism that concludes that whoever owned the horse and didn't keep it penned up is liable for the damages. But the justice's own comments during the hearing suggest that instead of starting from this "first principle," he has arrived at it, after an informal review of the case, as the only one that would exonerate Eck. Despite his pretense of hearing the facts of the case for the first time, the justice has reasoned "by what I know myself from these last four weeks" (*TH,* 365). He has learned that although everyone heard Hipps give Eck the horse by oral announcement, no physical transaction took place.

Therefore, Eck never really owned the horse: "In the law," he explains to Mrs. Tull, "ownership cant be conferred or invested by word-of-mouth. It must be established either by recorded or authentic document, or by possession or occupation" (*TH*, 365). Thus Mrs. Tull loses her case, but it is clear that the odds were against her at the outset, when the justice asked Eckrum, "What is the defendant's position? Denial of ownership?" (*TH*, 364). This defense had never occurred to Eck, but it seems the justice has been considering it, ever since Buck Hipps left Frenchman's Bend, as the only "first principle" that would reassert the order of the law over the chaos of this story.

The justice's reasoning in the second case illustrates the complaint of the realists in the 1930s that in the everyday practice of the law justice operates according to contingency and the predilections of judges rather than by preexisting principles and legal truths. Despite the elaborateness of his formal reconstruction of a city courtroom, and his implicit belief in an autonomous jurisprudence, the justice is complicit in the informal laws of the Bend, which ultimately privilege white males over blacks and women. The internal contradictions in the justice's practice register the fact that in the years Faulkner spent composing these stories, legal formalism was at odds with the ideas and practices of legal realism, a set of legal principles and assumptions that can be observed in the arrangement of Oxford's other legal space, its county courtroom. Oxford's county courtroom contrasts starkly with its city courtroom. It more resembles a theatrical stage, on which laws are constructed as a process of exchange and negotiation between the players involved, than a church building where the rules preexist each congregation. The observers' benches in the county court, curved as in a rounded theater, no longer imply a reverence for the rule of law but instead suggest a theater where the audience's response is as crucial a part of the performance as the judge's. The border between the spectators and the participants, because it is made of the same material as both the observers' benches and the litigants' tables, blends together, rather than separates, these two spaces. This effect is heightened by the proximity of the litigants' tables: whereas in the city courtroom the space between this border and the space of adjudication is significant, in the county room it is negligible. The litigants' chairs push right up against the curved, wooden rail. Finally, the adversarial quality of the

American system dominates Oxford's county courtroom, where what really happened in a case is performed and enacted before an audience of jurors rather than merely presented to the bench.[10]

This arrangement of space and authority is conducive to the realists' belief that the facts of a case need to be established in the process of legal decision making, with a broader definition in mind of what counts as relevant, "legal" information, and with the question of which precedents apply to a case left open. Briefly, we can observe some of these principles in Ratliff's efforts regarding the "Spotted Horses" episode of *The Hamlet*. Ratliff understands that Flem's trickery depends upon not letting anyone know who really owns the horses. "I'd sholy like to know just exactly who I was giving my money to," he says on Varner's gallery the day before the auction; "Seems like Eck here would tell you. Seems like he'd do that for his neighbors, dont it?" (*TH*, 307). But to Ratliff's repeated approaches, Eck Snopes's only response is "I dont know" (*TH*, 308). Two days after the auction, again on the porch, Ratliff's cross-examination is directed toward another of Flem's cousins, Lump, the store clerk. Amid the casual storytelling regarding the calamitous finish to the auction, Lump incautiously interjects that had Flem known how readily the men would buy the horses, he might have brought some tigers and monkeys from Texas as well. Ratliff immediately interjects, "So they was Flem's horses" (*TH*, 342). This effectively kills the conversation until Lump clumsily retracts his statement.

Lump can't see that more is going on here than casual talk until he has committed the grievous error of jeopardizing his powerful kinsman. "You town fellows are smarter than us country folks," he says (*TH*, 342). Throughout this scene, Ratliff is practicing a kind of law that establishes the facts of a case along the way in an attempt to block the formalist strategy of seeking precedents and premises that will exonerate the village's empowered citizens (such as Flem Snopes) at the expense of its women. Ratliff is frustrated in these efforts, however, partly because this model is not as familiar to the villagers as the formalist model, and partly because Ratliff is unable to produce himself as a figure of authority within this second model. In the early detective stories of *Knight's Gambit*, Gavin Stevens is much more effective than Ratliff at developing and manipulating the signifying operations of the county courtroom model, in which power and authority are no longer the stable possession of the bench but must be won through negotiation and rhetorical accomplishment. Stevens is able to determine the way law works rather than the way it ought to work according to the prescribed rules of jurisprudence. In the *Knight's Gambit* stories of the 1930s and early 1940s, Stevens's developing concern as a county lawyer is to fashion himself as a figure or sign of legal authority that he can "publish" throughout the county, thus displacing the legal formalism that otherwise mediates the relation between rural populations and the law.

That discussion, however, must begin with a story in which Stevens is actually an adherent to the formalist method. In "Tomorrow," we will see Stevens learning from mistakes he made as a follower of the formalist model—mistakes that cause him eventually to assimilate the principles and practices of legal realism into his own performances as a lawyer.

Legal Realism and the Early Gavin Stevens Stories

The realists' faith in extralegal information has its source in the innovative legal practices of Louis Brandeis in the first decade of the century. In *Muller v. Oregon* (1908), Brandeis set a new standard for argumentation before the Supreme Court when he submitted a brief packed with nonlegal information and statistics, from sources as various as "government labor statistics, reports of factory inspectors, and testimony from psychological, economic, and medical treatises."[11] Brandeis's use of outside information was not intended to reverse the Court's decision of three years earlier, in *Lochner v. New York,* that the state could not pass maximum work hours legislation because it had no compelling motive to interfere with employees' "liberty of contract," or with their freedom to bargain freely with their labor. Instead, Brandeis's reports and treatises focused upon the effect of long work hours upon women, because the *Muller* case dealt specifically with the state's right to limit the work week of women in laundries and factories. Brandeis's extralegal material was presented to the Court to demonstrate the specific effects of extreme labor conditions upon women workers. He asked the Court, in other words, to examine the facts of the case within the context of these women's working conditions and home environments, rather than simply refer to legal precedent and constitutional law. Although Brandeis's method was slighted in the majority opinion, he won his case primarily because he was able to convince the Court that extralegal factors could constitute enough compelling interest for the state to justify intervention in the labor policies of private business.[12]

An interesting parallel exists between the value of extralegal information for Brandeis as he argued *Muller v. Oregon* before the Supreme Court and for Gavin Stevens in "Tomorrow." "Tomorrow" is set earlier than any other story in *Knight's Gambit*, before Stevens is first elected county attorney. Its opening paragraphs are laced with intimations of the obscurity of this time in Stevens's life: his career prior to becoming county attorney "had lasted for such a short period that only the old men remembered it, and even some of them did not. Because in that time he had had but one case" (*KG*, 85). Stevens's first case is in defense of Bookwright, who has killed Buck Thorpe for seducing his seventeen-year-old daughter. Although Bookwright has confessed to the murder, "everyone believed the trial would be a mere formality" (*KG*, 85) because, as Mr. Holland tries to explain to Jackson Fentry (the lone juror dissenting from a vote to acquit Bookwright), Buck Thorpe "was not only no-good but dangerous" (*KG*, 89). Holland, in effect, is arguing from the same first principle that Stevens, Bookwright's defense lawyer, had taken in his summation before the jury: "All of us in this country, the South," Stevens says, "have been taught from birth a few things which we hold above all else" (*KG*, 87). Although he begins with an argument that would suggest an "eye-for-an-eye" finding against Bookwright, in fact Stevens applies his first principle, "that only a life can pay for the life it takes" (*KG*, 87), to Buck Thorpe's "taking" of Bookwright's daughter (who "was incapable of her own preservation" [*KG*, 88]).

With this reasoning, Stevens expects to exonerate his client because he knows that this form of argumentation should appeal to the conservative morality of the jury. Moreover, the syllogism of this argument for retributive justice against Thorpe is complemented by a second argument, which is based upon the "first principle" of a person's right of self-defense. In this case, Stevens's use of formalist rhetoric equates Bookwright's right to defend his daughter's honor with the community's right to defend its investment in the idea of purity and innocence at the center of southern regional character. Just as the story's first page contrasts "a swaggering bravo calling himself Buck Thorpe" to the "solid, well-to-do farmer, husband and father, too, named Bookwright"—and just as Holland later tries to persuade the recalcitrant Fentry to convict Thorpe by describing Thorpe as a contaminating threat to the community—Stevens, in his summation, depicts Thorpe's questionable "character and the morality of the act he was engaged in" as an affront to the moral values of a small southern community (*KG*, 85, 87). The effectiveness of Stevens's formalist strategy resides in the fact that it allows the jury to plead self-defense—the defense of the community's core values from this "outsider's" efforts to defile them—at the same time that it ratifies Bookwright's plea of self-defense in murdering Buck Thorpe, despite the fact that Thorpe never presented any real threat to Bookwright's physical health.

When Stevens is forced by his hung jury to travel out into the county to learn more about the hold-out juror Jackson Fentry, he learns that Fentry had married Thorpe's mother just before she died while giving birth to him. At the story's end, Chick remembers telling his uncle that he would have voted to free Bookwright, even if he, like Fentry, had been Thorpe's one-time father, "because Buck Thorpe was bad" (*KG*, 104). But at this point Stevens adamantly contradicts Chick:

> "No, you wouldn't," Uncle Gavin said. . . . "It wasn't Buck Thorpe, the adult, the man. He would have shot that man as quick as Bookwright did, if he had been in Bookwright's place. It was because somewhere in that debased and brutalized flesh which Bookwright slew there still remained, not the spirit maybe, but at least the memory, of that little boy, that Jackson and Longstreet Fentry, even though the man the boy had become didn't know it, and only Fentry did. And you wouldn't have freed him either. Don't ever forget that. Never." (*KG*, 104–5)

Stevens's reaction to Chick's naiveté is so forceful because, by the story's end, he has learned the value of information-gathering in the legal process. After accumulating more information about the case than its bare, courtroom facts suggest, Stevens is convinced that no one in Fentry's position would have voted to acquit Bookwright.

For Stevens, a trial lawyer, the lesson is invaluable: jurisprudence may be the sum of all legal principles and the skillful rhetorical use of them in a final summation before a jury, but adjudication consists solely of what a specific body of jurors will do at any one time. "Tomorrow" can thus be read as an interesting case study of how extralegal information worked its way into American legal discourse early in the twentieth century. Commenting upon this phenomenon, John W. Johnson characterizes legal developments of the early twentieth century as adhering to an "informational paradigm": the practice of law in America developed toward legal realism as information became more available to lawyers and judges. "Tomorrow" registers this paradigm shift in the lesson Stevens takes from his first legal case: knowledge of the rule of law is useful, but extralegal information—of the sort used in Brandeis's briefs—is equally, and sometimes more, important. If Stevens had explored the story of his juror's one-time parenting of his defendant's victim before the case had come to trial, he could have avoided the eventual declaration of mistrial, and thus the "loss" of this first case.

Another part of the development of legal discourse according to an informational paradigm for which there are parallels in Faulkner's text is the "good roads" propaganda of the New Deal in the 1930s.[13] For Faulkner's legal figures, the development of the highway system opened the frontier of rural America. In one sense, the growth of legal realism depended upon the progress of the highway projects of the New Deal: the amount of sociological information required to construct a Brandeis brief was made possible through improved commerce between rural and urban America. In "Tomorrow," the story of Stevens's first case, the system of roads that will effect this change is under construction: on the way to the home of Fentry's father, Chick tells us, "the roads we followed [were] less than lanes, winding and narrow, rutted and dust choked, the car in second gear half the time" (*KG*, 90). For his part, Stevens is fully aware of the extent to which his ability to collect the information he needs to solve his case depends upon the condition of rural roads. He declines a dinner invitation from the Pruitts because "it's thirty miles to Varner's store, and twenty-two from there to Jefferson. And our roads ain't quite used to automobiles yet" (*KG*, 97). And by the end of this story, Stevens is looking forward to the future "when all the main roads in Mississippi would be paved like the streets in Memphis" (*KG*, 104).

This relation between good roads and Stevens's legal reach is noted in other stories of *Knight's Gambit* as well. In "Monk," for instance, Chick imagines the lawlessness of the rural counties twenty-five years earlier, when they were "without roads almost and where even the sheriff of the county did not go . . . until a few years back when good roads and automobiles penetrated the green fastness" (*KG,* 40–41). In "An Error in Chemistry," the extension of good roads into the rural South provides Joel Flint's motive for a double murder: he turns himself in for killing his wife, then escapes from jail, murders—and then disguises himself as—his father-in-law, Wesley Pritchel, all in order to reap the profits of the sale of Pritchel's farm to northerners interested in a clay pit located at the center of the farm. This is no ordinary pit: the northerners will pay top dollar because they plan to "manufacture some kind of road material out of the clay" (*KG,* 115). One way or another, good roads make the law, and stories about the law, a real presence in people's lives and in Faulkner's fiction: "It was the good roads and the fords," Chick explains, "which not only brought Monk to Jefferson but brought the half-rumored information about his origin" (*KG,* 41). Good roads connect the rural counties and the urban centers, creating a larger area for Gavin Stevens, the representative of the law, to inscribe the law's presence. This allows Stevens to distribute himself as a figure of authority in an increasingly mobile legal system, but it also makes available to him the sort of extralegal information he needs to win cases in the courtroom (as lawyer) and to solve the mysteries (as lawyer/detective) that baffle conventional legal figures.

In "Hand upon the Waters," Stevens travels Yoknapatawpha's good roads to solve the murder of Lonnie Grinnup, but it is clear that his purpose is also to extend the reach of his authority as a legal figure. In this story, Boyd Ballenbaugh drowns Lonnie Grinnup so that Tyler Ballenbaugh, Boyd's brother, can collect on a $5,000 insurance policy. The murder occurs outside Stevens's jurisdiction: "As county attorney he had no business there, even if it had not been an accident" (*KG,* 65). Nevertheless, Stevens drives the eight miles on the new highway to the grist mill beside the country store—another of Faulkner's impromptu legal spaces—where the inquest is held. For Stevens, this country setting furnishes a new space in which to punctuate his legal authority, to make the law something that can happen in any corner of the county, not just in official courtroom spaces.

The inquest is crowded with the people who elect him every year, "even though they did not quite understand him, just as they did not understand the Harvard Phi Beta Kappa key on his watch chain" (*KG*, 67). It is true, as Jay Watson argues, that much of Stevens's effectiveness depends upon his colloquial skill, his ability to speak to rural folk "in their idiom" (*KG*, 16).[14] But Stevens, as we see here, is also capable of using language in a manner that baffles his interlocutors, and not just, as we might expect, those whose guilty confusion Stevens wishes to take advantage of. Instead, Stevens interjects the foreignness of legal language and its symbols into people's lives in order to make the law a constant, sometimes puzzling, presence. Thus, although Watson correctly praises Stevens's colloquial manner in "Tomorrow," his "art of listening" which encourages his rural informants to tell the story of Jackson Fentry, at other times, such as when Stevens is interrogating Pruitt, the narrator specifically notes that Stevens obtains information despite his conversational clumsiness: "And Pruitt told him, even though at that time Uncle Stevens would forget now and then and his language would slip back to Harvard and even to Heidelberg" (*KG*, 91). Rather than fostering the comfortable situation of the storyteller, Stevens's presence, in many of these rural scenes, is intimidating. He represents the law—which has not served everyone equally—and the law's extended reach. Fentry's father, far from being mellowed into easy conversation by Stevens's country accent, orders Stevens and Chick off his property precisely because his family has felt the brunt of this development: "You've badgered and harried him enough!" he screams, referring to the legal papers the Thorpes once used to take the child Buck from Jackson Fentry after the death of Buck's mother (*KG*, 91). Stevens must be aware of his propensity to confuse and alienate these rural folk. Indeed, he often benefits from it, constantly "spinning and unspinning around his finger" his Phi Beta Kappa key, as a mesmerist might dangle a watch from a string (*KG*, 111).

Stevens's journey from city to country inscribes the law in Faulkner's detective stories as a figure of extension. Much as the Agricultural Adjustment Administration (AAA) was installing county extension agencies throughout the South during the Depression in order to speed agricultural modernization, the New Deal's good roads extended the reach of the law into rural areas. Each of Stevens's journeys into the hinterland thus maps new territory for the law to occupy. In "Hand upon the Waters," Stevens extends the map as far as Lonnie Grinnup's fishing camp, the scene of Grinnup's murder, where Stevens surprises the Ballenbaughs as they look for any incriminating evidence Boyd may have left in Grinnup's cabin. Stevens stops along the way to publicize his presence: "I'm going in to Mr. Lonnie Grinnup's camp," he yells in the direction of a cabin along the way; "If I'm not back by daylight, you better go up to the store and tell them" (*KG*, 74). This is a self-protective maneuver, but it is also an unofficial broadcast to the cabin's inhabitants: expect the law to reach anywhere at any time. In this case, the message is also racially inflected; this is a "Negro" cabin, and the wife of the man who lives there suggests that at least part of Stevens's intention is to inform black rural residents of the ubiquity of the white power structure: "You come away and let them white folks alone!" she tells her husband (*KG*, 75). As a figure of the law, therefore, Stevens fills a role that is more than just "colloquial." In these stories, he represents the law as it functions in people's lives, and as it has historically privileged some groups of citizens over others.

The New Deal's good roads made extralegal information more available to courts and judges and allowed figures of the law like Gavin Stevens to publish the signs of their authority throughout rural America. This could explain a slight deviation from the genre of detective fiction made by popular American writers during the 1930s. This is the mobility of these writers' hard-boiled heroes compared to their prototypes, Conan Doyle's Holmes and Poe's Dupin.[15] To be sure, these earlier detectives venture into the world to investigate crimes and catch criminals, but their deductions generally proceed from information brought to them in their chambers by prospective clients. One senses that Holmes, for instance, has already begun to solve his cases' puzzles before he even visits their crime scenes. Hard-boiled American detectives, on the other hand, are more likely to stumble across the cases they solve and to reason inductively as they struggle to put the pieces of a puzzling case together. As John Cawelti observes, whereas the classic detective story begins in "the charming bachelor apartment of Holmes and Watson, or the elegant establishment of Lord Peter Wimsey," the American detective story of the 1930s more often begins with the hero "already in motion to the scene of the crime, on his way to visit a client, or, like

Philip Marlowe in the opening to *Farewell, My Lovely,* simply sucked violently in." Accordingly, the circular pattern that describes many of Holmes's cases—beginning in his drawing room, carrying him out to the scene of crime, and formally closing again within the personal space of the drawing room—is reversed in Raymond Chandler's *The Big Sleep* (1939; film adaptation, 1946), the screenplay which Faulkner wrote in collaboration with Leigh Brackett at the end of 1944. Chandler's story opens, not in Marlowe's drawing room or office, but in the mansion of his client, General Sternwood, the grounds of which turn out to be the scene of both Rusty Regan's murder and the novel's conclusion. Throughout this story, moreover, Chandler appears self-consciously to be contrasting the methods of his hero with those of his predecessors: "I'm not Sherlock Holmes or Philo Vance," Marlowe says at one point. As I read it, the early Gavin Stevens stories, such as "Monk," "Hand upon the Waters," and "Tomorrow," register a minor generic deviation—the detective who emerges from the traditional space of deductive reasoning in order to assemble information previously unacknowledged by the law—because this deviation is itself related to the substitution of legal realism for legal formalism as the country's dominant legal paradigm. Detective fiction, including Faulkner's early *Knight's Gambit* stories, had to make this change in 1930s America, in order to continue to make sense to a culture experiencing radical change in its way of understanding the effect of law in people's lives.[16]

"Knight's Gambit" and the Postwar Neoformalism of Gavin Stevens

The title story of *Knight's Gambit* registers a second turn—this time away from the realist paradigms that inform the collection's earlier stories and toward a resuscitated formalism in a variety of discursive regions. This return to formalist models—in particular, of legal and literary discourse—is apparent, first, in Faulkner's use of the classic model of detective fiction to manage Gavin Stevens's entry into the central mystery of this story: Max Harriss's attempted murder of an Argentinean captain named Gauldres, his mother's (and sister's) would-be suitor. Whereas the early stories in *Knight's Gambit* deviate from the classic detective stories of Poe and Conan Doyle in that Stevens moves out into the county to establish the "unofficial" facts of a case rather than simply relying upon information brought to him by prospective clients, in "Knight's Gambit," which Faulkner began in the early 1940s but revised substantially in 1948 and 1949 to conclude the *Knight's Gambit* collection, Stevens remains in his office nearly the whole time, relying upon deduction and syllogistic reasoning, the devices of logic advocated by his detective-predecessors as well as by the legal formalists.[17]

"Knight's Gambit" opens with the abrupt entrance into Stevens's study of Max Harriss and his sister (who remains nameless throughout the story). From this visit Stevens and his nephew Chick Mallison learn that Max has developed a murderous hatred of Gauldres, and that this hatred derives from Gauldres's amorous attentions to Max's mother and sister. After Stevens refuses Max's request either to arrest or deport Gauldres, the brother and sister leave. But Stevens has deduced that there is more to the Harrisses' story and that more will be forthcoming that very evening. Indeed, the sister returns, providing more information regarding the mystery of Max's hatred: Gauldres has also seduced Max's lover, a rural girl named Cayley. More details emerge from this second interview, but the point is that Stevens has no intention of investigating the case any further than his own doorstep. Even the story's most crucial information, that Max Harriss has purchased a notoriously dangerous horse from Rafe McCallum, is uncovered accidentally by Chick and brought to Stevens in his office, where the elder lawyer deduces Harriss's plan to substitute McCallum's horse for a favorite of Gauldres's, which the Captain rides only at night.

This return to the formal conventions of the classic detective story establishes a pattern in "Knight's Gambit" that continues through *The Town* and *The Mansion,* in which the modernist impulses of the earlier Gavin Stevens stories are displaced by neoformalist paradigms of both law and literature. The most salient change in Stevens's practice as a lawyer/detective is his unexplained relinquishing of his legal-realist practice of establishing for himself what "counts" as legal information. He becomes content, like the formalists of a previous era, to rely upon an established set of rules and principles to guide his actions and determine his conclusions. But this shift in his practice is only a symptom of a broader shift in American society and politics, and in American judicial history in particular following World War II. As Wilfred Rumble has observed, in this early cold war period, amidst increasing national hysteria over socialist and communist influences in American politics and society, the legal realism movement "tended to lose its dynamic force," and the formalists' emphasis upon precedent and basic legal principles was reasserted.[18] This recuperation of a formalist paradigm in American legal practice coincided with the anti-Communist crusades of the McCarthy era, which Watson, following Grimwood, sees reflected in the willingness of Yoknapatawphans in *Knight's Gambit, The Town,* and *The Mansion* to isolate and often punish foreigners who attempt to infiltrate their communities.[19] But while the anxieties of these characters over foreigners are real, there is also an increase, in Faulkner's postwar novels, in the presence of "outsiders" who represent city, state, and federal legal structures (corresponding, historically, to a period of increased governmental intervention in what southern whites perceived to be "local" matters related to education, interstate transportation, and civil rights laws). It is important to note that Stevens's "ineffectualness" as a sleuth in stories written after the war is closely tied to his divided loyalties regarding this presence. Stevens is happy to allow agents of city, state, and federal governments to play a crucial role in thwarting Snopeses in *The Town*—for instance, when city auditors discover Flem's theft of brass parts at the power plant, and when federal regulators investigate the National Bank of Jefferson on the very day Byron Snopes has absconded to Mexico with bank funds—because these investigations (despite their "foreign" origin) support the ritual scorn of Snopeses which is an integral part of the dialectic of identity-formation that produces Stevens as a privileged son of Jefferson and of the modern South. At other moments, however, as in his long monologues in *Intruder in the Dust,* Stevens claims that the federal government's attempts to assert its jurisdiction over the racial order of the South are the primary threat to the region's (and, by extension, his own) "core" identity. Similarly, in *The Mansion,* Stevens ultimately rejects the FBI agent's request for assistance in enlisting Linda Snopes-Kohl as an anti-Communist informant. In short, in these postwar stories Stevens experiences a crisis in his understanding of himself as a representative of the law, because in the nascent anti-Communist and pro–civil rights era in which these stories were written, the law itself has changed as a discourse that "produces" its subjects in certain ways.

Stevens's ambivalence toward the neofederalism of postwar southern society is represented in a number of ways in "Knight's Gambit," most apparently in a series of figures of recuperation in which a return to a more comfortable (for Stevens) conservatism is posited as the recuperation of a lost relation, and contrasted to a "polluted" modernist relation that has temporarily usurped its rightful position. Yet in each of these instances of recuperation, what is posited as the original is in fact an unsatisfying copy—a false ideal substituted for an existing relation in an endless effort to retrieve an imagined, "lost" unity that in fact never existed. Stevens's curious twenty-year effort to render "the Old Testament back into the classic Greek into which it had been translated from its lost Hebrew infancy" (*KG,* 207) is only the most obvious example of this rhetoric of reversion. Stevens's endeavor is founded upon a myth of original unity: the classic Greek, as the narrator observes, is itself just a version, a translation from a "lost Hebrew infancy." And even these Hebrew texts are translations of primarily oral stories and tales, passed on for generations before being written down and codified as texts of the Old Testament. As "Knight's Gambit" opens, Stevens has essentially spent the past twenty years playing with the idea of returning to a lost order of (Mosaic) law that in fact never existed in any official, originary form. By analogy, we might conclude that he has also played with the idea of returning to the formalist legal training he received in Oxford and at Harvard and Heidelberg. For Stevens, the only problem is that in the postwar South, his reversion to a formalist rhetoric of the law likewise requires his allegiance to the federal government's civil rights initiatives (based upon "first principles" of the Constitution), to which he, an elected official dependent upon rural county voters, is reluctant to commit himself. This crisis in Stevens's identity as a lawyer/detective establishes a pattern of imagined loss and fitful recuperation that is repeated in a number of ways in "Knight's Gambit."

The vicissitudes of the Backus farm, for instance, conform to this pattern. Described early in the narrative as "just another plantation raising cotton for the market," the farm becomes a north Mississippi "landmark" when the daughter of the plantation patriarch marries a New Orleans bootlegger named Harriss (*KG,* 135). Harriss turns the Backus farm into a modernist parody of a southern plantation: "a mile square of white panel and rail paddock- and pasture-fences and electric-lit stables and a once-simple country house transmogrified now into something a little smaller than a Before-the-War Hollywood set" (*KG*, 135). The many passages in "Knight's Gambit" that describe the "transmogrification" of the Backus farm focus upon Harriss's substitution of a polluted, modernist order for an order that is increasingly remembered as part of a classical, Attic past. For example: "It had been just a house, of one story, with the gallery across the front where the old master would sit in his home-made chair with his toddy and his Catullus; when Harriss got through with it, it looked like the Southern mansion in the moving picture, only about five times as big and ten times as Southern" (*KG*, 155). Ultimately, what is remembered as part of an ideal agrarian past becomes "a kind of mausoleum," one polluted for the moment by "electric wires and water pipes and automatic cooking and washing machines and synthetic pictures and furniture" (*KG*, 153). But the logic of recuperation that governs this narrative would suggest that although one model of a southern farm (Harriss's modernist parody) has overtaken a prior model (Backus's nineteenth-century homestead), this displacement can itself be reversed by the positing of the former model as part of a timeless, universal order, which only temporarily has been interrupted by polluting, modernist influences.

This return to a bucolic order will succeed only if ownership of the Backus/Harriss farm returns to an indigenous member of the community. As both Grimwood and Watson observe, "original" relations are posited in the stories of *Knight's Gambit* through the absence of strangers: when "outlanders" arrive, a degree of instability always occurs. The bootlegger Harriss introduces disorder when he substitutes himself for Backus, the local patriarch who "stayed at home and farmed his heritage and . . . sat through the long summer afternoons in a home-made chair on the front gallery, reading in Latin the Roman poets" (*KG*, 144). Everything is in place at the outset of this story for Stevens to install himself as the rightful successor to the Latin-reading Backus (Harriss has been murdered, leaving Melisandre as Jefferson's most eligible widow), and thereby return the farm to indigenous control. This explains why Stevens predicates his rescue of Gauldres (another foreigner, whose attentions to the Harriss women threatens to prolong the disorder begun by Harriss) upon Gauldres's promise to marry the Harriss daughter and leave the county. In this way, Stevens's substitution of himself for Gauldres as the suitor of Melisandre Harriss becomes an analogue of his effort to translate the Old Testament into classical Greek: the result of both endeavors is the reversion of one order of relations to an earlier one, which is then (dubiously) privileged as the "original."

This reversion of the Harriss farm back to local control is brought about when the narrative posits yet another "lost" relation to be recuperated: Stevens's betrothal to Melisandre Backus when she was sixteen years old. Indeed, Stevens's engagement and marriage at the story's end is presented as the recuperation of several "lost" relations: two lovers from Yoknapatawpha's classical past are reunited; the Harriss plantation returns to indigenous ownership and operation; and even the endogamous stability of the community is retrieved with the departure of Gauldres. However, just as the nineteenth-century farm undergoes a metamorphosis when it is represented as a classical principle in need of recuperation; just as the "foreignness" of both Harriss and Gauldres is predicated upon a dubious original unity within the "communities" of Yoknapatawpha and Jefferson; and just as, similarly, both the "lost Hebrew infancy" and the classical Greek translation of the Old Testament must be posited as recuperable, unified texts in order to dismiss subsequent versions as polluted translations, what is increasingly remembered as an "original" betrothal, a legendary romance from the chronicles of Yoknapatawpha which predates Melisandre's decadent life with the New Orleans bootlegger, is in fact a "thing which had never been more than a shadow anyway" (KG, 146), the ephemeral stuff of small-town rumor and gossip. This betrothal is only "a legend to or within or behind the actual or original or initial legend [of her marriage to Harriss]; apocryphal's apocrypha" (KG, 144). Far from the enduring love that the narrative ultimately constructs in order to make sense of Stevens's quixotic behavior regarding Max's attempted murder of Gauldres, this betrothal is really no more than "legend's baseless legend . . . born rather of a chance remark of her father's one day" (KG, 145). Nevertheless, the narrative posits Stevens's "return" to Melisandre as the recuperation of a unified past.

Melisandre herself is somehow purified of modernist contamination after Harriss's death. In letters from South America, she writes about her home, "not the monstrosity Harriss had changed it into, but as it had been before, as if, seeing again its site in space, she remembered its shape in time; and, absent from it, it existed intact again as though it had merely bided and waited for that; it was still as though, even approaching forty, she had less than ever any capacity for novelty, for experiencing any new thing or scene" (*KG*, 163). Both Melisandre and the farm begin to appear "transmogrified" into idyllic versions of themselves. And this conversion is consummated when Stevens drives out to the farm to make his second proposal: symbolically, not even the road that Stevens must travel to the Backus/Harriss farm has been modernized: "it (the road) was older than gravel too, running back into the old time of simple dirt red and curving among the hills" (*KG*, 230).

The apocrypha of Stevens's early romance with Mrs. Harriss is part of yet another figure of recuperation in "Knight's Gambit," one involving the degradation of narrative itself from a lost, classical order. This attenuation has already been represented in the plantation patriarch: after Harriss's arrival, "there was nothing left of the old man who had sat on the front gallery with his weak toddy and Ovid and Horace and Catullus for almost fifty years" (*KG*, 152). It is also represented through the degraded quality of books in general in the modern period: Chick muses about the library across the hall from his uncle's office, full of "sombre tomes," "the old yellowed volumes" teeming with "women who were always ladies and men who were always brave," to which the current "day of gaudy dust-jackets" compares unfavorably (*KG*, 142–43). Again, this representation of decline observes the paradigm of lost and recuperated origins. The tradition of literature, represented in the narrator's reference to Scott, Richardson, and other early romance writers, has been displaced by a tendency, in the very material of "Knight's Gambit," to unfold like a "story in the magazine installments" (*KG*, 143, 149). Grimwood argues that this tendency is reflective of the history of *Knight's Gambit*'s early stories, which first appeared as magazine fiction in popular periodicals. Faulkner's revision of "Knight's Gambit" in 1948–1949, according to Grimwood, was "a virtual repudiation of the commercial origins of the first five stories."[20] But if the formal structure of "Knight's Gambit" repudiates the earlier stories' commercial origins, it also repudiates their deviation from the classic detective formula of Poe and Conan Doyle; and therefore, it repudiates the influence of legal realism upon the genre of detective fiction, which was quite observable in the actions of Stevens in "Monk," "Hand upon the Waters," and "Tomorrow," but which has been repressed in Stevens's more conservative practice as a lawyer/detective in "Knight's Gambit."

In these ways, both the Stevens of "Knight's Gambit" and the narrative itself support a rhetoric of reversion in which certain traditions of the past (of agrarianism, of romance, of literature) are given priority over modernist substitutions. In his role as county attorney, Stevens continues this pattern as he relinquishes his role as one who decides for himself what will count as "legal" information and defers instead to a powerful (but absent) state or federal legal body of which he is only a representative, a single voice. Stevens defers to such removed legal presences in three skillful moves in the story's opening scene, when Max Harriss demands that Stevens find some way to prevent the Argentinean Gauldres from marrying either his mother or his sister. Stevens's first response is to identify his new office in the county: "I'm on the draft board here," he tells Max Harriss; "I don't remember your name in the registration" (*KG*, 137). The law appears to have a whole new purpose in this story that takes place on the eve of World War II: the federal registration of the country's male population, a project of which Stevens is but one part. To reinforce this new relation of part to whole, Stevens responds to Max's assertion that "You're the Law here, aren't you?" by saying, "I'm the County Attorney" (*KG*, 137). Stevens thus shifts the real force of law away from himself, onto a distributed legal system. Stevens would never have disabused a potential informant of his belief in Stevens's legal power in the earlier detective stories in "Knight's Gambit." Finally, Stevens completes this shift in the economy of legal power by restating Max's request in such a way that its focus is no longer himself, but the federal system: "I see. You wish to employ the deportation laws of the Federal government to avenge your sister on her jilter" (*KG*, 138). In each of these moves, Stevens relinquishes the devices of the legal realists, which posit law as the everyday occurrences of legal activity—devices he successfully manipulated in the earlier stories—and assumes a modified rhetoric of legal formalism, under which the law is a body of rules and practices very much out of the control of its individual representatives.

Stevens's rhetorical support of an external body of federal and state powers is one indication of his revised postwar role as a disseminator of a recuperated formalist paradigm of legal discourse among subjects of the law in Yoknapatawpha County. But this can only be a "modified" formalist rhetoric. The logic of recuperation set out in this story suggests that any attempt to transform legal discourse back into an "original" paradigm can only result in the creation of a new discourse of law, regardless of how it might simulate the practices of a prior formalism. This new legal formalism will not be based upon the model of the Church, as was the construction of legal space in Whitfield's Grove in *The Hamlet.* Instead, in the decade that separates the earlier Stevens stories from Faulkner's rewriting of "Knight's Gambit," Stevens has acquired a rhetoric that relies upon a widespread belief within the county in the stable, albeit sometimes belligerent, powers of state and federal governments. Stevens has given up his practice as one who wields the power of the law in his own hands, in deference to a larger system of the law that preexists his individual encounters with subjects of that system. This relinquishing of his practice as a legal realist corresponds roughly with the increased presence of federal legal initiatives in the South, which were based upon the principled application of constitutional protections, rather than on traditions of precedent and common law, which, as they were practiced in the South prior to World War II, were decidedly unconstitutional and undemocratic.

The impossibility of recuperating lost origins is not a new theme for Faulkner or Faulkner studies. John Matthews's extensive Derridean reading has shown how it informs Faulkner's plots and his use of language.[21] As I have argued, however, in his fiction spanning the 1930s and 1940s, the idea that language represents the ultimate absence of the concepts it purports to make present should be understood as a consequence of the discursive conflicts that inform Faulkner's texts. In the examples of *The Hamlet* and *Knight's Gambit,* we can observe the nation's turn toward legal realism in the 1930s, and its postwar conversion to a new kind of legal conservatism, to the extent that these texts are informed by alterations and transformations in the discourse of law during these years. If legal realism waned after World War II, it was because legal discourse, like any discourse, is subject to developments in the political and historical events that give it shape. Stevens's liberalism forces him to ally himself with the federal government that finally, in the late 1940s, began to enforce in southern states both the letter and the spirit of the Reconstruction amendments. To be sure, Stevens profits from this neoformalist practice of the law (he beats Gauldres in a contest of which Mrs. Harriss and her fortune are the spoils), much as the realists claimed that earlier formalists benefited from their supposedly objective application of legal principles. But because of the critique legal realism focused on the so-called "blind justice" formalism of the nineteenth century, we might also understand Stevens's new legal identity, "ineffectual" as it may be, as part of a movement to make the letter of the Reconstruction laws a real presence in the lives of all southerners, for the first time ever.

CHAPTER 3

Belaboring the Past in *Absalom, Absalom!*

S even chapters into *Absalom, Absalom!* readers are confronted with yet another example of the narrative play that makes this novel such a puzzle. Seduced into thinking that at last we will receive a full account of Thomas Sutpen's early biography—from the man himself—we find instead that the history of Sutpen's migration from Appalachia to tidewater Virginia, to Haiti, and then to Mississippi narrated in this section is neither authentic nor original because it, like so much in the novel, is the product of the narrative labors of three generations of Compsons, among others. Nevertheless, it is clear that Sutpen, when he tells his story to General Compson while the two men and their slaves hunt down the escaped French architect, wants to place a particular sequence of historical and biographical events "within the true," as Foucault would phrase it, and that we might understand the narratological efforts of the Coldfields, Compsons, and Shreve, as well as those of Faulkner's readers since the New Critics, as a series of attempts to reconstruct some version of Sutpen's biography that best approximates this "true."[1]

But what is the proper way to understand the series of discursive events represented in this novel, each of which, from Sutpen's own efforts in 1864 to those of Quentin and Shreve in 1910, seems to emphasize the difficult labor of telling Sutpen's story? In crucial ways, storytelling functions as a kind of labor that masks other, more exploitative forms of labor in *Absalom, Absalom!* Sitting before the campfire with Quentin's grandfather, Sutpen "labors" to produce an autobiographical narrative that will mask not only the brutality of the slave labor that at that moment is combing the woods for the fugitive French architect, but also the relations of labor that have degraded the French architect's prior status as a free worker.[2] Moreover, Sutpen's narrative of his youth represents a spectrum of labor positions (yeoman farmer, poor white worker, white overseer, planter, various forms of slave labor, and, most invisible of all, various forms of women's domestic labor, both black and white) within several labor economies (slave-based, share-based, and cash-based) but subsumes the inequities between these various positions and economies beneath a privileged discourse of "originary innocence" and the "grand design" that would effect its recovery.[3] Seduced by the rags-to-riches automythography thus established by Sutpen, the novel's subsequent narrators participate in this masking as they reproduce for each other, and for the reader, this early scene between Sutpen and General Compson as an "originary" moment in the dynastic history of Yoknapatawpha. Lost in these retellings is any stable critical apparatus that might explain the effect of changing labor relations upon these characters' lives—that might explain why the architect, for instance, as a free laborer, was not free to leave Sutpen whenever he wished, or that might detail the process of his degradation from free worker to indentured servant.

The practice of storytelling in this scene signifies one of the novel's discursive paradigms, according to which the value of free labor is subsumed beneath the ideology of individualism and the "legal" ownership of the labor of others. And critics who interpret Sutpen as an entrepreneurial capitalist only perpetuate this paradigm; for, although it is important to recognize that the availability to Faulkner of the language of 1930s monopoly capitalism does determine the novel's descriptions of Sutpen's rise to power and influence "from nothing," when we perceive only the surface narrative of Sutpen's "entrepreneurship" we lose sight entirely of the distance between its fictions of self-made men and the realities of exploited and degraded labor, black and white, a mile or two beyond the site of storytelling, as in the darkened woods of Sutpen's Hundred.[4] In other words, to accede to the terms of Sutpen's autobiographical narrative is simply to privilege the fictions of entrepreneurial capitalism which were a part of the discursive environment Faulkner occupied when he wrote this novel, but which were by no means the full extent of its formation with regard to labor, or capital, or economic subjectivity.

In response to this problem, Richard Godden proposes a closer analysis of slave labor and plantation ideology during the time represented in Faulkner's novel, especially the period 1820–70. Criticizing Cleanth

Brooks, Carolyn Porter, and Durk Kuyk for "producing" Sutpen as a combination New Dealer and ideologue of the American Dream, Godden observes that "such Sutpens bear no traceable relation to the boy of 1820, or indeed the man revising that boy in 1864." Yet surely Godden goes too far in his effort to separate Sutpen from Faulkner's era, for he ignores the historicity of Faulkner's own acts of storytelling, and the conditions and relations of labor that ultimately determined them. For Godden, it seems not Faulkner but an actual Sutpen and General Compson who "construct a story" in chapter 7; they are "two planters of similar social origin talking in 1835, four years after the Turner rising." Godden is correct to insist that "Sutpen is no capitalist because he founds his design on relations quite other than those between capitalist and free labor," but when he stresses further that planters like Sutpen and Compson "could not and did not perceive their activities through the language of bourgeois individualism," Godden is neglecting to consider the discursive context within which Faulkner the writer/storyteller wrote about these planters and their self-representations, a context that included not only the discourse of bourgeois individualism but also that of industrial, monopoly, and finance capitalism. This is an especially surprising omission in Godden, since he is otherwise so concerned with the effect of labor relations upon individual subjectivity, and since volatile labor relations are such an obvious subtext shared by both Sutpen's and Faulkner's personal history.[5]

As an alternative to Godden and the critics he addresses, I propose an analysis of Faulkner's representations of labor in relation to the conditions and relations of labor in which Faulkner himself participated while composing the novel. This analysis must begin by recognizing that "labor," like "history" and "law" as discussed in previous chapters, is not a stable and unitary concept but a discourse that is subject to radical discontinuities as a consequence of both national policy and local politics. At the time Faulkner was representing the various labors of Sutpen and others (that is, in the early 1930s), the rules of formation and exclusion that would determine the future of labor as an American discourse were very much under debate. In Faulkner's own state of Mississippi and in other southern states, workers were organizing against unhealthy workplace conditions and unfair labor policies set by mill and factory owners who had relocated to the region after local law enforcement agencies promised to prevent unions from organizing their towns.[6] Many of the sites of labor in Faulkner's novel replicate the poor working conditions protested by mill workers in Mississippi, and his representations of women laborers, especially, suggests the work of women in organizing southern workers. Likewise, while he worked over the final drafts of *Absalom, Absalom!* in Hollywood, Faulkner was surrounded by efforts on the part of studio workers to negotiate for improvements in pay, hours, workplace conditions, and crediting procedures, and on the part of studio executives to maximize profits and to control the unions. Again, Faulkner's position as a writer within the context of this labor history is observable in the labor positioning of the characters in his novel. Indeed, Sutpen's traversal of a number of labor economies throughout his life—economies based upon slave labor, tenant farming, and sharecropping—is analogous to Faulkner's own position as a laborer who moved back and forth between an economy offering him a "share" of the profits on his books realized by New York publishers, and the economy of the Hollywood studio system which offered him weekly wages and, sometimes, piecework. In short, the goal of this chapter is to demonstrate the degree to which Faulkner's representations of labor, capital, and, ultimately, economic subjectivity in *Absalom, Absalom!* are conditioned by disruptions in the discourse of labor contemporary with the novel's production.

If Faulkner's representations of labor in the American South before, during, and after the Civil War parallel the vicissitudes in his own position as a laborer and those in the discourse of labor in 1930s America, this is because both the mid-1800s and the decade from 1925 to 1935 witnessed a tremendous upheaval of the American labor force and a national debate over the proper role of the federal government in negotiations between workers, private companies and corporations, and states. Labor, then, is something of a "discursive link" between *Absalom, Absalom!*'s moment of representation (the Civil War) and its moment of production (the 1930s).[7] Although today the Civil War is most commonly understood to have been a battle over the morality of slavery and the constitutionality of secession, in the 1930s a number of scholars and historians were writing about the conflict as a revolution of the working classes in the North against a southern oligarchy which hoped, in the wake of the Kansas-Nebraska Act of 1854, to legalize slavery throughout the Union.[8] At stake especially were the new territories gained from the war with Mexico, which the South hoped to admit to the Union as slave states in order to expand their profits from slave labor and to increase slaveholders' representation in the Senate. Labor organizations in the North and in Europe feared that the combination of slave labor in the new territories and its legal importation into previously "free" states (following the Fugitive Slave Law of 1850 and the Supreme Court's decision in *Dred Scott v. Sanford* [1857]), would degrade opportunities for free labor throughout America. Indeed, it is possible to read Lincoln's greatest contests with Stephen Douglas as centering upon exactly this issue.[9] In the Marxist interpretation of events leading up to the war, then, the working classes organized against the South in defense of free labor.

While to some in the 1930s (as well as today) this would seem an implausibly retroactive analysis, Marx himself wrote as early as 1861 that, should the Confederacy be victorious, "the slave system would infect the whole Union. In the Northern states, where Negro slavery is in practice unworkable, the white working class would gradually be forced down to the level of helotry. This would accord with the loudly proclaimed principle that only certain races are capable of freedom, and as the actual labor is the lot of the Negro in the South, so in the North it is the lot of the German and the Irishman, or their direct descendants. The present struggle between the South and the North is, therefore, nothing but a struggle between two social systems, between the system of slavery and the system of free labor."[10] Labor leaders of the 1930s often drew upon the rhetoric of the 1860s to depict the fight for unionization and the right to bargain collectively as a struggle between a system of (wage) slavery and a system of free and organized labor. And just as slaveholders of the 1860s masked their efforts to maintain total control over their labor force with the doctrine of states' rights and the propaganda that northerners sought, through a "war of northern aggression," to deprive southerners of their individual liberties, so southern capitalists and their spokesmen in the 1920s and 1930s decried federal collective bargaining legislation as an infringement upon the "natural" rights of both workers and employers.[11] In the 1930s, in other words, the rules of formation and exclusion that determined labor as a discourse changed under radical pressure from labor interests, and this elicited from southern capitalists a reiteration and reformulation of the previous century's proslavery rhetoric regarding the "rights" of labor. Faulkner's novel demonstrates a similar phenomenon as it reverts to antebellum themes and rhetorical devices at a moment of crisis for labor in the 1930s. It follows that his representations of antebellum labor also would echo national debates of the 1930s over labor, federalism, and the doctrine of states' rights.

Fictions of Labor

Beginning with the novel's opening pages, scenes of storytelling in *Absalom, Absalom!* are infused with the themes of labor unrest in the 1930s. Issues of worker autonomy and control over the "shop" floor lie just beneath the opening chapter's description of the office where, for the past forty-three years, Rosa Coldfield has labored to produce the details of her version of Sutpen's story—struggling diminutively in the office's "too tall chair in which she resembled a crucified child" (*AA,* 4). This chair was provided by the equivalent of a shop manager (removed from the site of labor itself) who based his decisions upon suspect theories such as "that light and moving air carried heat and that dark was always cooler" and "that the cost of electricity was not in the actual time the light burned but in the retroactive overcoming of primary inertia when the switch was snapped: that that was what showed on the meter" (*AA,* 3, 70). When we understand that the labor most elaborately represented in *Absalom, Absalom!* is that of storytelling, we see that many of the scenes of such labor in the novel represent labor conditions unconducive to the work at hand: the freezing cold of Quentin and Shreve's dormitory room; the poorly lit porch where Quentin first reads Rosa's summons and from which Mr. Compson narrates his portion of Sutpen's story; the primitive campsite where Sutpen tells his own story to grandfather Compson.

Some of these scenes evoke specific concerns of labor/management negotiations in the southern textile mills. Like the cotton mill workplaces that, according to labor historian James Hodges, "were suffocatingly hot in summer and uncomfortably warm in winter" because cotton feeds better into the machines in a humid environment, Rosa's office is "a dim hot airless room with the blinds all closed" (*AA*, 3). And, like the mill workers who "complained of dust in the opening and carding rooms and lint in the spinning and weaving rooms, a lint that filled the air and covered everything," Quentin sees "dust motes" every-where, thinking of them as "flecks of the dead old dried paint itself" (*AA*, 3).[12] Dangerous because it is close, unventilated, and dusty, the atmosphere of Rosa's office causes Quentin to muse over the danger of paint particles suspended in the air, suggesting the threat of asbestos poisoning (also an explicit concern of Edwin Rolfe's 1928 poem "The 100 Percenter") as well as brown lung disease, caused by the millions of suspended cotton fibers that plagued weavers and loom operators every day.[13] Even the novel's first sentence suggests a grueling number of hours without break in Rosa's "shift" in the production of Sutpen's story, "From a little after two oclock until almost sundown" (*AA*, 3). In such scenes, "storytelling" becomes more than an act of narrative diegesis; it is a metaphor for labor, a "node" in which contemporary issues of labor and production are concentrated.

My point is not that Faulkner was directly commenting upon spe-cific labor actions (although in some instances it is likely that he was, as I will detail below), but that the discourse of labor "produced" him as a writer who could not represent conditions of labor without reproduc-ing the "languages" of labor available to him at the moment of his own textual productions. Even a seemingly insignificant episode such as Wash Jones's construction of Henry's coffin while Judith, eating supper, barks instructions to him through the dining room window, replays is-sues of worker autonomy and owner control which would have been familiar to an audience occupying the same labor environment as Faulkner when he composed these chapters. While much of Faulkner's language derives from the context of labor strife in southern cotton tex-tile mills, other representations of the labor of textual production derive from Faulkner's experiences as a screenwriter under the Hollywood stu-dio system. This system, too, was fraught with disorder as a conse-quence of battles over the unionization of Hollywood workers—and not just of screenwriters like Faulkner. Less celebrated workers such as lighting, film, and electrical technicians, carpenters and joiners, and building engineers fought for, and were fought over by, the various guilds and unions that sought to represent them in contract negotiations with the studios. As Janet Staiger writes, "In many instances, unions battled less against the owners and more against competing unions for jurisdiction of work functions." Indeed, the incoherence of the studio system was often exacerbated, rather than resolved, by inter-union squabbling: "An instance of the necessity to redefine lines . . . was the introduction of liquid rubber to replace textile padding of actors' bodies. . . . Such earth-shaking disputes were solved by the segregation of work functions to very specific job positions which, in turn, were allocated to particular unions."[14] These kinds of Hollywood labor disputes became part of the language of Faulkner's novel as he finished writing and revising it for final publication.

For example, the specific events of a strike called by the International Alliance of Theatrical Stage Employees (IA) in 1932, the year Faulkner began his work as a Hollywood screenwriter, can help us contextualize a puzzling remark of Quentin's during his first interview with Rosa, a scene we have already observed to be inflected with the rhetoric of southern textile industry labor disputes. Rosa frames her desire to tell Sutpen's story as an effort that will benefit Quentin: "Maybe some day you will remember this and write about it. You will be married then I expect and perhaps your wife will want a new gown or a new chair for the house and you can write this and submit it to the magazines" (*AA*, 5). But Quentin is skeptical of her motives and of her seeming dependence upon him as writer and craftsman: "*she dont mean that*," he says, "*It's because she wants it told*" (*AA*, 5). For Joseph Urgo, this scene suggests a Hollywood context, in that while Rosa *tells* the story of Thomas Sutpen, Quentin is *seeing* it, in pictures, in preparation for a treatment and screenplay he will eventually work up with Shreve.[15] In this sense, the scene represents issues of intellectual property and crediting rights that were important labor issues in the film industry. But the scene also evokes the atmosphere of distrust and suspicion in 1930s Hollywood labor relations that resulted from disputes over the distribution side of the industry. Just as Rosa avers that the success of her product (the story of Sutpen) is contingent upon Quentin's distribution of it in the magazines, studio leaders in the 1930s and 1940s claimed that they were at the mercy of the IA, which could use the threat of a strike among union projectionists in any contract negotiations.

Labor historians have generally accepted this understanding of the studios' disadvantage in collective bargaining with industry unions. But Denise Hartsough argues that IA leaders were unable or unwilling ever to call such a strike, and that by 1935, the studios had formed an alliance with IA leaders, who were actually members of the Chicago mob. Far from being powerless players against a team holding the ultimate trump card, studio executives were making regular cash payments to leaders of the IA to ensure that the union would enact policies and demand concessions agreed to in advance by the studios.[16] Faulkner probably did not know the intricacies of the studios' arrangements with the Chicago mob when he made Quentin suspicious of Rosa's professed dependence upon his agency as a distributor, but he would have known that the IA's threats before the mob takeover went unrealized in the union's loss of their 1933 strike, and he may have known that when the IA made its mob-financed comeback in 1935 (following passage of the National Labor Relations Act), its demands were seldom at cross-purposes with the needs of the studios. Hartsough's historical analysis reveals how studio executives used the story of their vulnerability to a projectionists' strike as a strategic power move. Claiming no control over the distribution end of the industry, they were able to capitalize on public sympathy and, we can assume, win some studio workers away from their comparatively radical union representatives. Similarly, Rosa attempts to conscript Quentin into the cause of producing Sutpen's story by pretending to hold no control over its eventual distribution.

Acknowledging the extent to which the relations of production that determined studio labor in the early 1930s affect the relations of labor in and around Faulkner's novel can also help us understand why so many of Faulkner's critics, following the early lead of Cleanth Brooks and Michael Millgate, continue to credit Quentin and Shreve with the primary responsibility for telling Sutpen's story. Although Olga Vickery astutely observed in 1959 how the different psychological conditions of Rosa Coldfield, Mr. Compson, and Quentin and Shreve determine their respective productions of the Sutpen story as gothic thriller, classical drama, or chivalric romance, it is more often the case that Faulkner's critics want to focus upon Quentin and Shreve's narrative and historiographical constructions, perceiving theirs to be most "plausible" (Brooks) and "both the richest and the most convincing version of the story" (Porter).[17] Even Urgo's excellent comparison of the stages of production under MGM's studio system to the various "treatments" of the story of Thomas Sutpen by the novel's many narrators moves reductively, in the end, toward a discussion of the narrative as a Faulkner/ Howard Hawks-like collaboration between Quentin and Shreve. Although motivated by their own desire to penetrate the complexity of Faulkner's novel, these critics are following a paradigm for recognizing labor that was established among studio laborers in 1932, and that continues to be "delivered" to film audiences and literary critics alike through apparatuses such as the Hollywood film and even by texts like *Absalom, Absalom!*

In 1932 screenwriters agreed upon official guidelines concerning crediting standards: "All writers on a script," Staiger writes, "would review the cutting continuity and final film and among themselves unanimously decide on one or two names for the credits."[18] This arrangement solved a problem that had developed alongside the studio system of production: as more and more writers contributed to each particular film, the relative value in terms of reputation and negotiating capital for each writer was depreciated. Under the new system, the one or two writers singled out as major contributors could trade upon their reputations, now officially entered into the narrative of a film's production, in seeking subsequent work. As a consequence, anywhere from five to ten additional writers' work went unrecognized in these official narratives. It is well known that Faulkner would find his name attached to only a few completed films, although Bruce Kawin's collection of Faulkner's MGM screenplays and Blotner's biography of Faulkner's Hollywood years both suggest that he worked on many more. The tendency among Faulkner's readers to seek out Quentin and Shreve as the two storytellers "really" responsible for the narrative of Sutpen's life reiterates this paradigm for attributing credit and recognizing labor that emerged from the material concerns of workers in the specific labor environment of Hollywood, California, in 1932.

Given the number of different scripts Faulkner was involved with during his Hollywood years, it is a little puzzling that he accepted the official narrative of his meager Hollywood contribution and only felt that he "earned" his salaries from MGM after Clarence Brown achieved critical success in his 1949 adaptation of *Intruder in the Dust.* "Ever since our mild fiasco of twenty years ago," Faulkner wrote Sam Marx in 1949,

"I have felt that accounts between me and MGM were not at balance, and my conscience hurt me at times. But seeing Clarence's 'Intruder in the Dust' here last night, the qualms have abated some."[19] How many other workers were made to feel that their contributions to the industry did not merit representation—in film credits or, for instance, in collective bargaining agreements—because of the industry's crediting procedures, which valorized the labor of a few and denigrated that of many others? This is a difficult question to answer, but we can understand the problem better if we look at *Absalom, Absalom!*'s competing strategies of acknowledging and eliding the labor behind the "production" of Thomas Sutpen's wealth and property.

Much of the labor that drives the economic development of Sutpen's Hundred has been erased before Sutpen himself even arrives in Yoknapatawpha County. This is the Haitian slave labor that produced the gold Spanish coin that Sutpen uses to record his deed to the hundred square miles of Indian land and that also pays for the "crew" of slave labor Sutpen brings with him upon his second arrival in Jefferson. From this moment onward, the story of Sutpen's Hundred is the story of labor universally extracted but only selectively credited. We know that Sutpen, the French architect, and the Haitian slaves "worked from sunup to sundown" and that Sutpen worked alongside his slaves as they carried the mansion "plank by plank and brick by brick out of the swamp where the clay and timber waited—the bearded white man and the twenty black ones and all stark naked beneath the croaching and pervading mud" (*AA,* 28). Yet the tendency of labor discourse in the 1930s is finally to distribute the credit for such labor unevenly, to make the labors of many invisible while it valorizes the labor of a few. Consequently, the Haitian slaves remain an undifferentiated mass of "still eyeballs," just as when they first arrived in Jefferson (*AA,* 27). Covered in mud, they become invisible to the curious, who might even "walk one of them out of the absolute mud like a sleeping alligator" (*AA,* 27). By contrast, Sutpen, although equally besmirched, can be distinguished "by his beard and eyes alone" and shortly by his assumption of the familiar role of labor manager: "as General Compson told his son, Quentin's father, while the negroes were working Sutpen never raised his voice at them, that instead he led them, caught them at the psychological instant by example, by some ascendancy of forbearance rather than by brute fear" (*AA*, 27, 28). It is even made clear at the start of this history of Sutpen's Hundred that the architect, by race a potential competitor with Sutpen for the accolades attached to the finished product, "was to advise though not direct" the labor at hand (*AA*, 26).

Thus the tendency of this section on the construction of Sutpen's Hundred is toward some statement crediting Sutpen with the whole: "inside of two years he had dragged house and gardens out of virgin swamp, and plowed and planted his land with seed cotton which General Compson loaned him" (*AA*, 30). Just as the diverse labor behind the production of a Hollywood film was always erased in those screenwriters' meetings where ultimate credit for a film was allotted to one or two writers, editors, technicians, whose names would then obtain an exchange value as they circulated in an economy based upon reputation and crediting procedures, we see Sutpen getting credit for all of the labor behind the construction of his plantation, despite the obviously fictional basis of this particular narrative of economic development. Similarly, Quentin and Shreve have garnered most of the credit paid out in Faulkner criticism for the production of Sutpen's story at the expense of the labors of Ellen, her children, Rosa, Wash Jones, and other Compson men, as well as of the hundreds of slaves and workers who "produced" Sutpen both before and after he arrived in Jefferson.

Fictions of Labor and Capital

Of course, the practice of crediting a single individual for the physical and creative work of many did not originate in the 1932 screenwriters' agreement. Nor are its lasting effects in the film industry limited to the listing of film credits at the end of even today's Hollywood productions. The entire phenomenon of the "auteur," the genius director whose creative vision is articulated through each film he or she "creates," dates back to the same labor climate that valorized the individual "captain" of industry at the expense of masses of workers. Hollywood's culture industry developed right along with the transition from early, industrial capitalism to monopoly and finance capitalism, and the fictions developed by the former to mask its exploitative relations of labor are therefore homologous with those that developed in the businesses and factories that thrived under the latter.[20] In other words, the same rhetorical strategies that valorized the inventive wisdom of a Carnegie and a Ford, while eliding the labor of the masses that built these industrialists' fortunes, were used to celebrate the creative genius of a Howard Hawks and to erase the labor that in fact built the films of the 1930s.

The strategies by which the labor of many is elided by the reputation of a few "tycoons" constitute what I would call the "fictions of capital" that union organizers had to dismantle each time they sought a fairer distribution of profits earned from the labor of their members. When a union went out on strike, local business and political leaders mobilized their rhetoric against such collective action, calling it a threat to the inherent rights and abilities of the "individual" worker. As a professional storyteller, Faulkner was always interested in the utility of such fictions and in exposing inconsistencies in the ideological narratives people use to support one version of reality over another. In the context of a worsening Depression, he would have seen the faults in capitalist America's rhetoric of entrepreneurship, which might have motivated lecture halls full of young business students listening to a speech by Andrew Carnegie in 1885, but which rang increasingly hollow as it passed through the mouth of Herbert Hoover on the eve of a decade of mass unemployment. Within this context, Faulkner's novel "stages" the debates over workers' and employers' rights as a series of dialogic encounters in which the most familiar fictions of capital, such as the fictions of entrepreneurship and of equality in contract, are asserted and then undercut by the narrative's subsequent play.

Capitalists of the late nineteenth and early twentieth centuries were fond of writing and speaking about how they achieved their millions. Predictably, the dominant themes of such narratives are hard work, discipline, and a single-mindedness of purpose. In a speech to students of the Curry Commercial College in Pittsburgh in 1885, for example, Andrew Carnegie summarized his business advice in this way: "Aim for the highest; never enter a bar-room; do not touch liquor, or if at all only at meals; never speculate; never indorse beyond your surplus cash fund; make the firm's interest yours; break orders to save owners; concentrate; put all your eggs in one basket, and watch that basket; expenditure always within revenue; lastly, be not impatient." Inevitably, the biographical narratives of these industrialists operate according to a serendipitous strategy that reifies and obscures the sources of these businesses' investment capital. In the context of wage negotiations, a capitalist like Carnegie or, later, Ford would write whole chapters on the shop floor, usually a metonym for physical labor, as the sole source of wealth for wages: "It is the workman who makes high wages possible," Ford writes; "it ought to be clear, however, that the high wage begins down in the shop." In narratives regarding their own "start," however, they would write of investment capital as cash simply available to any deserving man with the right idea at the right time. These men are so basically good that it makes perfect sense when a banker, an associate, or a friend invests capital in their concerns. According to Carnegie, "the first considerable sum" he ever made resulted from a local banker who could recognize a deserving man when he saw one. Carnegie recalls the man's response: " 'Why, of course I will lend it. You are all right, Andy.' " Ford, a generation after Carnegie, is similarly inconsistent in describing the connection between investment capital and personal wealth. In an early chapter of his autobiography, Ford writes that he had "determined absolutely that never would I join a company in which finance came before the work or in which bankers or financiers had a part." Yet, in a later chapter, he writes about the original capitalization of the Ford Motor Company: "The capitalization of this company was one hundred thousand dollars, and of this I owned 25½ percent. The total amount subscribed in cash was about twenty-eight thousand dollars—which is the only money that the company has ever received for the capital fund from other than operations." What these narratives have in common is a certain amnesia on the part of the autobiographer regarding his own past and the sources of his wealth, and it is this paradigm that Faulkner's novel, particularly its representation of Sutpen's rise to power, participates in while also revealing its inherent contradictions and inconsistencies.[21] Quentin's version of Sutpen's biography reveals Sutpen as something of an amnesiac regarding his own past. Even before he reached the tidewater with his family, Sutpen "knew neither where he had come from nor where he was nor why" (*AA*, 184). Similarly, the story of Sutpen's origins is silent about the six years between his departure for the West Indies and his defense of the "besieged Haitian room," eliding the labor of others which gave him both the opportunity and the cause to make this defense, and thus to produce himself as a worthy member of the planter class (*AA*, 199). As anxious to conceal his dependence upon the slave labor of the Haitians as he is to control the "free" labor of the French architect, Sutpen has attempted to produce himself *sui generis* through the apparatus of his autobiography, and the novel's subsequent narrators, like Quentin, ratify this self-construction in the portions of Sutpen's biography they individually relate.

It is precisely here that Carolyn Porter's reading of Sutpen as a 1930s-style entrepreneur is partially valid. Although, as Godden argues, Sutpen certainly is not a capitalist, in his willful forgetting of his own past, Sutpen is like the capitalists Faulkner would have known about as he wrote *Absalom, Absalom!*, those who did deny the ultimate sources of their wealth because these sources invariably derived from the public rather than the individual, and this fact always puts the lie to capitalist fictions of self-made men. As the embodiment of one of capitalism's dominant fictions, Sutpen is "available" equally to General Compson, the southerner who would have heard the same story of self-made men from the bankers and steel and railroad "barons" of the nineteenth century; to Quentin, who would know the New South boosterism of Henry Grady; and to Shreve, who as a Harvard undergraduate would have been familiar with the work ethic of Andrew Carnegie. Shreve, for example, just knows that when Sutpen returns from the Civil War, "his plantation ruined, fields fallow except for a fine stand of weeds, and taxes and levies and penalties sowed by United States Marshalls," the first thing he would want to do is "set out to try to restore his plantation to what it used to be" (*AA*, 146). This is because, as I have already observed, the discourse of labor in Faulkner's novel has already marked Sutpen for economic supremacy; when he "abrupts" upon the scene (again, of storytelling) in Rosa's office in the first chapter, it is as the leader of men, with a specific enterprise in mind: that of overrunning "suddenly the hundred square miles of tranquil astonished earth" (*AA*, 4). The tendency of capitalist discourse to promote the individual, in other words, has already placed Sutpen above the rest ("man-horse-demon"), with the labor upon which he depends "grouped behind him" in diminutive postures (*AA*, 4).

The tendency of capitalist ideology to promote the interests of the individual over those of the collective constitutes a large part of James

Cobb's *The Selling of the South,* a history of the incentive system that southern states used to persuade northern industry to relocate in their impoverished communities. According to Cobb, although "the practice of granting subsidies was already a common practice by the Depression years," dating back to the railroad barons of the nineteenth century, Mississippi business leader Henry White pioneered the use of state-funded incentives to entice out-of-state businesses as a solution to economic stagnation in the early 1930s, and his early, moderate successes propelled him to the governorship in 1936. While governor, White converted the strategy into state policy in a program called Balance Agriculture With Industry (BAWI). Under the BAWI plan, local communities desperate for any industry that could generate a payroll began to offer a number of incentives, including a term of tax exemption, free electric power and water, free land, and sometimes, free buildings. In many cases, prospective employees were even made to sign a contract in which they agreed, if employed, to relinquish 5 to 6 percent of their future pay in order to finance construction of a building that would be occupied by the courted industry. Such desperation made these communities vulnerable to any number of disreputable swindlers who would realize short-term profits from the state's surplus labor force and then betray these workers by pulling out before their communities could realize any long-term payroll benefits. Cobb writes of one case, for instance, in which a necktie operator, "after occupying a rent-free building and using the services of city-paid trainees for thirty days, pulled out with enough ties for the Christmas buying season." In a 1935 case from Ellisville, Mississippi, which Cobb reports "received considerable publicity," local officials used over $26,000 in WPA funds to construct a "vocational school" on the campus of the Jones County Agricultural High School and Junior College: "This new training addition was actually operated by the Vertex Hosiery Company, which had fled Weissport, Pennsylvania, after a siege of labor troubles. Vertex generously agreed to install thirty-six knitting machines in the Ellisville School and to furnish all the raw materials and 'instructors.' The company also committed itself to training Jones County student workers for twenty-five years, during which time it would pay no rent and would enjoy the tax exemption given to all the state's educational institutions." As this scheme was repeated in Brookhaven, Mississippi, officials became worried that it would fuel criticisms of much-needed WPA programs, so they finally "decided it was best to admit that the establishment was nothing more than a garment plant."[22] Needless to say, such practices put the lie to fictions of self-made men when the northern capitalists who ultimately profited from such schemes were obviously making their fortunes by exploiting desperate southern politicians, merchants, and workers. What may not be so obvious, because of the way the 1930s practices are "mapped" onto Faulkner's representations of Mississippi's antebellum communities, is the degree to which public opinion of 1930s investment schemes is reflected in public reaction toward Sutpen when he enters Jefferson with wagons full of wealth whose source of extraction is not entirely clear. Just as Mississippians developed a skepticism toward "entrepreneurs" of the early 1930s, which abated only when White came to power and organized his official BAWI programs for attracting business to the region, Faulkner's Jeffersonians, regardless of class, are antagonistic toward Sutpen until his long-term "design" for Sutpen's Hundred and its economic promise for the region become clear to them.

When Sutpen makes his first return to Jefferson, Mr. Compson tells Quentin, "his position had suddenly changed . . . he was in a sense a public enemy" (*AA*, 33). Mr. Compson ascribes this changed position not to the likelihood that Sutpen had committed numerous felonies to accumulate his new wealth, "his chandeliers and mahogany and rugs," but to "the town's realization that he was getting it involved with himself" (*AA*, 33). Unlike the antebellum Mississippians Carolyn Porter would have us believe in, who presumably would have recognized and celebrated the "entrepreneurial" spirit motivating Sutpen's economic alliance with Mr. Coldfield and others, Faulkner's townspeople are inherently skeptical of new wealth extracted from unknown sources and used as an enticement for local investment. The people of Jefferson, in other words, are more like Faulkner's neighbors and fellow Mississippians of the early 1930s who had been burned by out-of-town sharpers like the necktie merchant and hosiery manufacturer. Whether of the aristocratic, merchant, or working class, the attitudes toward Sutpen represented in this early moment of the novel, which Mr. Compson summarizes as "public opinion in an acute state of indigestion," are homologous with those of the various classes of Faulkner's own time following the business-friendly agreements that sapped credibility from the political class, investment capital from local business and civic interests, and all but indentured the relatively powerless working class (*AA, 35*). The fiasco of Sutpen and Ellen Coldfield's wedding further demonstrates this connection: Sutpen is snubbed by moneyed and unmoneyed classes alike, the first because of its reluctance to "get involved" with another out-of-town huckster, who may well intend only to extract more wealth from this location before moving on; the second because of its enforced involvement with his type in the past, through disadvantageous contractual agreements in which they had little or no bargaining power. It is not only the women of Jefferson, in other words, "who on the second day after the town saw him five years ago, had agreed never to forgive him for not having any past" (*AA, 40*).

Sutpen, instead of representing any historically "lost" class of self-made entrepreneurs in the South, is instead a representation of 1930s debates over the role that government should play in regulating the practices of both labor and capital in the South. These two readings are easily confused because of Faulkner's placing of Sutpen within the historical moment of the region's previous cataclysmic debate over this issue, the Civil War. "Appearing from nowhere" as he apparently does, Sutpen represents the fiction of the self-made man; but Faulkner's text consistently reveals the lie behind this fiction by indicating the strategies of elision by which the labor of slaves and poor whites is erased, and by making the prehistory of Sutpen the crucial information one needs to solve the novel's various mysteries. Moreover, by placing labor at the center of this novel about the Civil War, Faulkner's narrative counters the rhetoric of states' rights, which sought, in his time, to mask the cause of the Civil War—the worldwide demand for free labor—with a quasi-enlightenment ideology of worker self-determination. At the same time, it participates in a dialogue over the role of federal intervention in contemporary labor disputes, which in many ways was a repetition of issues fought out on the battlefields seventy years before.

That Sutpen is ultimately tolerated within the community of Jefferson simply confirms the basic contradiction of the southern position on labor as it developed in the 1930s. Although the schemes of fly-by-night operators left many Mississippians disaffected, the policy of using public funds to entice northern industry was eventually regulated and implemented successfully under White's BAWI programs. Though it was clearly a form of "social engineering," its supporters, paradoxically, were vehemently antiunion, and often charged that "the spread of labor unionism threatened free-enterprise capitalism."[23] Similarly, as long as Sutpen occupies the marginalized position of a "public enemy," he is anathema to all classes of Yoknapatawphans. After he is established in the county, and especially after he demonstrates his loyalty in the war (this, in effect, constructs a "past" for him), his various exploitations of the working class are taken as the normal order of business. It is not simply that Sutpen simulates the planter "design" closely enough for his neighbors to recognize themselves and their approved manner of living in his money, house, plantation, slaves, family, and wife. Rather, the town learns to tolerate Sutpen when, at the level of the landed and merchant class, they find that their collective, albeit largely involuntary, investment in Sutpen begins to pay off, through the exploited labor of the slave and white working classes.

Because Sutpen's labor identities are constructed from the "languages" that comprised the discourse of labor when Faulkner wrote *Absalom, Absalom!* it follows that Sutpen would function as a register of multiple ideological positions regarding labor articulated in the 1930s. The mysteries of Sutpen's personal history signify inconsistencies in the rhetoric of "entrepreneurship," *and* the threat posed to vulnerable rural towns by dishonest business practices, *and* the masking effect of ideological narratives that privilege some forms of labor while eliding others. Yet it is true that Faulkner did celebrate, in his own way, the self-reliant individual, however aware he appears to have been of its masking function in the ideological battles of his time. As his numerous mental accounts of his financial debts to Random House and MGM suggest, he had a similar love affair with a second fiction of capital, the concept of "equality in contract," although to read in Blotner about his decades of near-indenture is to be made aware that Faulkner was seldom in any position to bargain on equal terms with any of his employers. Accordingly, Faulkner's representations of contract obligations in *Absalom, Absalom!* evidence an ambivalent attitude toward the concept of "equality in contract," on the one hand celebrating contract as a potential equalizer of class, gender, and racial differences; on the other, exposing the concept as a fiction generated by those who inevitably occupy the privileged position in such agreements.

As a youth, Sutpen was socialized to revere the idea that all men are equal under the law of contract. He simply cannot understand that he has been turned away from the tidewater planter's front door, when he "had actually come on business, in the good faith of business which he had believed that all men accepted" (*AA*, 188). As many of Faulkner's critics have recognized, although his experience of rejection at the planter's door causes him to aspire to correct such breaches of faith in his own reconstruction of the southern "design," he finds he cannot help but reproduce its assumptions about the inherent inequality of members of the working class, of nonwhites, and of women. Again, this ambivalent attitude toward ideological constructs can be understood as a register of the rhetorical use made of "contract" by opposing forces in the discourse of labor in the 1930s.

In a speech quoted by James Hodges, Bernard Cone, an owner of several cotton mills in North Carolina, articulates the common use of the concept of contract among antiunion businessmen: "I believe a man who is fortunate enough to have acquired or built a cotton mill, in this free country of ours, has the right . . . to invite other free men to come and work in his mill at prices he feels he can afford or is willing to pay." If the worker thus "invited" subsequently becomes dissatisfied with Cone's terms of employment, Cone says, "let him quit. Let him go elsewhere and seek another job more to his liking. Do not let him stand at the mill door and seek by violence to keep others from working who want to work and are satisfied with the terms."[24] In expressing the position of owners regarding the "freedom" workers should enjoy in contract agreements, Cone employs two of the strategies of elision we already observed in the automythologizing of Carnegie and Ford, and which union leaders of the 1930s would immediately isolate as contradictions in the arguments of owners. Cone's phrasing acknowledges, probably against his will, that the mills he "acquired" were in fact "built" by the labors of workers and financed through bonds and investments secured by the availability of a local labor force. And just as he attempts to substitute "built" for "acquired" and thereby mask his ultimate reliance upon social compacts rather than his own enterprise, he later conflates "what he can afford" in wages with what he "is willing to pay," thus disguising his profits from the labor of others under the cloak of operating expenses. These strategies were familiar to unions and workers alike and certainly did not disappear after federal labor legislation of the 1930s guaranteed the worker's right to collective bargaining regardless of what local laws and ordinances had been passed under the rubric of states' rights.[25]

Absalom, Absalom! is replete with characters who operate according to assumptions of equality in contract but finally are forced to recognize their inherently unequal bargaining positions. Bon is in such a position when he expects an "instant of indisputable recognition" from Sutpen, because he understands patrimony as a kind of contract whose terms require mutual recognition (*AA*, 255). It is the echo, too, in Wash Jones's refrain, "Well, Kernel, they kilt us but they ain't whupped us yet, air they?" (*AA*, 223). Both Bon and Jones know that society has marked them (by racial and class categorization) as inherently unequal, yet each believes that Sutpen can be held to certain responsibilities according to a "blood" or "class" compact which is no less binding for the fact that it is unwritten and unstated. When they feel that Sutpen has failed to honor his end of their respective agreements, each also seeks redress in one form or another. Sutpen, in other words, is much like the mill owner who uses contract as an ideological fiction but dispenses with it when those whom contract law is designed to protect seek to force him to honor his commitments.

As the history of the labor movement demonstrates, however, owners were not the only ones to use the ideology of contract in this way. In particular, women workers, an integral force in the labor movement in both the North and the South, consistently found themselves underrepresented by their putative leaders in contract negotiations. True to its function as a register of the contemporary debate over labor, Faulkner's text recognizes both the importance and the socially degraded status of women's labor—describing, for instance, Sutpen's sister's labor over the family's dirty clothes as "brutish and stupidly out of all proportion to its reward: the very primary essence of labor" (*AA*, 191). But more than this, the novel makes reproduction, a metaphor for other forms of women's labor, the essential, contradictory element in Sutpen's attempts to revise the design that "produced" him as a youth. Sutpen pledges to reconstruct the southern "design" but finds it is im-

possible to complete the list of its elements—"money, a house, a plantation, slaves, a family"—without including "incidentally, of course, a
wife" (*AA*, 212). His attempt to elide the "operative" most crucial to his
plan (reminiscent of Cone's efforts to obscure the manner of his acqui-
sition of his mills and his actual ability to compensate the labor that
built them) also signifies the use made of women's reproductive "functions" by both capital and labor throughout American labor history to
deny equal bargaining protection for women. In many instances, the
patriarchalism of the unions conspired with the paternalism of mill
owners in subordinating women's rights and concerns in labor disputes
to those of men, precisely because women carried the additional "labor"
responsibilities of bearing and raising children. Philip Foner's exhaustive history, *Women in the American Labor Movement,* makes clear the
crucial role of women in organizing and supporting a number of walk-
outs throughout the South in 1929, to protest stretch-out policies and
to demand better working conditions and equal pay for equal work. Yet
Foner also demonstrates that organized labor, especially the AFL, was
slow to support southern women workers. When the AFL did help organize women workers, Susan Lehrer writes, it "defined women almost
universally in terms of their functions within the home as wives and
mothers, and saw their work force participation as temporary or as in-
terference with their primary place within the home." Thus, although
women suffered the worst of both workplace and strike conditions in
order to improve working conditions in the textile industry, women's
labor concerns remained underrepresented by those "contracted" to
represent them.[26]

The unequal status of women workers in the labor movement is reflected in the various "contracts" Sutpen enters into with his first wife
in Haiti, with Ellen and Rosa Coldfield, and with Milly Jones. Sutpen
understands his relations with these women in terms of an agreement
that requires them to provide a certain kind of "labor" for him—
specifically, the labor that will produce white male offspring. Sutpen
feels justified in putting his Haitian wife "aside" when he learns that she
has misrepresented her ability to fulfill the racial clause of this agreement. Sutpen's caution in subsequent attempts, with Rosa and Milly
Jones, to pursue the same agreement attests to his continued belief in
"contract" as the ground upon which human relationships should be

built. For her part, Rosa knows enough to be suspicious of such pretensions. She admits she might have slept with Sutpen after his oblique proposal had he not added the clause conditioning their marriage upon her reproductive ability. Reproduction, as Susan Lehrer has demonstrated, was all too commonly the grounds upon which the assumption of women's inherent inequality was reasserted in contract negotiations. This fact becomes most clear in Wash Jones's attempts to negotiate his granddaughter's sexuality as though it were his own property, an appropriation that is confirmed when he feels personally affronted by Sutpen's insult toward the product of Milly's "labor." In each of these cases, because of the primacy attributed to their role as reproductive laborers, these women's rights as humans and as fellow workers are neglected, "masked" by a prevailing trope of equality in contract that serves in fact to privilege Sutpen, as well as his twentieth-century avatars on *both* sides of the labor debate.

Fictions of Labor, Capital, and Subjectivity

The fictions of labor and capital that are produced and reproduced in *Absalom, Absalom!* speak volumes about the opportunities for self-fashioning that are made available by volatile discursive environments. The economic crises of the 1920s and 1930s made available a wide range of new labor identities to owners, who could use them to promote themselves as self-made millionaires and entrepreneurs, and to workers, who were equally prepared to portray themselves as heroic producers of the nation's wealth. When we encounter these identities in Faulkner's writing, however, they appear as works in progress rather than as coherent, complete entities. Incoherence and internal irrationality are the inevitable result when one attaches one's sense of self to one's identity as a worker or owner, especially at a moment of convulsive change within the prevailing economic system. As much as we all might want to represent ourselves as coherent individuals, in fact our economic subjectivities are marked by kernels of irrationality, the "residue" of our chaotic economic histories. We can observe such kernels of irrationality within the narrative of Sutpen's various labor identities at moments of intense economic crisis, when Sutpen is forced to "slough off" one outmoded subjectivity after another or suffer the consequences for refusing to do so. But it is not only Sutpen's biography that has come to us in a form that demonstrates this phenomenon. Faulkner, too, has been constructed by his biographers as an opportunistic economic subject, willing to transform himself into various kinds of worker in order to survive the volatile economic environments he faced throughout his life. If Sutpen appears as one who is aware of the new labor positions made available by changing relations of production in his lifetime, this is because he has learned the lessons Faulkner learned in his own (chaotic) career as a laborer, which we can see him working through in his representations of Sutpen's various economic identities.

Sutpen enters into at least two different relations of production in *Absalom, Absalom!*, beginning with his family's move from the Appalachian Mountains to tidewater Virginia. Here he is introduced to a social formation based upon slave labor, and he begins his struggle to occupy the position of slaveholding planter. In Quentin's telling, the relations of production in a society based upon slave labor are totally foreign to the child Sutpen: "he had never even heard of, never imagined, a place, a land divided neatly up and actually owned by men who did nothing but ride over it on fine horses . . . while other people worked for them" (*AA*, 179). Sutpen had never imagined that there existed so many objects to be possessed, "or that the ones who owned the objects not only could look down on the ones that didn't, but could be supported in the downlooking not only by the others who owned objects," but also by those who didn't and never would (*AA*, 179). Clearly, this is an environment in which one's economic identity is constructed out of one's relation to other economic subjects. When Sutpen learns that he (as a white male) can have the land and the slaves and the fine house, provided he models himself after the planter ideal and first serves the necessary apprenticeship as an overseer on the Haitian plantation, he leaves immediately for the West Indies (*AA*, 192). It would seem that Sutpen simply imagines himself in the role of a planter/slaveholder and thereby overcomes the economic and social limitations of his prior labor identity. But this act of self-fashioning is predicated upon a certain availability of scripts derived from the economic base: it is only *after* Sutpen is introduced to the relations of labor and production of a slave economy that it is possible for him to imagine a different economic subjectivity for himself.

Thus, any interpretation of Sutpen's character—as antebellum planter, as postwar landowner, or as modern entrepreneur—must begin from the assumption that character is an effect of the prevailing economic structure, but also, with the caution that one's prior economic identity (the residue of a prior economic structure) might, at any moment, "abrupt" onto the scene in the form of incoherent behavior. This kind of eruption leads ultimately to Sutpen's murder, because it is the cause of Sutpen's fatal miscalculation with regard to Wash and Milly Jones.

Sutpen's economic subjectivity changes as a result of the South's defeat in the war. He can no longer occupy the position of a slaveholding planter because the relations of production that produced that subjectivity have been replaced by relations based upon "share" rather than slave labor. His contemporaries, those who "with pistols in their pockets gathered daily at secret meeting places in the towns," want to perpetuate the old relations, which is the same as saying they want to retain their advantageous roles as economic subjects in the region's prior economy of subject/object relations (*AA*, 130). But Sutpen again sloughs off his old economic identity. While he waits for another to be offered to him by the revised relations of production in the postwar economy, Rosa tells us, "he wasn't there. . . . Not absent from the place . . . only from the room . . . and that because he had to be elsewhere . . . himself diffused and in solution held by that electric furious immobile urgency" (*AA*, 129). Eventually, Sutpen's economic subjectivity becomes reconstituted, and he occupies the position of landowner and store operator in the new relations of production that have also created the economic roles of the freedman and, as Shreve tries to express it, "What is it? the word? white what?—Yes, trash" (*AA*, 147). The economic convulsions that Sutpen must now navigate are perhaps best represented by the fact that in the postwar South's new economy, his relation to Wash Jones can no longer be imagined as that of "baron to retainer" (*AA*, 221). Jones is now Sutpen's employee at the store, and this revision of labor relations is ultimately fatal for Sutpen when Jones, who feels improved as a subject in the new economy, retaliates for Sutpen's breach of a contract that Jones believes Sutpen has established with him and his daughter Milly. Jones knows that Sutpen "will make hit right" between himself and Milly, but when Milly bears Sutpen a daughter rather than a son, the irrational kernel of Sutpen's economic subjectivity, the residue of his prior identity as an antebellum planter, expresses itself in the only way it can—by denying his daughter's rights and by canceling the implicit contract between himself and Jones and Milly (*AA*, 228). Ironically, while Sutpen's final gesture as an economic subject—his rejection of Milly and his daughter by her—is thus an expression of an anachronistic economic subjectivity, Jones's response—he never would have thought to murder Sutpen in his role as Sutpen's "retainer"—is only possible as a consequence of his revised labor positioning.

Faulkner's handling of Sutpen's character in the midst of economic instability demonstrates his awareness of the possibilities of resignification that accompany discursive change (in this case, changes in the discourse of labor) and of the narratives of legitimation which seem the inevitable by-product of one person's exploitation of another. This is, in part, the result of convulsions in Faulkner's own Depression-era South, which occasioned the transformation of Sutpen's postwar "share" economy into a cash economy in the 1930s and after. As Richard Godden writes, this transformation was accelerated when landowners of the 1930s learned they could increase their profits by paying wages at planting and harvest time instead of "sharing" the government's relief money according to agreements with sharecroppers on their land.[27] These Depression-era changes in the economy of labor relations in the South made available a wide array of subject positions which Faulkner, himself a small landowner both supporting and supported by a number of tenants, had to negotiate. But then, in his primary vocation as a writer, Faulkner already was experimenting with new labor identities in the 1930s and, like Sutpen, trying to capitalize upon the new opportunities for production and profit made available by them.

I mean, again, the relations of production under Hollywood's studio system. That Faulkner was immediately aware of the significantly different labor possibilities made available by Hollywood's mode of production compared to the economy he previously inhabited as a Mississippi writer dealing with New York editors and publishers is evident in an analogy he developed in a letter to Ben Wasson in 1933: his own position was like "that of a field hand: either of us (me or MGM) to call it off without notice, they to pay me by the week, and to pay a bonus on each original story."[28] As a writer, Faulkner saw himself making a transition from share to cash labor similar to that made by agricultural workers in his home state under changes brought about by the New Deal. On one hand, this comparison exposes Faulkner's blindness to the kinds of exploitation suffered by agricultural workers in the South, to which he was not exposed as a celebrated writer in Hollywood. But it is interesting that Faulkner described this new arrangement as a liberating one for both himself and MGM, even though Blotner's biography demonstrates that Faulkner was at a disadvantage in many of his contractual agreements as a screenwriter. Clearly, when he wrote this letter to Wasson, Faulkner hoped to cast himself as an independent contractor, liberated, in some way, by an agreement that allowed MGM to fire him at any time. This is exactly the kind of freedom in contract that mill owners and other capitalists wanted to ensure (for themselves) against labor's demands for certain worker protections. Likewise, it is precisely the kind of "free" relationship between the states and the federal government fantasized by those states' rights advocates who used their doctrine to denounce the National Labor Relations Act in 1935.[29] In this respect, Sutpen is an expression of Faulkner's own efforts to navigate the chaotic economic environment of the 1930s.

It is important to recognize, of course, that the demands of southern textile workers were not the same as those of Hollywood studio workers, and that neither of these labor contexts evokes precisely the same arguments as those produced over slavery the century before. But labor protest in both regions would have demonstrated to Faulkner the same lesson we have observed in Thomas Sutpen: workers are empowered most when they recognize their position in the economy of labor relations available to them, and recognize as well that other, possibly better positions would be made available if radical change were brought about in the social formation's dominant relations of production. This is certainly the lesson Loosh has learned when, as I argued in chapter 1, he dismantles Bayard and Ringo's representation of the southern order, in order to force the production of new subject positions to be occupied by him and other freed slaves in a reconstructed South. It is also important to recognize that storytelling, as a kind of labor, is often employed by those in possession of the means of production to mask the relations of labor that privilege some workers over others. Sutpen demonstrates his understanding of this when he masks his enslavement of "free" labor during his pursuit of the French architect, with the story of his own rise to power "from nothing." And Faulkner, throughout this novel, demonstrates his own understanding of the "masking" function of narrative as he persistently calls our attention to the fictions of labor and capital that privilege some forms of subjectivity over others.

CHAPTER 4

Ethnographic Allegory and *The Hamlet*

In order to share the shock of contact with a strange situation, I should like to wipe my vision clean of the effect of wont and habit and to see Southerntown again afresh as I first visited it.

 —John Dollard, *Caste and Class in a Southern Town,* 1937

Old City and Old and Rural Counties are located in the heart of the "deep South." . . . Before the Civil War, great plantations flourished here. Many of the planters made cotton fortunes, built great houses, and lived in feudal grandeur.

 —Allison Davis, Burleigh Gardner, and Mary Gardner, *Deep South:*
  A Social Anthropological Study of Caste and Class, 1941

Frenchman's Bend was a section of rich river-bottom country lying twenty miles southeast of Jefferson. Hill-cradled and remote, definite yet without boundaries, straddling into two counties and owning allegiance to neither, it had been the original grant and site of a tremendous pre–Civil War plantation, the ruins of which—the gutted shell of an enormous house with its fallen stables and slave quarters and overgrown gardens and brick terraces and promenades—were still known as the Old Frenchman place.

 —Faulkner, *The Hamlet,* 3

The unstated premise of many "cultural" readings of *The Hamlet* is that Faulkner's text can be read as a "thick description" not only of Frenchman's Bend but also of Faulkner's Mississippi, something like an ethnographic account of a group of people and a way of life no longer available to us, except through the stories they told about themselves or that others told about them. This anthropological approach to the novel follows James Clifford's observation that "much ethnography, taking its distance from totalizing anthropology, seeks to evoke multiple (but not limitless) allegories." Reading *The Hamlet* as something like an ethnographer's field notes, these cultural critics have produced some startling observations about the governing myths of Frenchman's Bend; its political and social organization and division according to kinship, race, class, and gender; and its evolving modes of communication and exchange, from storytelling, trade, and barter to Flem Snopes's calculated profits from interest loans and credit capitalism.[1] Generally, these analyses are extremely helpful, but they neglect the relation between Faulkner's "ethnographic attitude" in *The Hamlet* and the contemporaneous development of the ethnographic method within the discourse of anthropology. Accounting for this relation will involve interpreting *The Hamlet* as a meta-commentary upon the practice of ethnography itself, one that represents both the problems of Victorian-era anthropological discourse and the solutions to these problems introduced by the ethnographic method.[2]

The ethnographic approach to the study of other cultures developed in significant ways in the 1930s and early 1940s. Until the 1920s, anthropologists had been guided by the principle of evolutionary progress. Their texts were framed as narratives of the development of mankind from "primitive" superstition and darkness toward the modern, rational creatures that Victorian audiences (both English and American) could recognize in themselves. But Bronislaw Malinowski's description of the ethnographic method in *Argonauts of the Western Pacific* (1922) called for the suspension of grand narratives of evolutionary progress and for a focus instead upon isolated cultures and the goal of presenting them "from the native's point of view." Thus, while "armchair" anthropologists of the nineteenth century depended heavily upon "traveller's accounts, colonial records, and missionary scholarship for firsthand data," Malinowski called ethnographers to position themselves within the culture of study; as James Clifford describes it, "on the one hand grasping the sense of specific occurrences and gestures empathetically, on the other stepping back to situate these meanings in wider contexts."[3] In Foucault's more expansive terms, ethnography emerged as one of the "great mutations of science" in the 1920s—a new form of the "will to truth" within the discourse of anthropology, carrying its own rules of formation and exclusion, and determining in differently articulated ways "the manner in which knowledge is employed in a society, the way in which it is exploited, divided and, in some ways, attributed." Although for Foucault the emergence of a new discipline is not the result of a founding subject, it does imply the production of new subject positions, because a new discipline introduces restrictions or "conditions under which it may be employed," just as it imposes "a certain number of rules upon those individuals who employ it."[4] The emergence of ethnography in the 1920s demonstrates this because it was precisely when Malinowski and his followers championed the role of the "participant-observer" that anthropologists became compelled to critique their own positions as subjects in the representational narratives they produced about other cultures. My primary goal in this chapter, then, is to observe symptoms of a similarly autocritical attitude within the narrative voices of *The Hamlet* in order to gauge the degree of contiguity between the academic discourses of anthropology in the 1920s and 1930s and Faulkner's literary discourse—especially his "literary" representations of southern culture—in roughly the same period.

In many ways, the ethnographic method was inherent in traditional anthropological discourse, especially in its alternating use of what Mary Louise Pratt calls anthropology's "personal" and "scientific-objective" voices. In the genealogy described by Pratt, western conventions for representing other cultures date back to the first European narratives of exploration, conquest, and colonization. From these, and from the writings of missionaries that followed European colonization of America, Africa, and Asia, Victorian anthropology developed as a discourse whose written texts relied heavily upon the tropes and narrative conventions of the earlier "travel" narratives. As a consequence of these hybrid origins, Pratt writes, "personal narrative persists alongside objectifying description in ethnographic writing." Although the tension between personal and scientific forms of authority has been present since the founding of anthropology as a science, it became "especially acute since the advent of fieldwork as a methodological norm" because the result of fieldwork, the ethnographic text, reverts so overtly to the conventions of nineteenth-century travel narratives.[5] Pratt's observation suggests that the introduction of the ethnographic method within the "science of Man" made it impossible to continue to repress the bifurcation of the speaking subject of anthropological discourse. It is precisely this splintering of the speaking subject that we can observe in *The Hamlet* and other efforts to "tell about the South" in the 1930s, especially at moments of incoherence and inconsistency in the voices these texts use to represent southern culture.

The emergence of ethnographic practices within anthropology in the first half of the twentieth century thus provides another opportunity to observe a connection between subjectivity in Faulkner's texts and the historical discontinuities in the discourses of culture that produce, modify, and sometimes destabilize it. Faulkner's experiments in *The Hamlet* with the literary conventions of realism and modernism juxtapose, on an allegorical level, the two categories of voice ("personal narrative" and "objectifying description"), which, according to Pratt, competed with one another for representational authority at the moment of emergence of ethnographic practices in anthropological discourse. This interpretation of Faulkner's experiments with voice suggests a certain homology between Ratliff's position as an "authorizing" subject within Faulkner's literary discourse and that of several ethnographers and sociologists of the 1930s who took the South as their object of study and who produced ethnographies detailing their fieldwork. Put simply, Ratliff, as well as Faulkner's other narrating subjects, encounter problems of representation that are similar to those encountered by modern-era ethnographers. Faulkner's modernism, in this context, cannot be explained solely by his position as a literary modernist. His experiments with conventions of literary discourse (such as the pastoral, romance, and various forms of modernist irony) throughout his career, and especially in *The Hamlet,* signify a moment of transformation in the discourses of culture in the modern period that extends beyond the boundaries of literary history. They are indicative of, and are reciprocally influenced by, the experimentation with voice that occurred in other modern discourses, such as the discourses of historiography, law, labor, and—as I will now argue—anthropology.

Two Voices of Anthropology in *The Hamlet*

We can begin this examination of the emergence of the ethnographic method in anthropology, and of Faulkner's experiments with voice in

The Hamlet, by looking at book 3 of *The Hamlet,* "The Long Summer." This text is commonly understood to alternate between two narrative perspectives: the first is determined by Ratliff's modernist ironic stance toward the people and events of Frenchman's Bend; the second is most evident in the section that chronicles a day in the life of Ike Snopes and Jack Houston's cow, which parodies nineteenth-century conventions of romance and the pastoral.[6] The juxtaposition of these two narrative perspectives suggests the problems of representation inherent in nineteenth-century modes of literary narration and, analogously, in Victorian anthropology's conventions of "objectifying description." It also suggests the role of irony as a solution to these problems in both literary and anthropological contexts. Yet this juxtaposition also reveals the new set of representational dilemmas that attended the emergence of irony as a trope of modernism in both literary and anthropological (ethnographic) texts.

Ike Snopes is devoid of interior subjectivity. His thoughts are available to us only in the mediated form of his nearly constant moaning and drooling, or in the narrator's frequent surmises about what he is "probably" attempting or "perhaps" thinking, or what "nobody ever knew" about Ike (*TH,* 184, 185, 187). Unable to speak for himself, lacking any real subjectivity—unlike, for instance, Benjy of *The Sound and the Fury,* to whose complex interior we are permitted access—Ike also is devoid of motivation and agency except as these devolve from primitive desire and instinctual behavior. Ike is always progressing "backward into time," living in a primitive world in which he eats "things which the weary long record of shibboleth and superstition had taught his up-right kind to call filth," and always acting on "pure instinct" (*TH,* 196–97, 202).

The obstacles that Faulkner's pastoral parody places in the way of a reader seeking access to Ike's subjectivity are homologous with those produced by the narrative structures of Victorian "evolutionary" anthropology, and therefore signify dilemmas of nineteenth-century modes of representation that cross formal disciplinary boundaries.[7] Faulkner's location of Ike within an early moment of a "long record of shibboleth and superstition," for instance, signifies nineteenth-century anthropology's insertion of cultural Others into the early stages of its narrative of evolutionary progress toward "ever higher standards of rationality." It also represents the problem of the metaphor of "salvage" within anthropological texts. Edward Said's *Orientalism* locates the origins of "salvage" tropes in the narratives produced by Western colonization of the East, in which the Western (narrating) subject is active while the (represented) Eastern Other is typically passive. Originating in the rhetoric of Western colonization and conquest, the metaphor of "salvage" was incorporated into the narratives of Victorian anthropology, and as James Clifford has observed, it survived the emergence of the ethnographic method in the 1920s, so that even in the experimental ethnographies that followed Malinowski in the 1920s and 1930s, "it is assumed that the other society is weak and 'needs' to be represented by an outsider (and that what matters in its life is its past, not present or future)."[8] Signaled in anthropological texts of both the nineteenth and twentieth centuries by a sudden shift to what has been called the "ethnographic present tense," the structure of salvage is reproduced in "The Long Summer" when Faulkner tropes Ike's affair within a temporal framework that is timeless and that seems to move inexorably toward destruction: "At the same moment all three of them cross the crest and descend into the bowl of evening and are extinguished" (*TH*, 205).[9] In sum, just as Victorian conventions of anthropological discourse represented other cultures as inhabiting an early, primitive stage in the historical evolution of mankind, and just as the modern ethnographic method reinscribed this trope in its deploying of a timeless present tense when it attempted to record cultures "from the native's point of view," Faulkner's representations of Ike and his cow are conditioned by a pervasive "rapid twilight" that "effaces them from the day's tedious recording." Thus it inscribes Ike within a chronological space when "yesterday was not, tomorrow is not," a space devoid of any possibility of coherent subjectivity, of any meaningful history, and foreclosed from any practical future (*TH*, 183, 205).

We must keep in mind, however, that Faulkner's experiments with literary conventions are often attempts to seek a way out of the epistemological limitations of any given language or literary mode. Richard Moreland's close attention to Faulkner's experiments with modernist irony and humor are instructive in this regard, for it is precisely in the recognition of the subjectivity of the Other that, according to Moreland, Faulkner's characters potentially have a way out of the debilitating traditions of irony available to them (and to Faulkner). Faulkner's revisions of the "Barn Burning" material for the opening chapter of *The Hamlet*, for instance, impute possibilities of agency and subjectivity for Abner Snopes, despite the traditions of irony which lead Jody Varner habitually (and destructively) to assume Abner's total (feudal) subjection before the Varner family. Trading on his power as a known arsonist, "Abner seems now neither the condemned object of Jody's innocent judgement, nor the object of Abner's own ironic recognition of that same judgement: Abner must be instead another unpredictably resourceful subject."[10] Moreland's insight into Faulkner's use of irony as a mode of representation suggests a second homology between Faulkner's experiments with literary conventions (in this case the conventions of modernist irony) and the contemporary "moment" of ethnographic emergence in the human sciences. Drawing upon Hayden White's analysis in *Metahistory* of tropes of historical narratives in the nineteenth century, George Marcus and Michael Fischer observe a convergence upon irony as a dominant mode of representational discourse across the human sciences at the turn of the century. "During the nineteenth century," they write, "there had been a sustained series of efforts to find a 'realist' mode of description. All ended in irony, however, because there were a number of equally comprehensive and plausible, yet mutually exclusive conceptions of the same events."[11] Irony thus allowed the narratives of cultural experience produced within the human sciences to represent competing cultural perspectives—to recognize, in other words, the agency of all participants in a given social event. It is precisely this embracing of irony—and the developing of new ways to deploy it in the representation of Others—that Faulkner attempts in *The Hamlet*, with the effect, as Moreland observes, that this text insists upon the recognition of the subjectivity of traditionally marginalized characters, such as the rural poor farmer Abner Snopes.

As Moreland's reading of *The Hamlet* recognizes, such moments of insistence center upon the character Ratliff, whose narrative perspective I would read as an analogue of the ethnographic perspective developed within anthropology at the time of Faulkner's composition of this novel's individual stories. As Moreland has discovered, Ratliff's revised perspective upon cultural experience in *The Hamlet* produces narratives that represent the agency and subjectivity of the marginalized poor more completely than the nineteenth-century conventions of romance, pastoral, and realism, whose failures as modes of discourse on the Other are signified by Faulkner's insistent parodies and exaggerations (in his depictions of Ike, Houston's cow, Eula, etc.). Like the new ethnographers of the 1920s and 1930s, Ratliff speaks from what Mary Louise Pratt describes as "a moving position already within or down in the middle of things, looking and being looked at, talking and being talked at."[12] For instance, when Faulkner's parody of literary pastoral gives way again to Ratliff's encounter with Ike and the cow behind Mrs. Littlejohn's barn, "it was as though it were himself inside the stall with the cow, himself looking . . . at the row of faces watching him" (*TH*, 217). Like the (hybrid) ethnographic position, however, Ratliff's stance in *The Hamlet* is subject to the same dilemmas of nineteenth-century representation that created the conditions of its emergence as a mode of discourse on the Other—the dilemma of the "salvage" metaphor, for instance, which caused nineteenth-century anthropologists to assume the inevitable extinction of weaker, "primitive" cultures following contact with more powerful Western ones, and which emerges again in *The Hamlet* when Ratliff approaches Abner Snopes's farm and perceives a "cluttered desolation" inhabited by "the two last survivors of a lost species which had established residence in it," who make sounds to one another "the very apparent absence from which of any discernible human speech or language seemed but natural" (*TH*, 52). Indeed, just as the ethnographic method reproduced old dilemmas of representation while simultaneously introducing new ones, we can observe in Ratliff's "fieldwork" in Frenchman's Bend a number of representational blind spots which distort his various accounts—especially those that concern the "rural poor" Snopeses.

One of these blind spots results from the problem of bias in information gathering, which has attended the practice of ethnography since its emergence, not least in ethnographic projects in the South in the 1930s. John Dollard's *Caste and Class in a Southern Town*, one example of the many ethnographic studies of specific southern societies conducted in the 1930s, contains the following anecdote in a chapter entitled "Bias":

> One hot summer morning I made bold to present a letter of introduction to a well-known southern writer. He met me on his porch and,

after an exchange of formalities, inquired what I was doing. I told him briefly. He responded at once that I had little chance of learning anything about the personality of Negroes; he had lived among them for years and had not learned much; so what hope could there be for me? Since I had heard this before, I did not take it too seriously. Then he said something, however, which made me angry but which eventually I took very seriously. I had the idea in the back of my mind, he told me, that he was prejudiced and untrustworthy, and I came prepared not to believe what he had to say. I assumed unconsciously that he was blinded by race prejudice, as it is called in the North. I must feel this way, he said, because all northerners come south with this idea, no matter what their formal protestations may be.[13]

It is possible that Faulkner was the "well-known southern writer" Dollard refers to, since "Southerntown," it turns out, is Indianola, Mississippi, about an hour and a half's drive from Oxford.[14] Regardless, the issues of racial bias signified in this anecdote resonate in Ratliff's representations of race and class in the stories he narrates in *The Hamlet*. A first example of this occurs in Ratliff's narration of material previously published in the short story "Barn Burning"—most evidently in those portions of the story that Faulkner revised for the novel. Ratliff is not a character in "Barn Burning." His removal from the events of that story requires him to rely upon a number of informants to construct his inaugural narrative about the Snopeses in *The Hamlet*. Yet he both effaces and anonymizes these informants even as he appropriates their authority as highly credible participants in the events of the story.

In "Barn Burning," the story's omniscient narrator can attend to Sarty's thoughts at the moment of his and his father's rejection at the door of De Spain's house: "The door opened so promptly that the boy knew the Negro must have been watching them all the time, an old man with neat grizzled hair, in a linen jacket, who stood barring the door."[15] In the version of this story that opens *The Hamlet*, Ratliff's authority as narrator is dependent upon the house servant's participation in, and later retelling of, the event. Yet Ratliff's appropriation and re-narration of this material details neither the servant's experience of the event nor any facts about the moment of transmission of the story from the servant to Ratliff: "the nigger said Abner stepped in it [the horse manure] on deliberate purpose. Maybe the nigger was watching them through the front window. Anyway . . ." (*TH*, 16). The servant's loss of agency in Ratliff's version, from one who certainly had been watching Abner and Sarty, to one who "maybe" was, is paralleled by his linguistic demotion from "Negro" (in "Barn Burning") to "nigger" (in Ratliff's narrated speech). Moreover, as Ratliff's story continues, it becomes clear that his source of information regarding Abner's history of barn burning is not the crucial issue "anyway"; what matters most to Ratliff is the telling information about the Snopeses over which he now has total control.

Another example of the problem of information gathering signified by Ratliff's re-narration of the "Barn Burning" material is Ratliff's effacing of a firsthand witness to De Spain's arrival at the torched barn: "De Spain got there on his mare about the same time," Ratliff says, "because somebody heard him passing in the road" (*TH*, 18). Later, Ratliff knows that De Spain hurried to Abner's house, "according to the gait the fellow heard him passing in the road" (*TH*, 19). Again, details about the transmission of this information are subsumed beneath the more important project (for Ratliff) of producing himself as an authority upon this event. Although Ratliff's construction of an authoritative position for himself in his relation of the "Barn Burning" material mesmerizes Jody Varner ("Varner's suffused swollen face glared down at him" [*TH*, 17]), his method of piecing these fragments together reproduces fallacies inherent in an ethnographic attitude that relies upon the experiences of actual participants but fails to inscribe within its narratives a believably human agency or subjectivity for those participants. At such moments, ethnographers necessarily fall back upon their own positions as outsiders and contaminate their narratives with their own cultural/professional prejudices, assumptions, and purposes.

Examinations of the manner in which ethnographers met Malinowski's challenge to represent other cultures "from the native's point of view" have led to intense scrutiny of what Renato Rosaldo calls the "politics of domination" governing relationships between ethnographers and their informants. Rosaldo especially calls attention to how this politics of domination might contaminate informants' willingness—or even ability—to represent themselves and their villages, as well as ethnographers' capacity to comprehend informants' self-representations. Rosaldo argues convincingly that one way ethnographers construct their own positions of authority is by detaching the information they collect from the sometimes oppressive contexts within which it is collected, thus obscuring the relations of power and knowledge that govern such moments of information exchange. He observes, for instance, that in some of the reported interviews in *The Nuer* (1940), E. E. Evans-Pritchard elides the historical context of colonial terror, leading him to interpret an informant's reluctance to state his name and the name of his lineage as an admirable example of "European" bullheadedness and as evidence of a perverse desire to obstruct knowledge, rather than as a canny avoidance of self-incrimination in the village's recent confrontation with colonial soldiers.[16] We can observe similar issues related to the production of authority (whether ethnographic or, in the case of Ratliff, narrative, economic, and eventually political) in *The Hamlet* if we interpret the character Ratliff as a vehicle of ethnography's modernist-ironic voice, and if we scrutinize his methods of constructing his position of authority over the local narratives of Frenchman's Bend.

Ratliff's authority to tell about the events of "Barn Burning," in which he was not a participant, is an effect of his appropriation of information from firsthand agents who are then effaced or otherwise unacknowledged. A similar instance of appropriation occurs in his relation of material first published as "Fool about a Horse." This story's original narrator is an unnamed child of Abner Snopes. Faulkner's substitution of Ratliff for the original participant/narrator Snopes again has the effect of reinforcing Ratliff's "ethnographic" authority in Frenchman's Bend. Ratliff, in *The Hamlet*'s version, has barely begun to narrate Abner's experiences with Pat Stamper when he is interrupted by a skeptical voice: "How did you find all this out? I reckon you was there too"; Ratliff's credentials, in response to this challenge, are impeccable: "I was," he says, "I went with him that day to get the separator" (*TH*, 33).[17] Faulkner's revision thus underscores the imperative of firsthand experience for a narrator/ethnographer (Ratliff), even as it participates in the substitution of a privileged speaker for the voice of an indigenous subject (the unnamed Snopes of "Fool about a Horse").

Indeed, many of Faulkner's revisions of previously published material for *The Hamlet* heighten Ratliff's practice of using local narratives to assert the priority of his own perspective over the experience of others. In the original of "Lizards in Jamshyd's Courtyard," for instance, the transmission of narrative is a secondary concern for Ratliff (in his previous incarnation as Suratt), not even worth relating in its totality. He begins one story—"Let me tell you what I heard about one of them Grimms down there last month; it might be Eustace they tell it on"— only to be interrupted (and superseded) by the story's omniscient narrator: "He achieved his anecdote skillfully above the guffaws."[18] In *The Hamlet,* such opportunities for the assertion of Ratliff's proprietorship over local information are not left unnarrated. Here, too, there is a greater emphasis upon Ratliff's storytelling *voice.* Whereas in "Lizards in Jamshyd's Courtyard," Ratliff/Suratt merely has "a gift for anecdote and gossip," Faulkner's introduction of Ratliff in *The Hamlet* stresses the qualities of a storyteller's voice, "pleasant, lazy, equable," "pleasant and drawling and anecdotal" (*TH,* 14, 17, 138).

Ratliff's is the voice of modern ethnography straining to tell about cultural experience from the native's point of view but manufacturing that view from personal prejudices and assumptions when it is not directly available to the fieldworker. If, as Marcus and Fischer observe, ethnographers gained professional legitimation from such encounters, Ratliff gains in reputation, professional contacts, increased contracts, and ultimately higher profits (from the sale of sewing machines, and from his other money-making schemes). Another benefit of successful storytelling shared by both Ratliff and ethnographers in the South in the 1930s is access to other, more powerful informants. In the case of John Dollard, for instance, chance conversations with working-class informants on the streets of Southerntown would often lead to interviews with members of the upper classes of civic, political, or religious organizations. But this could lead to another problem of bias, as Dollard is aware: "Undoubtedly many researchers who have gone south unaware of this bias have been seduced by the hospitality of the middle- and upper-class southern white people, have formed agreeable ties with them, and have there-upon been pulled into the southern mode of perception of the racial problem." Dollard, on the whole, is quite self-conscious in this regard. He devotes two chapters of his account to questions of methodology and bias, and he is wary throughout of the potential color bias any white ethnographer might develop. Nevertheless, as he relates his informants' understanding of social life in Southerntown, Dollard leaves uncorrected an obvious demographic limitation of his study. In all, he tells us, he had "fifty or sixty informants, that is, persons with whom I had at least three or four conversations of some length"; yet, eight pages earlier he has admitted that only nine of these are black, three women and six men. Despite his burdened efforts to be conscious of bias, Dollard never explicitly addresses this racial imbalance in the pool of informants from which he draws his sociological conclusions.[19]

Both *Caste and Class in a Southern Town* and *Deep South,* another sociological study conducted during the 1930s, focus on race and class relations in "typical" southern cities. But since the fieldworker in the first case is white, and in both cases they belong to what they themselves would classify as the "upper" class, they encounter immediate difficulties in accessing each of the categories they wish to describe. The ethnographers of *Deep South* are less self-conscious than Dollard about their sources of information, with the result that their account of life in "Old City" is disproportionately weighted toward the experiences of middle- and upper-class whites. In their analysis, the white caste is broken into upper, middle, and lower classes, and each of these, in turn, is divided into upper and lower halves. As they describe the characteristics of each of these six groups, their information becomes increasingly sketchy and circumstantial: the initial description of "upper-upper" and "lower-upper" whites, for instance, occupies four and a half pages, is supplemented by several direct quotes, and is accompanied by a chart which clearly sets this group apart from the middle and lower classes. The "upper-lower" and "lower-lower" classes, in contrast, take only a page and a half to describe, and these contain no direct quotes. This brief introduction to the white class system in "Old City" is followed by over one hundred pages of in-depth information about the social organization of whites. But fewer than fifty pages are devoted to black social organization, and much of this information, the writers note, comes to them from "newspaper records of social affairs, lists of the members of churches and associations, and records kept by the field workers of clique activities"—not, it seems, from intensive, one-on-one interviews. Reading *Deep South,* it becomes obvious that its collaborators' ability to represent a whole social world was limited by their own caste, and especially class, identities.[20]

Ratliff's use of anonymous and underacknowledged informants to insinuate himself into the more powerful families of Frenchman's Bend similarly compromises his objectivity as a narrator of cultural experience there. For in the process of establishing his authority by retailing the stories of other informants, Ratliff gains access to the most privileged "informant" in the village: Will Varner, local land baron and "the fountainhead if not of law at least of advice and suggestion" (*TH*, 5–6). Ratliff appears to have cornered the market on Varner as an informant. Everyone else is wrong in guessing Varner's thoughts as he sits in front of the old mansion, "since it was only to an itinerant sewing-machine agent named Ratliff" that he ever confided them (*TH*, 7). Likewise, scattered throughout *The Hamlet* are more oblique references to Jody as the source of much of Ratliff's information—about Jody's first impression of Flem Snopes on the road outside Abner's house, for instance, "which Varner was to remember and speculate about only later" (*TH*, 24)—presumably, to Ratliff. As a consequence of his conscription into the Varners' privileged circle, much of Ratliff's narrative in *The Hamlet* reifies the social stratification of Frenchman's Bend, and for the same reason that the ethnographic attempts of the 1930s fall short of their aim to present a balanced account of life in specific southern societies. In each case, the primary sources of information are members of the class and caste whose status in the community most depends upon the objectification and marginalization of others. One result for *The Hamlet*, as James Snead has observed, is that the novel's "classical realist narrator" follows the local (white) custom of denying that blacks even exist in Frenchman's Bend—and consequently, of maintaining that race presents no problem of representation there—despite evidence to the contrary embedded within the narrative itself.[21]

A more direct indication that Ratliff's perspective as (occasional) narrator has been compromised by his induction into the worldview of the ruling class of Frenchman's Bend occurs in the final scene of book 1, in which Jack Houston makes his fatal demand to Mink Snopes of a dollar a day impound fee for Snopes's wandering cow. "I warned you," Houston tells Mink.

"You know the law in this country. A man must keep his stock up after ground's planted, or take the consequences."

"I would have expected you to have fences that would keep a yearling up," Snopes said. (*TH,* 100)

Ratliff is present on the gallery of Will Varner's general store when this exchange takes place, but because of his itinerant status, he finds that he has entered into the middle of a conversation for which the only discursive references immediately available to him are to animal husbandry, and to a familiar (and local) legal convention. So his first reaction, once Mink and Houston have left, is to seek from the other men on the gallery the several layers of information that might make the event more understandable:

"I dont quite understand about that fence. I gathered it was Snopes's yearling in Houston's field."

"It was," the man who had spat said. "He lives on a piece of what used to be Houston's land. It belongs to Will Varner now. That is, Varner foreclosed on it about a year ago."

"That is, it was Will Varner Houston owed the money to," a second said. "It was the fences on that he was talking about." (*TH,* 100)

With this information, Ratliff can reread the exchange between Snopes and Houston, and recognize in it the additional discourses of modern banking and usury, and, more importantly, of class distinctions as they are articulated in land ownership. This additional information clarifies Mink's response: "I see," Ratliff says; "Just conversational remarks. Unnecessary"—unnecessary, that is, because the land rented to Mink is now Varner's, and thus the only person "wronged" here, according to Ratliff's view, is Jack Houston, who is within his rights to keep Mink's cow penned up until Mink claims it (*TH,* 101).

This scene is interesting not only for its representation of the several discourses that inform cultural experience in Frenchman's Bend, but also for Ratliff's response, his uncharacteristic blocking-off of narrative play when the exchange between the two men is described more "thickly" for him by others on the gallery. When Ratliff believes a Snopes or some other marginalized poor white has acted dishonestly, he is eager to "unpack" the humor of the situation, to explore all the mental maneuverings that might have preceded a particular event. His comment about Flem "grazing up" the village, for instance, follows a playful interpretation of I.O.'s appointment as schoolmaster; and his prophecy that "Snopes can come and Snopes can go, but Will Varner looks like he is fixing to snopes forever" follows a humorous exchange between Ratliff and Bookwright about I.O.'s representation of Mink's case against Houston (*TH*, 77, 179). But here, where a more objective observer might be critical of a system that forces tenants to build fences on their landlord's property or risk losing their livestock, he is silent. By this moment, apparently, Ratliff has become so immersed in the episteme of the Varners that the plight of those at the mercy of this dominant family seems irrelevant to him. Structurally, this blindness is similar to his inability to criticize the patriarchalism that motivates Henry Armstid's abuse of his wife in the "Spotted Horses" episode; Ratliff does not see Armstid's abuse of his wife, only his "laziness" (*TH*, 346). In each of these cases, Ratliff (to borrow Dollard's phrasing) has become "seduced by the hospitality" of a group (the Varners, the patriarchs of Frenchman's Bend), and as a consequence his various narratives about life in the village are contaminated in much the same way as Dollard's and the *Deep South* authors'.

Ratliff's role as the vehicle of anthropology's emergent voices suggests both the advantages of the ethnographic method and the extent to which ethnography introduced new dilemmas of representation while also reproducing those of nineteenth-century anthropology. Like the anthropologists we have observed, he strives to maintain a balance between participation and observation, but like these contemporaries, he carries with him a great deal of ideological baggage that makes this ideal stance impossible. If this were only an "academic" problem—an incapacity of scientific languages to comprehend cultural experience—it is possible that Faulkner's narrative apparatuses would not mimic the fallacies of anthropological discourse so closely. But in fact, in the 1930s the ethnographic attitude toward the South conditioned the practice of representation not only in the "academic" disciplines (such as anthropology), but in other discursive regions as well. This is true of Faulkner's literary discourse, and it is true of the many governmental agencies created during the New Deal to communicate to Americans the federal response to the crises of the Depression.

One example of a government-funded project that reiterates both the goals and fallacies of the ethnographic method is *These Are Our Lives* (1939), a collection of "life histories" put together by the Federal Writers' Project under the regional direction of W. T. Couch. In Couch's words, this series of interviews with victims of the Depression was meant to provide "faithful representations of living persons . . . a fair picture of the structure and working of society." In Couch's praise of the life history as *"written from the standpoint of the individual himself"* (italics in original), we can hear an echo of anthropology's new goal of presenting other cultures "from the native's point of view." Yet the stories in this collection are fraught with the problems of representation that we have already observed in Ratliff's attitude toward Frenchman's Bend: they purport to be authentic representations of "real" southerners, yet every story is written by an "author," and many, Couch admits, were edited by a third party. In addition, these "authentic" histories have been fictionalized: "All names of persons have been changed, and where there is any danger of identification, places also." Like the sociological studies, which inadvertently weighted the experiences of the upper classes more heavily than those of others, and like Ratliff's own immersion in the Varners' perspective on Frenchman's Bend, this volume's focus offers the longest life history in the "On the Farm" section for the "landlord." Finally, despite Couch's attempt to inscribe these "life histories" within the conventions of social-scientific discourse, they clearly perform an ideological function as they rehearse the hardships of the Depression, and move toward some celebration of the Roosevelt administration's response. "Get Out and Hoe," for instance, quotes one informant: "It seems like that man in Washington has got a real love for the people in his heart, and I believe it's due to him and his helpers that the poor renters are goin' to get a chance." And in the collection's final history, "Weary Willie," a worker in the Civilian Conservation Corps, gushes: "This is better clothes than I ever got at home . . . before I got to the CCC." The dilemmas of representation that attended the shift toward ethnography in the 1930s, then, were hardly unique to the "academic" texts of anthropology. They permeated these texts, but they also are "refracted" in the structures of representation deployed by others who sought to "tell about the South" in the 1930s, from Faulkner's literary texts, to the texts produced by agencies of the federal government in the midst of the crisis of the Depression.[22]

Ethnography, Photography, and Other New Deal Apparatuses

As it reproduces tensions both within and between the "scientific-objective" and "modernist-ironic" voices of anthropological discourse, *The Hamlet* offers its readers competing stances toward cultural experience in the South in the 1930s. These can also be understood as competing subject positions, each carrying its own ideological framework of assumptions about racial and economic identity, regional history, national politics, and so forth. As Bakhtin writes, "Our ideological development is . . . an intense struggle within us for hegemony among various available verbal and ideological points of view, approaches, directions and values" (*DI,* 346). Literary apparatuses (such as novels) participate in this struggle over one's ideological development by offering readers positions "from which the text is most 'obviously' intelligible," to use Catherine Belsey's phrase. But Belsey's point is not that narratives simply "interpellate" readers once and for all. Rather, they situate the ongoing process of subject-formation (what Bakhtin calls "our ideological development") in a moment of reading that is saturated with identitarian pressures. Individual subjects are not finished products during, or even after, the moment of reading or writing; rather, they are "perpetually in the process of construction, thrown into crisis by alterations in language and in the social formation, capable of change."[23] Indeed, the substitution of twentieth-century ethnographers (and the participant-observer's doubled voices of "personal experience" and "scientific objectivity") for nineteenth-century anthropologists (and the science of Man's evolutionary narratives of "progress") can be understood as one effect of this dynamism in the process of subject-formation—as long as we recall the corollary from Foucault, that what matters in such substitutions is not the concrete (speaking) individual, but rather the "subject-effects" of discourse, potentiated spaces that only temporarily are occupied by actual (concrete) individuals. Thus Faulkner's literary discourse in *The Hamlet* does more than simply represent alternative ways of approaching culture derived from the emergence of ethnography in the 1930s. It organizes the subject-effects of anthropological discourse as competing, and sometimes newly emerging, ideological worldviews, as interpretive perspectives from which the narratives of local experience told by Ratliff (and others) can be "most 'obviously' intelligible."

Perhaps the most popular source of such perspectives on the South produced in the 1930s was not written texts at all. They were the photographs produced by agents of the New Deal and disseminated throughout the country in a government-sponsored campaign in support of the Roosevelt administration and its policies of relief and agricultural modernization. These photographs were part of the southern dialogue on the rural poor, and as such are represented in *The Hamlet* in ways that further complicate the relations of contiguity between Faulkner's literary discourse in this novel and other discursive efforts to represent the South in the 1930s.

Photographers played a crucial role in the Roosevelt administration's campaign for an organized federal response to the crises of the Depression. As agents for the Farm Security Administration (FSA) and the United States Department of Agriculture (USDA), photographers such as Dorothea Lange, Walker Evans, and Margaret Bourke-White were sent to the South and West and into urban areas with specific instructions from their project directors. At the FSA, project director Roy Stryker assigned his photographers the task of capturing the suffering of farmers and workers in order to demonstrate to better-off Americans the need for relief programs sponsored by the Roosevelt administration. USDA photographers, on the other hand, were charged with depicting New Deal programs at work. Intended to demonstrate prosperity brought about by agricultural modernization, USDA photographers avoided the images of suffering and despair that dominated FSA photographs, instead picturing farmers who had benefited from modernization assistance or extension agents demonstrating new equipment and methods.[24] These agencies' photographers were skilled at positioning their subjects in relation to the camera lens so as to construct a perspective that would force "readers" of the photographs into a sympathetic position vis-à-vis the plight of hard-hit Americans, as well as the government administrators who sought to help them.

In this way, photography was used by agents of the federal government as an Althusserian apparatus, interpellating subjects as an effect of the perspectives created by the photographers' cameras. However, just as the literary text does not interpellate the individual reader once and for all but participates in what Belsey calls "the process of construction" of the subject, photographs of the New Deal should be understood as offering competing perspectives upon the economic crisis of the Depression, rather than compelling a single ideological framework for understanding that crisis. Indeed, as Maren Stange observes, photographs of the New Deal often conveyed contradictory interpretations of the events of the Depression, because at the same time that FSA photographs told the story "of displacement, migration, and forced resettlement" in the Depression South, USDA photographs indirectly located the causes of this displacement in the very farm modernization programs promoted by the Roosevelt administration.[25] Whereas Althusser would argue that an ideological apparatus such as photography compels or "hails" its subjects as interpellated individuals, Stange's reading of New Deal photographs suggests they could foster what Gramsci calls a "contradictory consciousness" in their viewers, reproducing "official" knowledge about the benefits of agricultural programs but also confirming many Americans' "practical" skepticism about the government-compounded problem of homeless and itinerant agricultural workers.

The contiguity between New Deal photography and Faulkner's representation of southern experience in *The Hamlet* is observable on a number of levels. FSA photographers often focused on their subjects' eyes and facial expressions, seeking there a look—what William Stott calls "*the* look: mournful, plaintive, nakedly near tears"—that would make social problems, and the need for social programs, real and accessible to the readers of the magazines in which these photos appeared.[26] This is the "language" of FSA photography, and we can see it represented in many of Faulkner's prose descriptions of rural characters in *The Hamlet*. This happens in his depiction of the Armstids, for instance, as they approach the scene of the "Spotted Horses" episode. The narrator introduces Henry Armstid as "a thin man, not large, with something about his eyes, something strained and washed-out, at once vague and intense," and soon we see that his wife's eyes "were a washed gray also, as though they had faded too like the dress and the sunbonnet" (*TH*, 320, 323). Like Dorothea Lange's famous "Migrant Mother," who officially remained nameless for decades because Stryker was more inter-ested in the "universal" than in the particular, Mrs. Armstid remains anonymous throughout this scene: Henry is immediately named, but she is referred to only as "the woman," "the wife," and "the missus." Moreover, like the black-and-white photographs of the New Deal, there is neither color nor movement in the narrator's portrayal of Mrs. Arm-stid: constantly described in shades of gray, "framed" by her gray sun-bonnet, she is perceived in terms of stillness—even when she is obeying Henry's command to follow him into the lot to catch his pony: "she moved without inference of locomotion, like something on a moving platform, a float" (*TH,* 325). Unlike the subjects of most FSA photo-graphs, Henry and Mrs. Armstid are not migrant workers; they have a house, and "chaps in the house that never had shoes last winter" (*TH,* 322). But much of the language used to describe them represents the iconography of migrant workers made famous by Lange and others—beginning with their wagon, "battered and paintless," reminiscent of the contraptions Oklahoma drought victims pieced together to make the journey to California.

Faulkner's text represents the processes of modernization in the South most fully when it reproduces an icon such as the battered wagon and then offers competing perspectives (subject positions) from which this "text" can be intelligible to readers. One place this occurs is in book 1, "Flem," when Trumbull, the village's blacksmith for twenty years, is displaced by Eck Snopes in one of Flem Snopes's modernization schemes, "the first of his actions in the village which he was ever seen in physical juxtaposition to" (*TH,* 73). After installing the incompetents I. O. and Eck Snopes in Trumbull's position, Flem builds a new black-smith's shop in the village and equips it with the latest machinery. He hires Trumbull's old apprentice, attracts all of I. O. and Eck's business, and then sells the new concern to Will Varner under an arrangement that allows Flem to sell all the equipment from the old shop, move the new concern into the old building, and then sell the new building to a local farmer. Flem's stated purpose in all this is "so that people could get decent work done again" (when Flem was the one who installed his incompetent kinsmen in the first place!) (*TH,* 73). Like the New Deal programs that promised more efficient and profitable practices for southern farmers but in effect profited landowners at the expense of displaced tenants, Flem's scheme profits himself and a few others (Eck and Trumbull's apprentice, to whom Eck becomes apprenticed at the conclusion of the scheme) at the expense of the "original" tenant, Trumbull, who in the midst of Flem's machinations can be seen driving "through the village with his wife, in a wagon loaded with household goods" (*TH*, 72–73).

Rather than compelling one ideological stance toward Depression-era conditions, however, this scene, like the photographs discussed by Stange, would confirm the contradictory consciousness of contemporary readers toward New Deal modernization plans (as well as toward the iconographic images that represented them) by forcing readers to observe both the value of modernization and the human consequences of the programs that implemented it. Hence the narrator's emphasis upon what the local observers of Flem's modernization scheme *see*. When Trumbull drives his wagon through town, some of the men on Varner's gallery, those who "had waited about the store to see what would happen when he arrived," are already aware of the injustice done to him (*TH*, 72). They want to *see* how Trumbull plans to redress this injustice. The narrator quickly informs us, however, that nothing happens as Trumbull drives past Varner's store (which is directly opposite the old smith shop), and that those waiting on the store's front porch "never saw him again" (*TH*, 73). The implication here is that their concern for Trumbull's welfare diminished as the new shop entered into the discourse of "progress" that small southern towns relied upon to survive the Depression. As the narrator subsequently notes, "All they saw now was that they had a new blacksmith" (*TH*, 73). Indeed, it was all but inevitable that these observers of Trumbull's displacement would repress the memory (or rewrite it as an inevitable effect of "progress"), because it is from the perspective of their own economic dependence upon Will Varner (symbolized by their ensconcement upon the front porch of Varner's store, which furnishes their own livelihoods as tenant farmers) that they observed the scene of Trumbull's ousting in the first place. They have been inducted into Varner's perspective, much as Ratliff, at other moments in this text, assumes Varner's habits of understanding the economic experiences of the poorer residents of Frenchman's Bend. Meanwhile Trumbull, Joad-like, is forced to relocate as a worker despite his twenty-year tenure as the village's black-smith.

The presence in Faulkner's novel of subjects (and subject positions) made widely available from FSA photography indicates at least a few degrees of contiguity between these two discursive domains. But this contiguity emerges only if we think genealogically about the appearance (or "utterance") of such iconic images. Take, for example, Dorothea Lange's famous image "Plantation Owner" (1936), which depicts a proud-looking white man standing with his foot on the bumper of his automobile in front of what seems to be the store from which he "fur-nishes" the black sharecroppers sitting on the store's steps. This photo-graph resonates with audiences today, as in the 1930s, because of the multiple discursive registers it evokes. One of these is the era of western expansion's rhetoric of rugged individualism, which is supported in the photograph by the dominance of the white man and by his metaphori-cal "possession" of the scene, signified by his literal ownership of the store and the automobile. The image also evokes the earlier rhetoric of the Puritan work ethic, which hierarchizes labor and creates permanent classes of rich and poor, and which is supported in the photograph by its representation of rigidly stratified labor roles and by the angle of the camera, which forces anyone viewing the photograph to look "up" to the white landowner and then "down" at the black workers. But the photograph also resonates with its "readers" because of its representa-tion of internal inconsistencies within these rhetorical traditions. Al-though the framing of the photograph produces for the plantation owner a position of almost feudal power (analogous to that assumed by Jody Varner in his first exchange with Abner Snopes in the Varner store), this position is undercut by the manifold presence of black workers. This man clearly depends upon the labor of others to prop him up financially, just as he depends upon their presence and the products of their labor (the store, the automobile) as "props" in the drama of racial and economic superiority played out in this photo-graph.

Some subsequent history of the uses to which Lange's photograph was put in the 1930s supports this "doubled" reading. Two years after "Plantation Owner" was taken, Archibald MacLeish used it in his heav-ily ironic juxtaposition of photographs and an extended poem, *Land of the Free* (1938). MacLeish's cropping of the photograph emphasizes the white man's domination of the scene by cutting out most of the black workers. Yet a single head remains in the background of MacLeish's version of the photograph, between the plantation owner and his automobile. A longer exposure in the processing of MacLeish's image also has darkened the man's facial features, again suggesting the effort of dominant whites to erase the black presence that supports them. But both MacLeish's book and Lange's photograph are powerful precisely because of their ability to seduce readers into recalling ideologically charged myths (such as the myth of rugged individualism) and then to remind them, as with the faceless head of the black worker, of their internal inconsistencies.

What, then, is the relation between Lange's and MacLeish's uses of the iconic image of the plantation owner and Faulkner's representation of it in the figures of Jody, and especially Will, Varner? First, it is important to recognize that this relation is one of reciprocity rather than simple "reflection." Lange's photograph is itself a response to prior representations of sharecropper exploitation in both photography and literature. By November 1937, Stott writes of another study of the tenant system, "the problem it treated was known to virtually everyone who read the book." Among others, Erskine Caldwell had become famous for his novels about agricultural poverty, and in 1937 he published *You Have Seen Their Faces,* featuring the photographs of Margaret Bourke-White, which, like Lange's, emphasized unequal relations of power between workers and landowners. Neither "Plantation Owner" nor the character Will Varner in *The Hamlet* were "original" in this sense, but rather repetitions and quotations of power relations in the South that preexisted even the agencies of the New Deal. Will Varner is both a reiteration of these earlier relations and a reformulation of his photographic representation in "Plantation Owner" and other FSA photographs. But it is not just the position of the ruling class vis-à-vis the working class that is represented (reciprocally) in such "utterances." The mechanisms of exclusion by which the Varners maintain their power in *The Hamlet*—the habitual refusal to acknowledge the presence of blacks as part of Frenchman's Bend's social body—are themselves prefigured in MacLeish's ironic cropping out of all but one of the sharecroppers in Lange's photograph. And even this mechanism of elision had been prefigured by the policies of some of the federal agencies that employed photographers in the first place. As Pete Daniel writes, the "official" story of black tenant farmers, as depicted in New Deal photographs, was manufactured by USDA photographers in "command performances," in which photographers asked blacks to pose in their Sunday best while extension agents demonstrated the latest tools and techniques of agricultural modernization. Even more often, the story of black agricultural labor was elided entirely: "black extension work," Daniel writes, "was never a priority of the agency." Rather than simply reflecting figures and events already familiar to readers from newspapers, magazines, and films, Faulkner's literary discourse in *The Hamlet* both constitutes, and is constitutive of, the subject-"effects" of those discourses of culture (whether photography, ethnography, or others) that also sought to represent the experience of poverty in the South in the 1930s.[27]

Given the reciprocal energies between Faulkner's literary discourse and other discourses of culture in the 1930s, it becomes more difficult to explain Faulkner's role as the author of his books in terms of ownership and proprietorship, as when he labeled himself "sole owner and proprietor" of Yoknapatawpha County in the map included in *Absalom, Absalom!* in 1936. If it is true, as Bakhtin writes, that "in the everyday speech of any person living in society, no less than half (on the average) of all the words uttered by him will be someone else's words" (*DI,* 339), then surely we need a new model of authorship in order to understand the relation between Faulkner's evident genius and the texts that bear his name. Here, too, we can benefit from further investigation into the reciprocal relationship between Faulkner's literary discourse and the use of photography as both a tool of ethnography and as an ideological apparatus in the 1930s.

Lange's "Plantation Owner" makes one other perspective available to its readers, one that is easy to overlook because it is extremely marginal and often cropped out in reproductions of the image. This is the position of Lange's husband, Paul Taylor, at the left of the image, where he casually smokes a cigarette while engaging the attention of the plantation owner. Lange has clearly instructed the plantation owner to look in the direction of her husband, but the ocular exchange that results, as it exposes the reliance of the white man's position upon another's ratifying gaze, deconstructs the very position of superiority that, for the plantation owner, is ostensibly under construction in the photograph. The black workers, for their part, are studied in their avoidance of the racial drama taking place between the two white men. Their attention, instead, appears to be on the camera lens's construction of their own (subordinate) position. The exchange between these workers and Lange's camera is more available to Paul Taylor than it is to the plantation owner, who stands oblivious to the workers' gazes projecting from behind his back. In fact, the black workers' studied indifference toward the white plantation owner is more available to Taylor than to Lange herself, who, after all, can only perceive it as one part of the larger composition she seeks to produce. Taylor's position in the margins of this image is thus multivalent: like the ethnographers of the 1930s (and thus like Ratliff), he is both a part of, and removed from, the various racial and economic dramas unfolding in the scene before him. The position from which he observes the scene captured by Lange's camera comprehends the landowner and the black workers, but also Lange herself and the mechanical nature of the photographic apparatus that will produce the image for later audiences. Faulkner's role as the author of his books is more like that of Taylor, in the margins of this image, than it is like Lange, because while Lange may be the ostensible "producer" of the image, Taylor is able to view even this position as just another subject-effect, one that, like his, exists only on the margins of discursive production.

The deep sense of irony with which Faulkner regarded his own position as a writer has to do with his sense of himself not as the "photographer," the literal recorder, of such moments of cultural experience, but rather as the bystander and (inevitably) ineffectual manipulator of the subject-effects of those discourses that intersect in any given moment of cultural production. This is neither the scientific-objective stance of nineteenth-century anthropologists (which *is* represented by the novel's "grandiloquent" narrator), nor the modernist-ironic stance of modern ethnographers (and which *is* represented in Ratliff), but something different from, and critical of, these preexisting, predetermined discursive "spaces." But it would be a mistake to attribute this perspective entirely to Faulkner's genius as the author of his "own" literary discourse. As Taylor's position in Lange's photograph indicates, the metacritical perspective upon the production of cultural experience is itself an effect of the production of cultural experience. Its appearance in Faulkner's literary discourse simply reiterates the reciprocal relationship that obtains between modern discourses at moments of emergence for the new subjects, and subject-effects, of culture.

CHAPTER 5

Race Fantasies: The Filming of *Intruder in the Dust*

I first visited Oxford, Mississippi, in June of 1991, to examine Oxford's city and county courtrooms and to consider how the formal construction of legal spaces in Faulkner's hometown might inform the writer's representations of the law, the most "official" of cultural discourses. While in Oxford, I learned to distinguish between the law as a prediscursive body of rules and regulations, and the law as one of several "delivery systems" that mediate the individual subject's relation to the symbolic order of culture. The manner in which apparatuses such as law, literature, newspapers, and film produce a particular reality for their audiences became especially interesting to me as I reread Faulkner's murder mystery *Intruder in the Dust*, viewed Clarence Brown's film adaptation of the novel, and attempted to learn more about the historical and cultural contexts of Faulkner's story about a lynching narrowly averted, by researching what the local paper, the *Oxford Eagle*, had reported of two events: the actual 1908 lynching of Nelse Patton, whose grisly story caused a sensation in Oxford when Faulkner was almost eleven years old; and MGM's filming of *Intruder in the Dust* "on location" in the spring of 1949.

I found very little on Nelse Patton in the *Oxford Eagle*: approximately two column-inches, six sentences in all, with the headline "Negro Lynched by Mob" and a short narrative in which a Mr. McMillin, serving a jail sentence, sends Patton to deliver a message to his wife.[1] According to the story, Patton had "remained about the place," prompting Mrs. McMillin to attempt to frighten him away with a revolver. This allegedly led to Patton's disarming Mrs. McMillin and then slitting her throat. I was struck by the absence of detail in this front-page story: for what crime had Mr. McMillin been jailed? What message did he send his wife? Why did he choose Patton to deliver the message?

What witnesses were there to tell that Patton "remained about the place"? Why would he do this? How do we know Mrs. McMillin pulled a gun on Patton or what her motives were? Why would Patton kill Mrs. McMillin? How was Patton captured? Who was in the lynch mob that took him from the jail? How did the mob overcome the jailers? Did they even need to? Finally (although this hardly exhausts the number of questions a motivated journalist might have pursued regarding the event), what had happened to Patton's body?[2]

The absence of these details makes more sense when we consider the story's ideological function as a rehearsal of the dialectic of racial subject-formation, in which white southern men are offered a position of superiority, what the narrator of *Intruder in the Dust* calls the "white man's high estate," over the black Other (*ID*, 134). The Nelse Patton of the *Oxford Eagle* story was no longer an actual person but the ideological figure of the Negro used by southern societies in the modern period to "stitch up" a basic contradiction within the fantasy-construction of white supremacy and white racial purity. Psychologically, segregated whites required the presence of a black Other to support the fantasy of uncorrupted racial boundaries, but they hated this dependence and entered into any number of delusions to disavow it. The newspaper story, like the lynching that preceded it, turned the actual Nelse Patton into an object of ritual scorn and mutilation, delivering for its readers a particular version of reality in which clear racial divisions exist between blacks and whites. To apply Slavoj Žižek's phrasing, the newspaper served as a support for the ideology of white supremacy, producing for its readers "an illusion which structures the effective, real social relations" of the segregated South. Gavin Stevens participates in such an illusion when he claims, in conversation with his nephew Chick, that "we alone in the United States (I'm not speaking of Sambo right now; I'll get to him in a minute) are a homogeneous people" (*ID*, 150). The absence of detail in the Patton story served to obscure the "insupportable, real, impossible kernel" of truth about the economic and psychological dependence of segregated whites upon blacks—a truth that is inconsistent with the illusion of a "fully" segregated society. Žižek's formulation of the process by which the Symbolic is mapped onto the unconscious is thus open to a concept of social antagonism, unlike the

Althusserian instance of interpellation, which for Žižek "never fully suc-
ceeds": "there is always a residue, a leftover, a stain of traumatic irrationality and senselessness sticking to it." In Stevens's ruminations on the
"homogeneous" South, this residue of inconsistency surfaces in the par-
enthetical reference to "Sambo." In the Nelse Patton story, it appears in
the irrational dependence of whites upon the moment of lynching for
the reassertion of their racial difference from blacks. Even the serial use
of lynching by whites is itself evidence of a fundamental irrationality in
the concept of racial purity (or "homogeneity") upon which segregation
ideology was based.[3]

I will occasionally refer to the Nelse Patton story as I explore events
surrounding the filming of *Intruder in the Dust* in the spring of 1949,
which also strikes me as an episode of racial and economic subject-
formation, one uniquely determined by alterations in the discourses of
culture available to white southerners after World War II. My primary
focus will be the elaboration of film as a vehicle for the fantasies of the
South's dominant classes, where this function had previously been performed in the discourse of American historiography and in the legal
rhetoric of Manifest Destiny.[4] Marxist analyses have long recognized
film's capacity to create, through the apparatus of the camera lens, the
illusion of mastery in the viewer-spectator. In this approach to film theory, the illusion reifies the relation between capital and labor, encourag-
ing the spectator "to desire and possess a consumable space from his or
her own perspective, a space in fact requiring the presence of 'an individual' for its lines (perspectival) to be justified."[5] While film's perpetuation of capitalist paradigms is an important consideration for any
discussion of film and American culture, we need to recognize that in
the segregated South, the same process would reinforce regional assumptions about racial difference, which legitimated, for white southerners, the practice of subordinating the experience of blacks to that
of whites. Although film theorists generally understand the illusion of
mastery as it is created for audiences viewing a finished film, in the context of the filming of Faulkner's story, I understand it as a deferred object of desire analogous to the endlessly deferred moment of racial
purity which is the impossible goal of the segregationist fantasy.

Film as Segregationist Discourse

American historiography of the Civil War and Reconstruction is replete with examples of the dialectic of dependence and disavowal, as it describes white attitudes toward the place of blacks in American society. In one example found throughout the literature, the Union's dependence upon black labor and black soldiers is disavowed through the perpetuation of proslavery stereotypes of the benevolent planter, the loyal slave, the rapacious carpetbagger, and the freedman quickly learning to miss the old days under slavery. Although revisionist historiographers such as W. E. B. Du Bois had corrected many of these misrepresentations by the late 1930s, by then they had become staples of American cinema and remained so until at least the 1950s.[6] Not only did the first American films rewrite *Uncle Tom's Cabin* in the same proslavery vocabulary that historiographers were then using to write American history, but America's first great film director, D. W. Griffith, who pioneered techniques of feature film making still in use today, directed and produced the viciously racist *The Birth of a Nation* (1915), and this, along with its virtual remake *Gone with the Wind* (1939), cemented proslavery ideology in white America's cultural imaginary.[7] Recognizing how profitable these earlier narratives had been with white audiences, MGM marketed *Intruder in the Dust* as the third installment of a southern trilogy beginning with *The Birth of a Nation* and *Gone with the Wind*.[8] Although Faulkner's narrative takes place in the late 1940s and not in the Reconstruction past, both it and Oxford's collaboration with MGM deploy the same dialectic of dependence and disavowal that both the discourse of New South historiography and these earlier films made available to white southerners.

For example, just as the southern plantocracy and its avatars historically have disavowed their dependence upon black labor, whites in *Intruder in the Dust* ritually scorn their economic reliance upon blacks. The novel registers this dependence in several places—not least in Lucas's annual payment of his property taxes. Yet Faulkner's narrator describes "the whole white part of the county" driving into Jefferson to witness Lucas's lynching, traveling the new roads to the town's jail and courthouse, all of which, in their minds, "existed only by their sufferance and support" (*ID*, 143). Moreover, each time Chick half-remembers something in this novel, he is recalling and then disavowing a similarly "traumatic residue" of the repressed facts of white dependence, as with the memory that Miss Habersham and Molly, Lucas's wife, had been "born in the same week and both suckled at Molly's mother's breast and grown up together almost inextricably like sisters, like twins" (*ID*, 86). Chick recalls this fact of local biography but immediately disavows its details: "here again something nagged at his mind his attention but already in the same second gone, not even dismissed: just gone" (*ID*, 76). This disavowal in the face of dependence predicates most of the violence performed or contemplated in the novel, and its essential role in the production of white subjectivity is always on the verge of exposure. In fact, most of Chick's education in this *Bildungsroman* is tied to his exposure of the dialectic he temporarily has refused to activate with regard to Lucas's lynching. "It seemed to him now," the narrator observes at one point, "that he was responsible for having brought into the light and glare of day something shocking and shameful out of the whole white foundation of the county" (*ID*, 135).

Chick's critical examination of the cultural and psychological processes that produce him as a southern white male contrasts with anything southern film audiences might have expected from Brown when he proposed filming Faulkner's novel in Oxford. As was the case with the earlier films by Griffith and David O. Selznick, audiences would have expected Brown's film to reproduce these processes as essentially "real" and natural. They could rely upon film as an ideological apparatus, in other words, to reproduce and thereby support the effective relations of existence under segregation. This is the "real" Oxford that Oxonians repeatedly claimed, in the *Oxford Eagle* and elsewhere, would be represented in Brown's film. Of particular interest in these accounts were the number of local buildings that would appear in the film and the percentage of finished product that would be filmed on location. Speaking of the "substantial resemblance" between Faulkner's "word picture" and the environs of Oxford, one writer for the paper continued: "That 'substantiality' and the 'character' that is real in these real scenes is what Mr. Brown says he hopes to capture in this film, a reality which he could not simulate in Hollywood."[9] Some articles even spoke of the "Oxford Method" of filmmaking, claiming that the more a movie is filmed where the story "takes place," the more accurate it will be.

The Oxford in both Faulkner's novel and Brown's film is a reflection of the white fantasy of a South whose black population is subject to erasure at any moment. On the Monday following Vinson's murder, the town of Oxford is devoid of the black labor that ordinarily keeps the town running smoothly; were it a Sunday, Faulkner's narrator muses, the town might have "accepted a day with no one to plug and unplug the humming sweepers and turn the buttons on the stoves . . . but this was Monday, a new day and a new week . . . yet still no Negro had they seen" (*ID*, 118–19). The absence of blacks in Jefferson strikes Chick suddenly; while driving Miss Habersham's car to the jailhouse (where she will spend the day fending off Crawford Gowrie and his cohorts), Chick notices the heavy traffic, and "that there had been no children in the schoolbus but only grown people and in the stream of cars and trucks following it and now following him where he had finally cut in, a few of which even on stock-auction Monday . . . should have carried Negroes, there had not been one dark face" (*ID*, 132). And throughout the novel, Chick ruminates upon the "simple and uncomplex" vocabulary available to the people of Jefferson and Beat Four for "the deliberate violent blotting out obliteration of a human life" (*ID*, 88).

Brown's film begins in the aftermath of this "blotting out" of Jefferson's blacks. "Where they all at?" the man looking for a shoeshine boy asks in the film's earliest lines; "seems to me I ain't seen one darkey in the road since yesterday." To emphasize the fact that Jefferson's blacks are hiding, Brown inserts a series of scenes that portray black fear of white retributive violence as Chick, Miss Habersham, and Aleck Sander travel to Caledonia Chapel. In one, a black woman covers her children with a bed cover; in another, three adults drink coffee in the dark; and in the third, a single man watches fearfully as Miss Habersham's car and Chick's horse go by. The succession of these scenes and images amounts to an obsession in Brown's film with the power of whites to remove the town's black presence. Chick's father, similarly obsessed, uses a metaphor of sanitation as he cautions Chick to "stay home until this thing is cleaned up—over, finished, and done with." Finally, Brown's film represents the racially "cleansed" town in a celebratory atmosphere: while the townspeople wait for the Gowries to lynch Lucas, they game, flirt with one another, and, as festive music is broadcast above their heads, generally enjoy a rare, all-white moment in Jefferson.

Intruder in the Dust's obsession with the power of whites to remove the black presence from a protected town square speaks volumes about the development of film as a discursive domain producing its audiences as racial subjects in the late 1940s. The sudden acceptance of Faulkner's story among his notoriously antagonistic neighbors in Oxford, Mississippi, suggests they were in need of some new apparatus to support the dialectic of white superiority that had sustained their vision of an Anglo-Saxon South since the days of Andrew Jackson. Cheryl Lester's thesis about black migration suggests one cause of this anxiety: migrating in droves since World War I, African Americans had been protesting the region's oppressive racial climate and asserting an agency denied them in white representations of the South and southern history.[10] In this context, the man whose desperate search for some black Other opens Brown's film represents the white South's anxiety over black migration, which threatened the dialectical foundation of its racial identity. But Brown's film also creates the reassuring fiction that blacks would always be available, once empowered whites created the conditions for their reemergence. In this, it follows Faulkner's text rather closely: "they were still there," Faulkner's narrator repeatedly suggests, "they had not fled, you just didn't see them" (*ID*, 95). In the context of black migration, then, the filming of *Intruder* evoked a mass nostalgia over a South that no longer existed by 1949. As several film theorists have noted, film has this delusional capacity to "fix" a particular view *as* historical reality.[11] For the residents of Oxford, film could project a segregationist fantasy that excluded blacks from a protected white center but maintained their availability as binary references in both the social and psychological construction of white racial identity.

As it came to represent the effective relations of whites and blacks under segregation, the filming of Faulkner's novel supported the everyday fantasies of white privilege. In fact, filming became a metonym for these relations, an "associated idea substituted" for segregation. Implicitly, every moment of filming referred to a future moment of viewing the film in segregated movie houses across the South. But MGM's presence in Oxford represented segregation most fully when it exposed the daily inconveniences and irrationalities of a racially divided society. Juano Hernandez, like the character Lucas Beauchamp he portrayed, forced Brown and others to confront many of these irrationalities. Hernandez obviously required lodging while in Oxford, but law and custom prevented his housing with other, white actors. The dilemma was resolved when prominent members of Oxford's African American community volunteered to house Hernandez and other black members of the MGM crew, but this solution only raised another difficulty when Faulkner found he could not invite Hernandez to the cast party he hosted at Rowan Oak. As Joseph Blotner reports, "He was a fine actor and a cultivated man, but if they invited him they would have to include the Bankhead family [his hosts] as well, and they felt that they could not do that." In addition to these high-profile instances, one can imagine the number of daily aggravations that the rules of a segregated society created for Brown's film—a film Brown himself had championed as "the most eloquent statement of the true Southern viewpoint of racial relations and racial problems ever sent out over the nation." The chamber of commerce, for instance, encountered difficulties casting local African Americans for the film's jail scene, because, as the *Oxford Eagle* reported, "the colored people don't appear to fancy being in the jail even in make believe." Like the system of segregation itself, producing *Intruder in the Dust* as a support for segregation ideology gave Brown and the residents of Oxford daily opportunities both to confront and to disavow their dependence upon blacks.[12]

Conflating Race in *Go Down, Moses* and *Intruder in the Dust*

One might think that the daily irrationalities of an ideological fantasy eventually would discredit it in the eyes of those experiencing them, but according to Žižek they actually ensure its "unconditional authority" by simultaneously deferring and making real the object of desire.[13] Instead of discrediting the segregationist fantasy, each example of white dependence upon blacks makes the desired future moment of racial division and disavowal more real—the moment of viewing Brown's film in a segregated cinema house, for instance; or the moment of lynching, in the case of Faulkner's characters, and of the mob that acted against Nelse Patton forty years earlier. Yet each time the promised moment of racial separation approaches, it immediately withdraws again as the impossible object of desire. *Plessy v. Ferguson*'s one-drop rule is an excellent example of this phenomenon, since it posited an impossible standard as the proof of racial purity and thus necessitated an absurd taxonomy of legal distinctions in order to support it.

Plessy was by no means the first legal decision to promise and then endlessly defer white southerners' desired object of racial homogeneity, however. The Indian Removal Act of 1830 generated an array of similar legal technicalities as the basis for deciding who would count as an Indian for the purposes of removal and, later in the century, land allotment in the West. Since the early nineteenth century, southern discourses of racial differentiation have tended to conflate Native Americans and African Americans as a single, threatening Other, because they have been motivated by a similar desire to remove racial Others from an imaginary, uncorrupted white space. In the 1940s, substantial changes in federal policy toward the white South's strategies of exclusion regarding these racial Others were a cause of heightened anxiety in the region. The unconstitutionality of Jim Crow laws received increased federal scrutiny in the 1940s, just as, according to Felix Cohen, there had run in federal Indian legislation since the 1930s "the motive of righting past wrongs inflicted upon a nearly helpless minority."[14] Again Oxford's taking up of Faulkner's story in the spring of 1949 can be seen in relation to anxieties caused by these historical events—in particular, in the ways both Faulkner's text and Brown's film offer the discourse of Native American removal as a way of canceling Lucas's claim to a white ancestry and fixing him firmly in the position of the Other.

One justification for reading race in *Intruder in the Dust* as a conflation of Native American and African American ancestry is Faulkner's use of Indian iconography in his earliest portrayal of Lucas Beauchamp. When we first see Lucas in *Go Down, Moses* (1942), he is hiding his still in an Indian burial mound so he can then tell the landowner, Carothers Edmonds, that George Wilkins, Lucas's aspiring son-in-law, is manufacturing liquor on his property. Lucas's digging unsettles the mound and it collapses, covering him in dirt and pottery, and depositing in his hand a single gold coin. This coin symbolically connects Lucas with the South's racial Other of a hundred years earlier—the Cherokee of Georgia and the Choctaw and Chickasaw of northern Mississippi—and with the desire for gold that motivated whites to dispossess Indians of their lands. In several ways, both Faulkner's novel and Brown's film continue this association of Lucas Beauchamp with America's historical treatment of Native Americans.

Repeatedly, both text and film express Lucas's outstanding characteristics in a vocabulary of wooden, unmoving, and tragically heroic figures once set aside for the "noble savages" of nineteenth-century discourse. This vocabulary surfaces in several places in Faulkner's text to describe Lucas's demeanor, and it bears an unmistakable resemblance to the stereotyped statues of cigar-store Indians once ubiquitous in the South and West. When Lucas emerges from sheriff Hampton's car, the narrator notes that his "face was not even looking at them, arrogant and calm and with no more defiance in it than fear: detached, impersonal, almost musing, intractable and composed" (*ID*, 43). This is an example of what Philip Weinstein has called the "framing" of Lucas: "Lucas hardly possesses legs in *Intruder in the Dust*. We see him mainly as in a portrait photograph, from the shoulders up."[15] While I agree with Weinstein that the immobility associated with Lucas's facial features makes this text complicit in Crawford Gowrie's frame-up of Lucas, if we neglect the moments when the narrator observes Lucas from toe to head we will miss the extent to which both Faulkner's text and Brown's film transform Lucas into an African American iteration of the cigar-store icon. In particular, I'm referring to the first time Chick meets Lucas, as Chick climbs out of the creek on Lucas's property and "up the bank until he saw two feet in gum boots which were neither Edmonds' boy's nor Aleck Sander's and then the legs, the overalls rising out of them and he climbed on and stood up and saw a Negro man with an axe on his shoulder" (*ID*, 6). In this scene and throughout Chick's visit to Lucas's cabin, Faulkner describes Lucas's presence as statuesque, "intolerant, inflexible and composed" (*ID*, 13). Likewise, in his film adaptation, Brown positions his camera at Hernandez's feet to emphasize Lucas's statuesque qualities. The camera's lens remains at ground level but sweeps up Lucas's legs to portray a larger-than-life, yet inanimate figure.

During Chick's visit to Lucas's cabin, the discourse of Indian removal appears much more explicitly, separating Lucas from the white South and marking him as essentially different. As Chick enters the sitting room of Lucas's home to dry off from his mishap at the creek, readers of the novel are presented with alternate frameworks for interpreting Lucas's racial identity. In one of these, Lucas is represented in a painting reminiscent of Grant Wood's *American Gothic:* "there looked back at him again the calm intolerant face beneath the swaggering rake of the hat, a tieless starched collar clipped to a white starched shirt with a collarbutton shaped like a snake's head and almost as large . . . and beside him the tiny doll-like woman in another painted straw hat and a shawl" (*ID,* 14). Near this portrait hangs a second framed image, a "lithograph of a three-year-old calendar in which Pocahontas in the quilled fringed buckskins of a Sioux or Chippewa chief stood against a balustrade of Italian marble" (*ID,* 10). In the revised American gothic, Lucas's claim to both a white and a black identity is undercut by the permanence of the frame surrounding his relationship with his non-white wife, Molly. The threat posed by Lucas's dual heritage is thus contained within this frame. At the same time, the historical figure of Pocahontas and her *actual* role as a uniter of races are repudiated in the insistence upon essential difference that dominates the *legend* of Pocahontas, and its representation in the lithograph of Pocahontas wearing "quilled fringed buckskins." While the framing of the Italian balustrade does suggest her voyage across the Atlantic, it marks her as essentially different in the same way that the portrait frame marks Lucas. Moreover, the lithograph of Pocahontas erases both her life with colonist John Rolfe and her symbolic crossing of racial and cultural boundaries among the British. Significantly, Chick's contemplation of these images precedes his own attempt to assert an essential racial barrier between himself and Lucas, when he paternalistically offers Molly coins in return for the meal that Lucas has provided as a gesture of hospitality.

In Brown's film, the containment of Lucas's threatening, biracial identity within the context of his marriage to Molly is enhanced by her position in front of the revised *American Gothic* when the camera first pans it. The novel's lithograph of Pocahontas is replaced in the film by a painting that represents Euro-American expansion in the nineteenth century. Although our view of the painting is obstructed by actors Claude Jarman Jr. and Juano Hernandez, we can just glimpse a team of horses pulling a covered wagon and a scout on horseback with his back turned in a gesture that indicates his responsibility to protect the white pioneers from Indian attack. Like the gold coin that drops into Lucas's hand in the Indian burial mound in *Go Down, Moses,* this painting subordinates Lucas's claim as a (partly white) southerner to the discourse of expansion and Euro-American domination of the continent. Moreover, just as each of these images placed in Lucas's home rehearses a particular fiction about America's European discovery and Euro-Americans' subsequent "manifest destiny," the scene acted out before them, Chick's demand that Lucas pick up the coins Chick has dropped on the floor, rehearses the ideology of white superiority, even in Lucas's own home.

In different but similarly motivated ways, then, Faulkner's novel and Brown's film modify nineteenth-century discourses of racial removal as they participate in the dialectic of dependence and disavowal that sustained white identity in the segregated South. This dialectic relies upon a rhetoric of purity at the center and threat at the margins, and it is Gavin Stevens's espousal of this rhetoric—his theory of a homogeneous South—that further explains Oxford's uncharacteristic sympathy with him, and with the project of filming Faulkner's novel, in the spring of 1949.

For Stevens, purity is evident in the ubiquity of Anglo-Saxon surnames, names like Workitt "that used to be Urquhart only the one that brought it to America and then Mississippi couldn't spell it" (*ID*, 146). This use of common names to prove the dominant culture's "pure" genealogy is echoed by a columnist in the *Oxford Eagle*, who, backing up Lafayette County's "historic contention that it is the most Anglo Saxon spot in the entire United States," notes that "among the hundreds of Oxford citizens who appear in 'Intruder in the Dust,' scarcely six non-Anglo-Saxon names could be found!" The southerner's interest in supporting the ideal of pure origins is indicated by the final line of this writer's story: "the Anglo-Saxon blood has been kept intact down the years." For both Stevens and this nameless columnist, proper names signify racial purity, a quality invoked in any justification of white hegemony. As James Snead has observed, this is why Lucas's name is so disturbing to whites in *Intruder in the Dust*. Already a sign of miscegenation whose physical presence repudiates the dominant culture's basic racial philosophy, Lucas is also very careful that people know the proper genealogical referent of his name: "I aint a Edmonds," Lucas corrects the sawmill lout who harasses him at the crossroads store, "I belongs to the old lot. I'm a McCaslin" (*ID*, 19). Lucas's presence thus denies Stevens and his community the right to tell itself stories about its pure, Anglo-Saxon identity. In response, they seek to rewrite Lucas's white ancestry in Native American terms, and thus exclude him from their vision of a homogeneous Anglo-Saxon South.[16]

Democrats, Dixiecrats, and the "Reversion" of Civil Rights

This desire to remove Lucas from the protected center of the white South, evident in both Faulkner's novel and Brown's film, suggests southerners' anxieties in the late 1940s over their losses in the national debate over segregation following Truman's desegregation of the military during World War II and his party's reelection in 1948 despite—possibly because of—the civil rights plank in its campaign platform. Edmund Wilson's statement, in his review of *Intruder in the Dust* in the *New Yorker*, that Faulkner's novel contained "a kind of counterblast to the anti-lynching bill and to the civil-rights plank in the Democratic platform" suggests that the southern fantasy was threatened by real fears of federally mandated desegregation.[17] The filming of *Intruder in the Dust* and its consequent removal of racial issues from the body of the "real," placed within the context of the Democratic South's political revolt in 1948, can thus be read as a local example of the region's strategic response to one more threat from a "belligerent" North.

If one could isolate a single event that launched the civil rights debate into the 1948 campaign it would be the skirmish that erupted at the Democratic nominating convention over the language of the party's civil rights plank. Truman had adopted civil rights as a party priority in 1946, when he created, through executive order, the Committee on Civil Rights, which published its findings in a highly publicized statement, "To Secure These Rights." On February 2, 1948, Truman delivered an address to Congress proposing action on several of the items listed in this document. Following strong opposition by southern members of the Senate, however, Truman backed off these proposals and along with members of his campaign team pushed for a moderate statement in the platform built at the 1948 convention. The drafting committee at the convention cooperated by crafting a moderate civil rights statement, asserting the following: "We again call upon the Congress to exert its full authority to the limit of its constitutional powers to assure and protect these rights." This ambiguous language was a concession to southern Democrats, who could read it as a recognition of the limits of federal jurisdiction, and of the validity of the doctrine of states' rights. However, when minority drafts were put to a floor vote, this language was replaced by the following statement: "We call upon Congress to support our President in guaranteeing these basic and fundamental rights: (1) the right of full and equal political participation (2) the right to equal opportunity of employment (3) the right of security of person, and (4) the right of equal treatment in the service and defense of our nation." This new language repudiated the doctrine of states' rights. As a consequence of its adoption, delegates from southern states, including Mississippi and Alabama, walked out of the convention, and on July 17 dissatisfied southern Democrats met in Birmingham, Alabama, to nominate Governor Strom Thurmond of South Carolina and Governor Fielding L. Wright of Mississippi for president and vice president on a states' rights ticket. In several southern states, including Mississippi, this ticket was listed on the official ballot as the nomination of the Democratic Party.[18]

One reason the story of Lucas's near-lynching in *Intruder in the Dust* might be read in relation to the Democratic split in 1948 is that this split was a culmination of southern opposition to federal antilynching legislation throughout the first half of this century.[19] Although Strom Thurmond was himself considered a "liberal-minded" governor because he was known to pursue the perpetrators of lynching in his state, "he always opposed a federal anti-lynching law as an unconstitutional invasion of states' rights."[20] Southerners like Thurmond and Wright had always resisted this legislation because of the precedent it would set for federal intervention in the South, especially in matters relating to segregation. While desegregation was thus the paramount consideration of the states' rights party, it had been articulated before World War II primarily through opposition to federal antilynching legislation, which, to the Dixiecrats, amounted to the unconstitutional extension of federal powers into state law enforcement. This connection between federal legislative pressures and reactionary southern opinion is directly represented in Faulkner's novel when a white farmer, upon seeing Sheriff Hampton driving out of town with two black prisoners, his car loaded with the shovels that will disinter Vinson Gowrie's coffin, shouts, "Aint you heard about that new lynch law the Yankees passed? the folks that lynches the nigger is supposed to dig the grave?" (*ID*, 137). Implicitly, however, a discursive link runs throughout both Faulkner's novel and Brown's film between the doctrine of states' rights and southern intransigence in the face of federal imperatives regarding both the system of segregation and the weakness of southern antilynching efforts.

Much of the lobbying on behalf of antilynching legislation was done by members of the Association of Southern Women for the Prevention of Lynching, and this political activism of southern women against the criminal actions of white men is also represented in Faulkner's novel in several ways.[21] Like the transformation of the African American into a rhetorical figure that is then always available as an object of erasure, the politically active woman is transformed by both Faulkner's novel and Brown's film into the stereotype of the passive "kinless spinster" always on the verge of political irrelevancy (*ID*, 75). "Good evening, sir," Chick says as he interrupts Miss Habersham's conference with his uncle; Miss Habersham is in his blind spot, but even when he acknowledges her presence he simultaneously can forget her: "He had dismissed her; he had said 'Excuse me' and so evanished her not only from the room but the moment too" (*ID*, 74, 77). Although Miss Habersham's role in freeing Lucas is crucial and does suggest the contemporary work of members of the Association of Southern Women for the Prevention of Lynching, the ludicrousness of the scene at the jail in which she passively resists Crawford Gowrie's attack shows that Faulkner's text is also blind to the active role of women in the battle against lynching. The ideological figure of the spinster, then, allows both the novel and the film to "stitch over" the "irrational" fact of activist white southern women with the socially acceptable image of a respectful white male (Crawford Gowrie!) dutifully observing the wishes of a venerable southern lady.

Beyond eliding southern women's protests against violence committed in the name of southern womanhood, Faulkner's novel, and MGM's proposed film adaptation, offered Oxonians the opportunity to respond to increased calls, on a national level, for civil rights reforms. In the novel, this regional response is articulated in Gavin Stevens's theory of the South's racial future, which both depends upon and disavows certain traditions within African American culture. On behalf of the white South, Stevens offers African Americans what amounts to a counter-proposal to W. E. B. Du Bois's offer, fifty years earlier, of a general theory for understanding the uniqueness of American culture. In *The Souls of Black Folk,* Du Bois had looked forward to a day when "on American soil two world-races may give each to each those characteristics both so sadly lack." Du Bois recites a long list of racial characteristics African America could offer the country and concludes with a celebration of black Americans' "simple faith and reverence in a dusty desert of dollars and smartness."[22] In what amounts to a counterproposal in Faulkner's novel, Stevens suggests a "confederation" between black and white southerners and likewise portrays the true enemy of the American citizen (regardless of race) in terms of a "mass of people who no longer have anything in common save a frantic greed for money" (*ID,* 153). But Stevens's offer is something less than a free exchange among equals; referring to the generalized "Negro," Stevens proposes that "We—he and us—should confederate: swap him the rest of the economic and political and cultural privileges which are his right, for the reversion of his capacity to wait and endure and survive" (*ID,* 153).

What does it mean for Stevens to ask, in this "swap" intended to atone for the historical effects of slavery, for the "reversion" of Lucas's (and of all African Americans') capacity to endure and survive?[23] Although it might appear that Stevens is simply asking blacks to teach whites the virtues of patience and survival, the OED's first definition of "reversion" has a strictly legal sense, of which Yoknapatawpha's county lawyer would certainly be aware: "the return of an estate to the donor or grantor, or his heirs, after the expiry of the grant."[24] If this is Stevens's sense, then his theory is that upon the establishment of the Jim Crow South, whites "granted" blacks certain qualities (the "capacity to wait and endure and survive"), in exchange for the social and economic privileges that adhere to the dominant group in a segregated society. According to the logic of his proposal, then, for blacks to coexist peacefully with whites in a post-Confederate southern society, for them to be given back their "economic and political and cultural" rights, these essences, constitutive of an "estate" (the "capacity to wait and endure and survive"), must be surrendered, reverted back "to the donor or grantor." In other words, blacks can keep their human "essences" only in the absence of economic and political enfranchisement; if granted these, blacks must sacrifice, at least in the eyes and minds of white southerners, those attributes that Faulkner himself, in his Nobel acceptance speech, considered most fundamental to human experience (the capacity to "endure and prevail"). The logic of Stevens's plan for southern renewal thus calls for exactly that "second slavery" Du Bois warned against. Because it is predicated upon the "reversion" to whites of all legal control over the "essences" of black humanity, it would necessarily reproduce the second-class status blacks already suffered under segregation.

While most of the details of Stevens's proposal are not directly represented in Brown's film, a second sense of "reversion," as "the right of succession to an office or place of emolument, after the death or retirement of the holder," does dominate Brown's understanding of Stevens's character and his rivalry with Lucas over Chick's racial allegiance.[25] In both novel and film, Stevens is astonished that Chick has disobeyed his command not to deliver Lucas's tobacco personally and is clearly motivated by this cut, this threat to his own "place of emolument," in his subsequent transactions with Lucas. As long as Lucas remains the prime suspect in Vinson Gowrie's murder, Stevens safely occupies the position of Chick's mentor, but once Lucas's guilt is in doubt—thanks to Chick's own actions—Stevens becomes anxious that Chick has learned to understand the world (more specifically, the world of race relations in the South) from Lucas's point of view, rather than his own. This is where Brown's camera *can* represent Stevens's anxieties over the increased influence of blacks upon racial policies in the South. Stevens remains fast by Chick's side from the moment Chick returns from the Caledonia Chapel, correcting his nephew's interpretations of the townspeople and of the likely future consequences of their actions.

These moments of verbal confrontation, by the end of Brown's film, have at least two effects. First, they transform the story of Lucas's near-lynching into a story of momentary white vulnerability followed by "redemption." Stevens tells Chick in one of the final scenes of the film, "We were in trouble, not Lucas Beauchamp." While Stevens thus participates in the white South's habit of substituting whites for blacks as the ultimate victims of the region's oppressive racial climate, he is also speaking personally, expressing his insecurity as an authority figure before Chick.

A second consequence of Stevens's concerted effort to re-indoctrinate his nephew is the rhetorical transformation of Lucas, once again, into the figure of the Negro. This is best observed in the final lines of the film, as Chick and Stevens see Lucas walking through the town square. Chick says,

> They don't see him, as though it never happened.
> They see him.
> No. They don't even know he's there.
> But they do. The same as I do. And they always will, as long as he lives. Proud, stubborn, insufferable. But there he goes, the keeper of my conscience.
> Our conscience, Uncle John.

Chick believes that Lucas has entered into the townspeople's "blind spot"—that they simply refuse to acknowledge Lucas's presence among them. But Stevens knows that the people of Jefferson have gone a step further, replacing the actual Lucas Beauchamp with the white invention of the Negro—"proud, stubborn, insufferable." And once again, Stevens assumes the role of the aggrieved white whose own victimhood supersedes that of Lucas's, because it is now Lucas who holds power over Stevens as the "keeper" of his conscience. That Chick once again acquiesces to Stevens's interpretation is signified by his appropriation of Stevens's language ("our conscience, Uncle John") and by his physical proximity to Stevens as the two observe Lucas on the town square at the film's conclusion. In each of these scenes, Stevens successfully imposes his perspective upon Chick, making Chick see things from his (white, middle-class) point of view and privileging it over Lucas's.

Film as an Apparatus of Race *and* Class Identity

Stevens's theory of reversion as the grounds upon which blacks and whites will coexist in the postwar South articulates the several layers of white response in the 1940s to pressures from the North for progress on race relations. He tells Chick that "people in the North believe it can be compelled . . . ," but the insincerity of his proposal, his call for an "exchange" of values between the races, simply restates the position of intransigent southerners who were in no mood to "give" on civil rights without receiving something in return, regardless of what pressures may emanate from Washington (*ID*, 152). Although Oxonians were often disaffected by Faulkner's commentaries upon race relations, they were sympathetic toward the ultimate conservatism of Stevens's position. Still, it took the city of Oxford some time to warm to the idea of Hollywood outsiders converging on their town to make a film about race. As Faulkner himself related in a conversation quoted by Blotner, "people were saying, 'We don't want no one comin' into our town to make no movie about no lynchin.'" And in an article for the *Oxford Eagle* that looked back to early concerns about the "public relations problem" of bringing nonsouthern black actors into Oxford, Phil Mullen writes, "Just at the time, racial tension throughout the country had been inflamed by the politicians. That certain type of red-tinged racial extremist could have created incidents which would have done great harm." Although the elections thus contributed to an atmosphere in Mississippi and in Oxford that was hostile to outsider commentary about racial relations there, this atmosphere dissipated when Brown and MGM pitched the idea to local merchants. Soon after Brown arrived in February 1949, to scout the area for filming in the spring, the local chamber of commerce met and voted to support Brown: the film would be "of great economic, cultural, and advertising value to Oxford," chamber of commerce president C. S. Haney claimed, as he pledged Oxford's full support. Oxford's merchants overcame their initial reluctance because it made good business sense, but their decision combined economics with a concern for the region's national image, apparently convinced by Brown that the film could be "a great credit to Oxford and to the South."[26]

We could say that Oxford's merchants saw an opportunity for profit in Brown's proposal and leave it at that. But I want finally to show how these merchants and professional men and women also were concerned that only a lower-class, bigoted view of southern race relations was reaching the North, and saw the presence of Hollywood's cameras as an opportunity to define the "real" South as primarily mercantile and middle class. "Class" thus describes an additional category of dependence and disavowal outlined by the discursive arrangements of Faulkner's story in Oxford in 1949. It is distinguished from the nineteenth-century removal of Indians to the western territories, and from the twentieth-century removal of both black-white interdependence and the political protests of southern women from the "real" South, primarily in the degree to which the removal of lower-class whites necessitated the simultaneous refashioning of white southernness. This, too, is in line with Stevens's theory of southern race relations, for in his construction of a "homogeneous" South, and in order to illustrate segregationist claims of "equal" racial treatment, he found it necessary to remove lower-class whites like the Gowries from the sphere of the privileged white southerner. If Lucas shouldn't be lynched for killing Vinson Gowrie, his theory implies, well, the wheels of southern justice will turn toward the next likely suspect, regardless of race. To be sure, the doctrine of a pure, Anglo-Saxon South is itself evidence of the dominant culture's self-constructions in relation to its underrepresented populations. But the process by which the white South is redefined in both Faulkner's novel and Brown's film as primarily middle-class, merchant, and professional is unlike these earlier episodes of subject formation because it involves the sacrifice of one whole class of whites in order to continue the illusion of a pure center threatened by hostile margins. While Faulkner's text illustrates how lower-class whites can be substituted for racial Others and thus removed from the center of the social body in similar ways, the events surrounding its filming—as well as those surrounding its "world premiere"—show how Oxford's dominant merchant class intentionally sought to remove itself from the image of poor, "benighted" whites in the South.

Not only were local merchants and businessmen, under the auspices of the chamber of commerce, responsible for the initial decision to welcome Brown, MGM, and the idea of filming in Oxford, they continued to pitch Faulkner's story to the rest of the town throughout the spring, summer, and early fall of 1949. The chamber of commerce became the studio's local casting office, finding roles in the film for over three hundred white and two hundred black county residents. More than anything, the chamber of commerce intensely advertised the film, both locally and in outside papers. The *Oxford Eagle* reports that Mayor Williams and the "World Premiere Committee" would host "the largest group (thirty) of notable newspaper editors ever to visit Oxford." And when the film debuted, the *Eagle* emphasized it as the town's opportunity to display itself to the North. "In Most Any Newspaper in the Country," reads the front-page headline of the world premiere edition, "May Appear Something about Oxford." Such widespread attention caused the people of Oxford to fall over themselves in their excitement at being projected upon the big screen: Mississippi's Governor Wright, the Dixiecrats' vice presidential candidate the previous year, named Clarence Brown an honorary colonel on his staff; the city organized the biggest parade in its history, with prizes for floats to be judged by Brown; the university scheduled a Premiere Ball; and a string band was commissioned for a free street dance, for which cornmeal was "scattered over the concrete to save the shoe leather." Significantly, the theme for parade floats was "The New South."[27]

If the film and its premiere provided Oxford the opportunity to advertise itself to the rest of the country, the image promoted was distinct from popular images of the Old South. Unlike the Agrarians' touting of the poor yeomanry in the 1930s, or *Gone with the Wind*'s portrayal of aristocratic landowners, the people behind the filming of *Intruder in the Dust* celebrated a middle-class, professional identity for themselves and their region. In the premiere edition of the *Oxford Eagle*, for example, the editors call attention to Oxford notes written by MGM publicist Barrett Kiesling and scattered throughout the nation's media. Most of these celebrate the realism of the film by noting, for example, its use of Oxford's own St. Peter's Episcopal Church, rather than a Hollywood set, in the opening scene. But the notes also stress the mercantile and professional image of Oxford that Brown's film would publicize across the country. "St. Peter's was built in 1851," one note reads; "it now joins the Lafayette County Jail, a college professor's home, a cotton farm, a dress shop, a drug store and a lawyer's office in the list of authentic settings which Brown used."[28]

Moreover, an anecdote printed under these notes suggests how class image was a pervasive undercurrent of the event of Brown's filming. Brown, looking for a local resident to portray the proprietor of Fraser's Store, found George Galloway at his own general store and cast him on the spot: "It disturbed [Galloway] that director Brown had thrust him before the camera just as he was, and somewhat mussed from moving merchandise. So at noon he went home, washed, shaved and changed his clothes. The shave could be obliterated with make-up . . . but it was necessary for store-owner Galloway to return home and don the togs in which he had been registered by the cameras during the morning!"[29] Just as local blacks had not wanted to cooperate with Brown by willingly jailing themselves, so this local merchant wanted to avoid being filmed in the trappings of the lower class, because of the separation of this class from the empowered (middle) classes that was occurring at the time.

Faulkner's novel is replete with middle-class success stories of the sort that would have appealed to Oxford's chamber of commerce. Most of these involve erstwhile farmers who, after a few years' residence in town, own property—sometimes their own homes—and are prospering as office workers or professionals. Such success stories of the middle class are represented in individual characters like sheriff Hampton ("He was a countryman, a farmer and son of farmers when he was first elected and now owned himself the farm and house where he had been born" [*ID*, 105]); and Jefferson's town marshal ("a Beat Four Ingrum come to town as the apostate sons of Beat Four occasionally did to marry a town girl and become barbers and bailiffs and nightwatchmen"[*ID*, 133]). But the phenomenon is also evinced in Faulkner's descriptions of neighborhoods "where the prosperous young married couples lived with two children each and (as soon as they could afford it) an automobile each and the memberships in the country club/and the bridge clubs" (*ID*, 118).

Following Faulkner's interest in Jefferson's changing class structure, the story of Brown's filming, as it is told in the pages of the *Oxford Eagle*, offers the city's mayor, R. X. Williams, as a symbol of the "arrived" middle class in the South. Williams figures prominently in the newspaper's stories as a promoter of the city, the owner of the local theater where the "world premiere" took place, and, as one *Eagle* photo caption reads, "practically the 'location manager' for the M-G-M film company."[30] He is also one of the city's residents chosen to play a character in the film, the role of Mr. Lillie, "a countryman," Faulkner's text reads, "who had moved to town a year ago and now owned a small shabby side street grocery" (*ID*, 46). The text dwells upon Lillie's house as a harbinger of middle-class suburbia: "a small neat shoebox of a house built last year between two other houses already close enough together to hear one another's toilets flush" (*ID*, 46). In the film, the story of a transplanted yeoman pursuing a nobler class identity for himself is further signified by the crisp new suit worn by Mayor Williams, seemingly out of place for someone watering his grass, but "coherent" in the sense that it suggests Lillie's long day at the office. Williams—and by extension, all the merchants and business owners who participated in the filming—thus performed roles both in Brown's film and in the story of the New South that grew out of Hollywood's presence in Oxford.

In the process of producing Oxford as a middle-class success story, Brown's filming followed Faulkner's text in sacrificing lower-class whites in order to project the illusion of equal racial treatment under segregation. As with the removal of black subjectivity in "southernist" historiography of the Reconstruction, we should recognize that the removal of poor whites from the image of the New South fashioned in both Faulkner's text and Brown's film is predicated upon a certain revision of the middle and upper classes' role in the South's racial past. After all, it was a former U.S. Senator from Mississippi, W. V. Sullivan, who asserted with pride to a reporter for the Jackson *Daily Clarion-Ledger* that it was he who had led the mob against Nelse Patton in 1908. And as late as 1950 Faulkner had identified a prominent banker as the author of a hate letter in response to Faulkner's advocacy, in a letter to a local paper, of integrated public schools.[31] Thus the dialectic of class identity-formation relies upon a process of dependence and disavowal similar to that in regard to race: the middle and upper classes depended upon their rural, agrarian past to demonstrate their own economic progress, but disavowed this dependence by explaining the South's remaining prejudices as a problem of the lower, unreconstructed classes.

As with any process founded upon artificial binary oppositions, Oxford's fashioning of a white, middle-class identity for itself is fraught with contradiction and irrationality. Within the contexts of both Faulkner's novel and Brown's film, the fantasy of a unified, white middle class is most vulnerable when it is confronted by the double-impossibility, according to its logic, of a black middle class. As the cotton farm included in the list of "authentic" film scenes suggests, the ownership of property—as Lucas owns the ten acres at the center of the antebellum McCaslin plantation—qualifies one for middle-class status in Jefferson as in Oxford. Lucas's final appearance in Faulkner's fiction, demanding a written record of the financial transaction he has conducted with Gavin Stevens—the most visible white professional in Jefferson—thus confirms his own "arrival" in the face of efforts by the white community in general, and by Gavin Stevens in particular, to exclude him. And as I have already suggested, Hernandez's Hollywood celebrity presented the people of Oxford with an analogous refutation of the system of exclusions upon which their segregated society was based.

I would not want finally to reduce these various instances of subject-formation to a *single* formula of dependence and disavowal, however. Doing so would participate in the same longing for order and cohesion this dialectic serves to support. Doing so would allow one to rationalize the white South's history of racial exclusion, for instance, as fundamentally the same as the wealthy white South's economic and political scapegoating of poor whites. It is true that middle-class whites have depended upon blacks, poor whites, and politically active women, and have disavowed this dependence in similar ways. But the consequences of the dialectic are different in these various situations. When Chick says the people of Jefferson will "make a nigger" out of Lucas, his phrase refers to the same process by which Nelse Patton became the figure of the Negro in the 1908 *Oxford Eagle* (*ID*, 31). In this process, the actual Lucas—with a home, a family, a history—would be transformed into an ideological object of scorn and mutilation, one which could be used in subsequent retellings of his lynching to reinforce the white fantasy of uncorrupted racial boundaries. When Crawford Gowrie emerges as the real murderer, however, the nearest thing to an ideological figure for the people of Jefferson and Beat Four to transform him into is a perpetrator of fratricide, understood in terms of the Old Testament. In the postwar context of Faulkner's story, this rhetorical transformation anticipates no communal violence against Crawford, as it does in the case of Lucas. Instead, Crawford conveniently is allowed to take his own life with comparative honor. A final, perhaps obvious difference between these cases is the speed with which the two objects of disavowal are inserted into the dominant class's dialectic of self-ratification. Lucas is immediately accepted as a suitable object of scorn and ritual erasure, whereas Crawford, still a visible reminder of the white middle class's own recent experiences, is only disavowed when the facts of Vinson's murder become undeniable.

This is only to say that one should avoid the temptation to reduce narratives of social injustice to a single plot without considering the differential spaces between them. Rather, we should seek to retrieve the details of cultural events that seem most impossible, most irreducible to a single narrative of symbolization. A final example from what happened to Faulkner's novel during Brown's filming will illustrate this point. Literally, we know that the body of Jake Montgomery gets lost somewhere between Faulkner's novel and Clarence Brown's film. In the novel, when Chick, Aleck Sander, and Miss Habersham disinter Vinson Gowrie's coffin, they discover that Gowrie's body has been replaced with that of Jake Montgomery, the agent to whom Crawford Gowrie had been selling the lumber he stole from his brother, Vinson, and his uncle, Sudley Workitt. Montgomery had known that Crawford had stolen the lumber he was selling, and that it was Crawford, not Lucas, who murdered Vinson. It was Montgomery who first dug up the body of Vinson Gowrie with the aim of using the forensic evidence it contained (the bullet from Crawford's, not Lucas's, gun) to blackmail Crawford. But Crawford ambushes Montgomery—bashes his skull and throws his body into Vinson's grave—and then disposes of Vinson's body in the nearby quicksand. This subplot of Faulkner's novel is left out of Brown's film; like the details of the Nelse Patton affair, which would have confused the formula of "white womanhood protected" for the readers of the *Oxford Eagle* in 1908, Jake Montgomery's connection to the Gowries, and the second corpse it introduces into Faulkner's narrative, would have complicated Ben Maddow's screenplay beyond the coherence of a Hollywood film. Yet, implicitly, Montgomery's body represents many of the irrationalities and inconsistencies in racial and economic ideology that the dominant group of any social formation would prefer simply to forget. Its elision from Brown's film, therefore, can serve as one final example of the phenomenon of disavowal I have explored in this chapter.

Montgomery's body is *the* evidence of Lucas's innocence. His murder occurs while Lucas is detained in jail and thus redirects the focus of Stevens's and Sheriff Hampton's investigation away from Lucas and toward Crawford Gowrie. Symbolically, when it is driven into town from Caledonia Chapel, Montgomery's body is also the evidence of the white townspeople's eagerness to disavow the facts of Lucas's case in favor of the dialectic that would allow them to lynch this "Negro" and thereby ratify their racial and economic identities. Chick is aware of the evidentiary value of Montgomery's body when, upon watching the town's response to the body's arrival, he recalls his uncle's statement that "they [the townspeople] could stand anything provided they still retained always the right to refuse to admit it was visible" (*ID*, 181). Faulkner's townspeople, in other words, are prepared to accept the facts of Lucas's innocence provided they can immediately disavow, or "stitch over," the visible evidence of such facts. And this is exactly what their counterparts in the actual town of Oxford, Mississippi, are invited to do when they collaborate with the filming of Clarence Brown's film, which leaves out altogether the "body" of evidence provided by the Jake Montgomery subplot of Faulkner's novel. As I hope to have shown, however, cultural events like the filming of *Intruder in the Dust* are best understood when we retrieve the incoherent details that others have determined to forget, and examine the processes of dependence and disavowal that lie behind their removal.

Rethinking Revision: "Zones of Contact" in Faulkner

Throughout his career, Faulkner produced a literary discourse remarkably contiguous with other discourses of his culture. Whether these emanated from academic disciplines (such as history, anthropology, or sociology), from professions (such as the law), from labor history, national politics, or national or regional economics, the discourses that shaped America from the 1920s through the 1950s are represented in the discursive architecture of Faulkner's novels. These texts do not reflect contemporary events in a simple, direct way, however, because the discursive structures of history, law, labor, and anthropology experienced moments of "eruption" during the period Faulkner wrote, moments in which existing paradigms were turned on their heads by the subjects (or subject-effects) they produced. These discourses of culture developed new rules of formation and exclusion in the modern period and consequently are observable in Faulkner's literary discourse at those moments of discursive contiguity—what Bakhtin refers to as "zones of contact" between the different social languages of society—which foreground the contingencies of historical experience.[1]

One key aspect of this approach to reading Faulkner is the connection it establishes between moments of revision in Faulkner's practice as a novelist and the representation in his novels of "revisionary" moments of emergence within these other discourses of culture. The preponderance of the evidence I have provided for a discursive reading of the novels is drawn from revised portions of these texts—usually from portions of the novels that were added to or changed in some way from a previous draft or published story. This would indicate that readers of Faulkner who are interested in the cultural/discursive contexts of his work should consider the contexts of his *revisions* to a much greater extent than they currently do. As I will argue below, it also indicates that any understanding of the "novelistic" qualities of Faulkner's writing should be based, at least in part, upon an analysis of his "novelistic" practices of revision.

Bakhtin considered the novel a unique genre because of its capacity to absorb other genres and, essentially, other languages of the social formation. The novel is not the tool solely of the dominant social groups; it is the staging ground for the lived conflicts that exist in any society between the "languages" of the various social groups. Key to Bakhtin's theory of the novel is the understanding that it is a *developing* genre: "The novel is the only developing genre and therefore it reflects more deeply, more essentially, more sensitively and rapidly, reality itself in the process of its unfolding. Only that which is itself developing can comprehend development as a process" (*DI*, 7). The novel contrasts with the "epic" genres precisely because in the latter what is represented is the distant past (Bakhtin often refers to this as the "national, hierarchical past"), and the moment of narration of these genres establishes an insurmountable gap between the narrator's audience and his or her "field" of representation. The epic past does not develop; audiences do not expect it to.

The novel, by contrast, is based upon a confrontation between audiences and the present "in all its openendedness" (*DI*, 19). When Bakhtin characterizes the novel as a developing genre, he is, of course, speaking historically. He is contrasting the unique ability of the western novel, since its emergence in the eighteenth century, to absorb all other genres, with "those genres that stubbornly preserve their old canonic nature" (*DI*, 6). However, there is no reason we should not consider moments of novelistic revision in works by Faulkner (or any other novelist) as particular moments in the development of the novel as a genre. We have observed the "novelization" of certain poetic images in Faulkner's transformation from poet to novelist when he revised conventional, pastoral imagery from his Mississippi poems into a dialogized representation of social conflict in *Flags in the Dust*. Such an approach to revision in Faulkner merely takes literally Bakhtin's statement that "only that which is itself developing can comprehend development as a process." But this understanding of Faulkner's practice of revision is further warranted when we observe that what Bakhtin considers the defining characteristic of the novel—its ability to represent the *heteroglossia* of society—is most true of Faulkner's novels in those portions he revised most heavily (often, from a previously published story) for textualization in the novels. Compared to his "novelistic" revisions of them, Faulkner's magazine stories are relatively monologic; they are "poetic in the narrow sense," for in them "the internal dialogization of discourse is not put to artistic use" (*DI,* 284). By contrast, in the novels "this internal dialogization becomes one of the most fundamental aspects of prose style and undergoes a specific artistic elaboration" (*DI,* 284). As I have defined it, this "internal dialogization" always involves some contiguous reference, some "zone of contact," with other discursive structures of society.

For example, much of the evidence I presented to demonstrate contiguities between *The Hamlet* and revisionist impulses within both legal and anthropological discourse comes from material Faulkner revised for the novel from the previously published short story "Spotted Horses." We observed in Faulkner's representations of the law in *The Hamlet* and *Knight's Gambit* evidence of a rebellion within legal discourse by adherents of legal realism, a movement that criticized formalist rhetoric about the rule of law and that advocated instead a more practical understanding of the everyday effects of the law in people's lives. The two pieces of evidence I used to demonstrate formalist paradigms in *The Hamlet* were not present in the earlier "Spotted Horses." Henry Armstid's faith in "precedent" as a guarantor of equal treatment under the "law" of the horse sale, for instance, is wholly missing from the original story. It is only in the novel's version that the Armstids arrive after Buck Hipps has offered Eck Snopes one free horse in exchange for starting the bidding on another. Similarly, Buck Hipps's use of the semiotics of religious space to compel the villagers of Frenchman's Bend to respect his authority as a horse trader is missing from the earlier "Spotted Horses," in which Hipps sits atop a fence post and conducts his sale in a relatively straightforward way. In each of these examples of Faulkner's revisionary practice, a conjunction between legal and religious forms of authority marks the revised "Spotted Horses" episode of *The Hamlet* as a "zone of contact" between Faulkner's literary discourse and contemporary discontinuities within American legal discourse.

These examples of discursive contiguity in *The Hamlet* are made possible by the most obvious change Faulkner made while revising "Spotted Horses" for the novel: his shift from the first-person narration of V. K. Surratt in "Spotted Horses," to the third-person omniscient narrator whose voice can more fully encompass the languages of the novel's "concrete social context" (*DI*, 300). While dialogization can occur within any single speech act, Faulkner's changing of Surratt's first-person account to a third-person omniscient narrator increases the novel's capacity to represent contiguous discursive activity. This becomes clearer if we recall the argument that Faulkner's representation of Mrs. Armstid contains "quotations" from the language of Farm Security Administration photography, and that this is so because of a more general representation in *The Hamlet* of the emergence of ethnographic practices within the discipline of anthropology. The emotive quality of the omniscient narrator's language would not have had the same effect had it emanated from the colloquial storyteller V. K. Surratt in "Spotted Horse." But in the revised, narrativized, and *novelized* scene in *The Hamlet*, it contributes to the novel's overall participation in national (and regional) debates about rural poverty, and the possibilities of a federal response to the problem.

The revisions Faulkner made to "Spotted Horses" and other previously published stories made them (and the novels) more *novelistic,* in Bakhtin's sense of that term. One reason for this is the presence of the trope of "laughter" at moments of revision in the literary discourse that Faulkner generated, as well as in contemporary discourses of culture as they experienced moments of revisionary emergence. Faulkner often scorned his commercial stories. He berated them and was eager for opportunities to revise them for integration into novels and *novelistic* story collections, such as *The Unvanquished* and *Go Down, Moses.* In a 1934 letter to Morton Goldman, he referred to previous versions of stories later published as *The Unvanquished* as "trash" and "a pulp series." Yet, after revising these stories, and writing "An Odor of Verbena" to conclude the new novel, his attitude toward the series changed, as signified by his use of *The Unvanquished* as a model for another story collection even dearer to him, *Go Down, Moses.* Michael Grimwood has written persuasively about this pattern in Faulkner's career, particularly in his argument that Faulkner's revisions of an earlier version of "Knight's Gambit" constitute a "gesture of repudiation and exorcism" for the "sins" Faulkner had committed in first publishing the other *Knight's Gambit* stories in commercial magazines.[2] Faulkner did not consider his published stories finished pearls; he was willing to rise up against them, to "laugh" at them, and, as Bakhtin writes of the novelistic impulse generally, to experiment with them.

Of laughter as a novelistic trope, Bakhtin writes, "As it draws an object to itself and makes it familiar, laughter delivers the object into the fearless hands of investigative experiment—both scientific and artistic—and into the hands of free experimental fantasy" (*DI*, 23). While it is easy to apply this language to Faulkner's attitude as a modern writer, it is important to note that a similar spirit of irreverent experimentalism characterizes each of the revisionary subjects of modern discursive systems discussed in the preceding chapters: W. E. B. Du Bois, whose revisionist historiography altered both the rules and practices of American historiography in the 1930s; the legal realists, who sought to alter the legal paradigm that determined Americans' understanding of the law, whether in the law schools of the Northeast or in courtrooms across the nation; the labor leaders of the 1930s, who lobbied in Washington and in factories throughout the country in favor of workers' rights over the rights of management and of factory and business owners; and finally, the ethnographers who, following the lead of Bronislaw Malinowski in 1922, altered the practices of anthropologists for the rest of the century. Each of these examples of discursive emergence can be characterized as a revisionary gesture attended by the laughter of the modern sensibility at the traditions (especially, at the traditions of exclusion) of the past.

A final connection to make between these moments of revision within a variety of modern discursive systems and contiguous moments of revision in Faulkner's practice as a novelist is that each moment of revision results in the production of new subjects (and subject-effects) of discourse, and that these are then newly available to discursive systems across a given culture or society. The emergence of legal realism in the early twentieth century created new subjects of the law who understood the effect of the law in fundamentally different ways when compared to people of the nineteenth century. The details of what "counts" as legal information were different, and therefore the ways in which people defined themselves (and were themselves defined) in relation to legal information changed as well. These new possibilities of subjectivity were then made freely available to the subjects of other cultural discourses, such as Faulkner, who could reproduce them in the literary discourse he produced—especially, as I have argued, in his representations of legal figures such as Gavin Stevens. In the early Gavin Stevens stories, we see him convert to the principles and practices of the legal realists of his time; in a fundamental way, this is possible only because of alterations in the discourse of the law that occurred contemporaneously with Faulkner's writing.

Modern discursive systems should always be understood within a context of emergence, however. Just as the novel itself is a "developing genre," the discourses of culture contiguous with the novel are constantly undergoing changes in their rules of formation and exclusion. Because the influence of legal realism waned shortly after World War II, Faulkner's representations of the law in the late 1940s necessarily reflected the diminished power of the legal realist paradigm in some way. As I understand it, the final version of "Knight's Gambit" does this by reverting to a more conservative, formalist paradigm in representing the legal maneuverings of Gavin Stevens.

Finally, we must consider the possibility that such discursive influences are reciprocal. As Bakhtin writes, it is the nature of the novel as a genre to offer authors (and readers) new subject positions from which to understand cultural experience. Indeed, this is the defining characteristic of the novel within the history of its own discursive emergence, as it places authors and audiences into a "zone of contact" with the depicted world: its "new positioning of the author," Bakhtin writes, "must be considered one of the most important results of surmounting epic (hierarchical) distance" (*DI*, 28). Therefore, it is always possible that the novel, or some discursive system other than the law itself, is partly or wholly responsible for the production of a new legal subjectivity, and that the same sort of reciprocity influences the production and reproduction of subjects (and subject-effects) within novelistic discourse (on one hand), and (on the other) historiography, anthropology, political economy, and other modern discursive systems.

In the end, it is precisely the issue of "causality" that makes any discussion of discourse in Faulkner difficult to pin down. This is a challenge rather than a curse. We no longer live in a time in which mechanistic theories of causality and influence will solve the puzzles either of modern America or modern American literature. We cannot explain "race" as an essential category of identity once we have understood it as a concept that developed in specific historical, economic, national, and international contexts; we cannot study the development of "blackness" without accounting for the simultaneous and contiguous development of "whiteness." And we certainly cannot examine such concepts in Faulkner's literary discourse without accounting for these relations of contiguity as best we can. Hence the substitution in cultural criticism, and in the preceding pages, of theories of "representation" for previous generations of critics' theories of reflection, source studies, and examinations of literary influence. These were predicated upon the assumption that texts, whether literary or extraliterary, are discrete units unto themselves, and that authors, also discrete, autonomous, and willful entities, make conscious decisions regarding the literary works they create, the events they depict. In very disturbing ways, "discourse" changes all this. It asks that we disregard the assumption of wholeness and instead consider texts contingent, incomplete, always unfinished. And it requires a similarly discursive attitude toward our own identities, as writers, as critics, as human beings. Blasphemously, a discursive approach to literary criticism asks us to relinquish our hard-won "selves" in exchange for identities based upon "relations." Left to negotiate our lives as readers and writers of texts on a purely contingent basis, we can only grasp nostalgically at the brass ring of coherence, which, on each round, we can only remember vaguely as once having been within our reach.

NOTES

Introduction: Voice and Discourse in Faulkner

1. Malcolm Cowley, comp., introduction to *The Portable Faulkner* (1946; repr., New York: Viking 1974), viii. Lawrence Schwartz locates Cowley's first effort to revise Faulkner's reputation in a 1940 review of *The Hamlet*. See *Creating Faulkner's Reputation: The Politics of Modern Literary Criticism* (Knoxville: University of Tennessee Press, 1988), 22.

2. Cowley, comp., *Portable*, viii, emphasis added.

3. William Faulkner, *"Helen: A Courtship" and "Mississippi Poems"* (Oxford, Miss., and New Orleans, La.: Yoknapatawpha Press and Tulane University Press, 1981), 153.

4. Minter argues correctly that writing this poetry was a valuable learning experience for Faulkner. For one thing, his ultimate rejection of the pastoral mode confirmed his solidarity with other modernists who were rejecting the dominant literary modes of the nineteenth century (*LW*, 36). This rejection also severed the lines that bound Faulkner to the monological world he was constructing in his poetry, and allowed him to discover his many "voices" as a novelist.

5. Richard Gray, *The Life of William Faulkner: A Critical Biography* (Cambridge, Mass.: Blackwell, 1994), 12.

6. Joseph Blotner, *Faulkner: A Biography*, vol. 1 (New York: Random House, 1974), 94.

7. For a discussion of lamentation in Faulkner as a rhetorical trope occasioned by the redistribution of wealth, see Rebecca Saunders, "On Lamentation and the Redistribution of Possessions: Faulkner's *Absalom, Absalom!* and the New South," *Modern Fiction Studies* 42 (1996): 730–62.

8. Noel Polk, *Children of the Dark House: Text and Context in Faulkner* (Jackson: University Press of Mississippi, 1996), xiii.

9. Michel Foucault, *The Archaeology of Knowledge*, trans. A. M. Sheridan Smith (New York: Pantheon Books, 1972); David Shumway, *Michel Foucault* (Boston: Twayne Publishers, 1989), 102.

10. Michel Foucault, "The Discourse on Language," in *Archaeology*, 222, 224.

11. Michel Foucault, "Two Lectures: Lecture One: 7 January 1976," in *Power/Knowledge: Selected Interviews and Other Writings, 1972–1977*, ed. Colin Gordon (New York: Pantheon Books, 1980), 81–82; Shumway, *Foucault*, 107.

12. Michel Foucault, "Nietzsche, Genealogy, and History," in *Language, Counter-Memory, Practice: Selected Essays and Interviews*, ed. Donald Bouchard (Ithaca: Cornell University Press, 1977), 140, 145, 147–48, 150–51; Foucault, "Discourse on Language," 227.

13. See John David Smith, *An Old Creed for the New South: Proslavery Ideology and Historiography, 1865–1918* (Athens: University of Georgia Press, 1991).

14. W. E. Woodward, *Meet General Grant* (Garden City, N.Y.: Garden City Publishing Co., 1928), 372.

15. David Lewis, introduction to W. E. B. Du Bois, *Black Reconstruction in America, 1860–1880* (1935; New York: Athenaeum, 1992), x; Foucault, "Discourse on Language," 224.

16. Michael Millgate, *The Achievement of William Faulkner* (1963; Athens, Ga.: Brown Thrasher, 1989), 14, quoting Faulkner. Millgate provides several reasons to distrust Faulkner's claim not to have read Joyce until late in his career; but as a warrant for assuming Faulkner was an attentive listener and that he made use of the sources of discourse available to him, the anecdote is still valuable.

17. Foucault, "Discourse on Language," 231.

18. In *Fiction's Inexhaustible Voice: Speech and Writing in Faulkner* (Athens: University of Georgia Press, 1989), Stephen Ross categorizes voice in Faulkner's texts as "phenomenal," "mimetic," "psychic," "oratorical," and "authorial." Although immensely helpful as a close reading of voice and dialect in Faulkner, in its conceptualization of these as "the original speech that the text itself generates," Ross's study commits a critical error lamented by Bakhtin, in which "an analysis of novelistic style is replaced by a description of the language of a given novelist" (*DI,* 263). In particular, what Ross leaves unexplored is the process by which the internally stratified languages of culture are transmitted to the Faulknerian subject—to Faulkner himself, to characters within his fiction, and to readers of his texts.

19. See Philip Weinstein, *Faulkner's Subject: A Cosmos No One Owns* (New York: Cambridge University Press, 1992), 64–81. In his study, the *historical* dimension of individual instances of subject-formation is often limited to the oeuvre of Faulkner's works. Prefacing his remarks on the "conflictual space" that produces subjectivity for Lucas Beauchamp, for instance, Weinstein rightly observes that this space is "conflictual, theoretically, because subjectivity itself is not an essence but a stance shaped by one's position within a signifying economy: as the economy alters, so does the subjectivity." Initially positing a broad horizon of "signifying economy" within which to understand Faulkner's representations of Lucas's subjectivity, Weinstein quickly delimits his investigation by interpreting Lucas solely within the closed economies of publication history and textual analysis. In this manner, *Faulkner's Subject* proposes to study the processes of subject-formation without recourse to the "deep" historical events surrounding Faulkner's literary production that contributed to or altered these processes.

20. See Jay Watson, *Forensic Fictions: The Lawyer Figure in Faulkner* (Athens: University of Georgia Press, 1993), and Susan Snell, *Phil Stone of Oxford: A Vicarious Life* (Athens: University of Georgia Press, 1991).

21. Paul Smith, *Discerning the Subject* (Minneapolis: University of Minnesota Press, 1988).

22. Stephen Ross has observed this weakness in Wesley and Barbara Morris's *Reading Faulkner,* which tends to totalize the concepts of race, class, and gender as "the root of all narrative" in Faulkner. See Ross, "Close Reading and Discursive Practice: A Review-Essay

on Faulkner," review of *Reading Faulkner,* by Wesley Morris and Barbara Alverson Morris, *Mississippi Quarterly* 43 (1990): 439. Ross's criticism notwithstanding, the Morrises do an excellent job of retrieving the many historical discourses that inform Faulkner's texts, and my reading of ethnographic discourse in chapter 4 is indebted to their discussion of *These Are Our Lives* and *As I Lay Dying.*

23. Although many of Michael Grimwood's observations (*Heart in Conflict: Faulkner's Struggles with Vocation* [Athens: University of Georgia Press, 1987]), for instance, take the kind of detour into historical context that I perform here in the analysis of discursive "descent" and "emergence," his insistence upon fitting Faulkner's works into a single template illustrating Faulkner's personal struggle over his identities as both writer and farmer is ultimately reductive. Richard Moreland demonstrates a similar willingness to explain the critical power of Faulkner's works through their revisiting of several "primal scenes." Immensely valuable in helping us to understand the centrality of these moments in Faulkner, *Faulkner and Modernism* nevertheless neglects to consider the relation between these moments of ideological pressure within the texts and the political and historical events of Faulkner's time that produced and arranged them prior to their textualization. The absence of this dimension in Moreland's work results from the lack of critical work generally on the relation between literary modernism and changing relations of production and distribution under modern and postmodern forms of capitalism, work that John Matthews has undertaken to perform. See John T. Matthews, "*As I Lay Dying* in the Machine Age," *Boundary 2* (1992): 69–94; and "Faulkner and the Culture Industry," *The Cambridge Companion to William Faulkner,* ed. Philip Weinstein (New York: Cambridge University Press, 1995), 51–74.

1. Revisionist Historiography, Agrarian Reform, and *The Unvanquished*

1. For Matthews, this effect of history in *The Sound and the Fury* signifies the ideological "work" of the novel, since it reflects strategies by which the dominant class suppresses the oppressions that have supported it in the past so that it can duplicate them in the present. John T. Matthews, "*The Sound and the Fury*": *Faulkner and the Lost Cause* (Boston: Twayne, 1991), 105.

2. Cowley, comp., introduction to *Portable,* viii; William Faulkner, *Selected Letters of William Faulkner,* ed. Joseph Blotner (New York: Random House, 1977), 78–79.

3. The original publication information for the stories that, after revision, comprise *The Unvanquished* is as follows: "Ambuscade," *Saturday Evening Post,* 29 September 1934: 12–13, 80, 81; "Retreat," *Saturday Evening Post,* 13 October 1934: 16–17, 82, 84, 85, 87, 89; "Raid," *Saturday Evening Post,* 3 November 1934: 18–19, 72, 73, 75, 77, 78; "Skirmish at Sartoris," *Scribner's Magazine,* April 1935: 193–200; "Riposte in Tertio," published as "The Unvanquished" in *Saturday Evening Post,* 14 November 1936: 12–13, 121, 122, 124, 126, 128, 130; "Vendee," *Saturday Evening Post,* 5 December 1936: 16–17, 86, 87, 90, 92–94. The stories are available in *Uncollected Stories of William Faulkner,* ed. Joseph Blotner (New York: Vintage Books, 1981).

4. Blotner, *Biography,* 364.

5. James S. Allen, *Reconstruction: The Battle for Democracy, 1865–1876* (1937; repr., New

York: International Publishers, 1937). For brief discussions of Faulkner's revisions, see Jo-anne Creighton, *William Faulkner's Craft of Revision: The Snopes Trilogy, "The Unvan-quished," and "Go Down, Moses"* (Detroit: Wayne State University Press, 1977), esp. 73–84, and Millgate, *Achievement,* 165–70. For a useful history of Civil War and Reconstruction historiography, see Smith, *Creed.*

6. Du Bois quotes Woodward, *Meet General Grant,* 372.

7. Faulkner, "Ambuscade," in Blotner, ed., *Uncollected Stories,* 5.

8. Foucault, "Nietzsche," 146.

9. Frank Lawrence Owsley, "The Irrepressible Conflict," in *I'll Take My Stand: The South and the Agrarian Tradition,* by Twelve Southerners (1930; repr., Baton Rouge: Louisi-ana State University Press, 1983), 62.

10. Foucault, "Nietzsche," 146.

11. This case is referred to in James Wilford Garner's *Reconstruction in Mississippi* (New York: Macmillan, 1901), 160. The full text of Justice Handy's decision is printed in the *New York Times,* 26 October 1866: 2.

12. Citing another example of this legal/rhetorical phenomenon, C. Vann Woodward notes how the 1873 Supreme Court, acting on public opinion and political necessity, read ambiguity into the words of the Fourteenth Amendment and "discovered that they did not at all mean what they seemed to mean, nor what their authors thought they meant." *The Burden of Southern History* (Baton Rouge: Louisiana State University Press, 1960), 84.

13. Howard Jay Graham, "The 'Conspiracy Theory' of the Fourteenth Amendment," in *Reconstruction: An Anthology of Revisionist Writings,* ed. Kenneth M. Stampp and Leon F. Litwack (Baton Rouge: Louisiana State University Press, 1969), 107–8.

14. James Allen, for instance, lamenting the failure of the National Labor Union to become an enduring postwar organization, writes that "its collapse was in no little measure also caused by failure to grasp the revolutionary significance of Reconstruction in the South and to utilize the full possibilities it offered for an alliance with the Negro people and the middle classes." *Reconstruction,* 165.

15. Albert Kirwan quotes the Vicksburg *Democrat-Commercial,* for instance, which claimed that "the Independent movement was an attempt of 'the old Radical party for a new lease of power.' It saw the movement as 'an effort to foist upon the people again, men who have heretofore been extremely obnoxious'" (*Rev,* 20–21). Kirwan is quoting from the Vicksburg *Democrat-Commercial* of 16 August and 29 October 1877.

16. The establishment of public schools in the South as a consequence of Reconstruc-tion is a major theme of Du Bois's *Souls of Black Folk* (1903). In *Black Reconstruction,* he reiterates that "public education for all at public expense, was, in the South, a Negro idea" (*BR,* 638).

17. On the political aspirations of the Agrarians, see Paul Bové, "Agriculture and Aca-deme: America's Southern Question," *Boundary 2* 14 (1986): 169–95.

18. Most readings of this story celebrate Bayard's ability to distance himself from his father's violent ways. John Sartoris may have participated in the bloody "redemption" of southern governments that ended Reconstruction in 1878, but Bayard, we are asked to

believe, has renounced violence as a political means. In my analysis, Bayard's enduring attachment to his father's class identity—and by the analogy I have pursued throughout this chapter, to that of the 1930s Agrarians—makes him incapable of fully participating in the more democratic South whose framework had been put in place following the Civil War, and whose promises were being demanded in the 1930s by revisionist historiographers, political reformers, and civil rights activists.

2. Figuring Legal Discourse in *The Hamlet* and *Knight's Gambit*

1. Graham, "The 'Conspiracy' Theory of the Fourteenth Amendment," 107–31.

2. John W. Johnson, *American Legal Culture, 1908–1940*, Contributions in Legal Studies 16 (Westport, Conn.: Greenwood Press, 1981), 22–23.

3. See Hans Kelsen, "The Pure Theory of the Law: Its Methods and Fundamental Concepts," *Law Quarterly Review* 50 (1934): 474–98; and Peter Goodrich, *Legal Discourse* (New York: St. Martin's, 1987), 11–81.

4. The appellation "legal realism" suggests a uniformity of practice and belief among judges and lawyers that did not always obtain. For an extended analysis of the legal realism movement, which nevertheless concedes this important point, see Wilfred E. Rumble, *American Legal Realism: Skepticism, Reform, and the Judicial Process* (Ithaca, N.Y.: Cornell University Press, 1968).

5. See Roscoe Pound, "The Need for a Sociological Jurisprudence," *Green Bag* 19 (1907): 607–15; and "The Scope and Purpose of Sociological Jurisprudence," *Harvard Law Review* 25 (1912): 140–68, 489–516.

6. Rumble unhelpfully attributes legal realism's diminished status after the war to "a new climate of opinion, the death of major realists, and various other factors." *American Legal Realism*, 3.

7. See Roscoe Pound, "The Call for a Realist Jurisprudence," *Harvard Law Review* 44 (1931): 697–711; and Karl Llewellyn, "Some Realism about Realism—Responding to Dean Pound," *Harvard Law Review* 44 (1931): 1222–63.

8. Although legal historians continue to debate Oliver Wendell Holmes's relation to the movement, Holmes does summarize the realists' position in this passage from *The Common Law*: "The life of the law has not been logic: it has been experience. The felt necessities of the time, the prevalent moral and political theories, intuitions of public policy, avowed or unconscious, even the prejudices which judges share with their fellow-men, have had a good deal more to do than the syllogism in determining the rules by which men should be governed." *The Essential Holmes*, ed. Richard A. Posner (Chicago: University of Chicago Press, 1992), 237.

9. For a generally untheorized application of law topics to Faulkner's texts and career, see *The Law and Southern Literature Symposium*, spec. issue of *Mississippi College Law Review* 4 (Spring 1984).

10. Jay Watson writes persuasively about "judicial theater" (*Forensic Fictions*, 26–31), but his approach assumes that all courtroom action is based upon the model of drama. My point is that while this is true of one model of the law, it is not the only model available, nor the only one whose operations are observable in Faulkner's text.

11. Johnson, *American Legal Culture*, 30.

12. The irony in Brandeis's application of patriarchal attitudes in a case that stands as a landmark in legal realism's debate with formalist jurisprudence is not lost on me. For my purposes, however, the importance of what has come to be known as the "Brandeis Brief" lies in its redefinition of legal and nonlegal categories, and in the shift in the country's dominant legal paradigm it brought about, moving that paradigm away from a model based upon precedent and formal legal principles, toward a model based upon a variety of information sources.

13. Grimwood (*Heart in Conflict*, 208) discusses "good roads" politics of the 1930s as a metaphor, in Faulkner's early detective stories, for the introduction of destructive, urban "outlanders" into the pastoral "center" of Yoknapatawpha. For more on the effect of good roads on the discourses of Faulkner's texts, see Morris and Morris, *Reading Faulkner*, 26–38.

14. See especially Watson's description of "Tomorrow" as containing "the purest, most sustained examples of colloquial detection in all of *Knight's Gambit*" (*Forensic Fictions*, 157).

15. For an extended account of "An Error in Chemistry" and "Knight's Gambit" in relation to the genre of detective fiction as it derives from Edgar Allan Poe, see John T. Irwin, "*Knight's Gambit:* Poe, Faulkner, and the Tradition of the Detective Story," *Arizona Quarterly* 46.4 (1990): 95–116.

16. John G. Cawelti, *Adventure, Mystery, and Romance: Formula Stories as Art and Popular Culture* (Chicago: University of Chicago Press, 1976), 144; Blotner, *Biography*, 460–62; Raymond Chandler, *The Raymond Chandler Omnibus* (New York: Knopf, 1964), 129.

17. Grimwood provides a useful summary of "Smoke," written in 1930 between the two versions of *Sanctuary*. It was later published by Harper's. Scribner's bought "Monk" in 1937; "Hand upon the Waters" was written in 1939 and soon after was bought by the *Saturday Evening Post*. The *Post* also bought "Tomorrow" in 1940, and "An Error in Chemistry" was published in *Ellery Queen Magazine* in 1945. Faulkner first sent the collection's title story to his agent, Harold Ober, in 1942, but his revisions continued until he turned the short story into a novella in late 1948 and early 1949.

18. Rumble, *American Legal Realism*, 2.

19. See Grimwood, *Heart in Conflict*, 200–13. Watson argues that Stevens's ritual scorn of Snopeses is the "local equivalent of a red scare," because it portrays Snopeses as "a creeping alien menace out to disrupt the American Way in Yoknapatawpha" (*Forensic Fictions*, 228).

20. Grimwood, *Heart in Conflict*, 188.

21. John Matthews, *The Play of Faulkner's Language* (Ithaca, N.Y.: Cornell University Press, 1982).

3. Belaboring the Past in *Absalom, Absalom!*

1. "In short, a proposition must fulfil some onerous and complex conditions before it can be admitted within a discipline; before it can be pronounced true or false it must be,

as Monsieur Canguilhem might say, 'within the true.'" Foucault, "Discourse on Language," 224.

2. In *"Absalom, Absalom!,* Haiti and Labor History: Reading Unreadable Revolutions" (*ELH* 61 [1994]: 685–720), Richard Godden argues persuasively that Sutpen's storytelling in this scene also helps him repress the knowledge that he is dependent upon both black labor and the black body as constitutive of his own subjectivity. See especially 714–15.

3. Godden usefully discusses the transitions between these three labor economies in Faulkner's South in *Fictions of Capital: The American Novel from James to Mailer* (New York: Cambridge University Press, 1990), 139–42.

4. Carolyn Porter interprets Sutpen as an early-twentieth-century entrepreneur in *Seeing and Being: The Plight of the Participant Observer in Emerson, James, Adams, and Faulkner* (Middletown, Conn.: Wesleyan University Press, 1981), 222.

5. Godden, "Labor History," 704, 687.

6. See James C. Cobb, *The Selling of the South: The Southern Crusade for Industrial Development, 1936–1980* (Baton Rouge: Louisiana State University Press, 1982), 23.

7. In his analysis of *Absalom, Absalom!* within the context of literary modernism, Richard Moreland identifies "irony" as a similar link between the novel's modern present and its antebellum past. Irony attempts to "reconcile" the contradictions within competing postures toward the southern past, which espouse, on the one hand, an aristocratic planter society and, on the other, a mobile population of yeoman farmers. As Moreland is aware, "this reconciliation resembled all too closely the New South boosterism which argued the continuity of the commercialized New South with the Old." *Faulkner and Modernism,* 24. Whereas Moreland is interested in the consequences of this historically particular form of modernist irony upon the psychological states of Faulkner's characters, I explore in more detail the rhetorical and political strategies that produced it, especially as these are determined by American labor history.

8. See, for instance, *BR* and Allen, *Reconstruction.*

9. In the first Lincoln-Douglas debate (Ottawa, Illinois, 21 August 1858), for instance, Lincoln warned that "it needs only the formality of a second Dred Scott decision, which he [Douglas] endorses in advance, to make Slavery alike lawful in all the States—old as well as new, North as well as South." *Selected Writings of Abraham Lincoln* (New York: Bantam, 1992), 96.

10. Karl Marx, "The Civil War in the United States," in *The Civil War in the United States,* Works of Marxism-Leninism 30 (New York: International Publishers, 1937), 81.

11. George Tindall discusses the use of the doctrine of states' rights as a response to federal attempts to preserve the integrity of "free" labor, in *The Emergence of the New South, 1913–1945* (Baton Rouge: Louisiana State University Press, 1967), 513.

12. James Hodges, *New Deal Labor Policy and the Southern Cotton Textile Industry* (Knoxville: University of Tennessee Press, 1986), 30.

13. For a firsthand account of the dangers of cotton fibers for weavers and loom operators, see Victoria Byerly, *Hard Times Cotton Mill Girls: Personal Histories of Womanhood and Poverty in the South* (Ithaca, N.Y.: ILR Press, 1986), 181–91.

14. David Bordwell, Janet Staiger, and Kristin Thompson, *The Classical Hollywood Cin-*

ema: Film Style and Mode of Production to 1960 (New York: Columbia University Press, 1985), 311–12. This history of clashing interests was abated somewhat in 1926, when the studios recognized five unions in the Studio Basic Agreement of 1926. For more on Hollywood labor history, see Murray Ross, *Stars and Strikes: The Unionization of Hollywood* (New York: Columbia University Press, 1941).

15. Joseph Urgo, "*Absalom, Absalom!* The Movie," *American Literature* 62 (1990): 56–73.

16. Denise Hartsough, "Crime Pays: The Studios' Labor Deals in the 1930s," in *The Studio System,* ed. Janet Staiger (New Brunswick: Rutgers University Press), 226–48.

17. Olga Vickery, *The Novels of William Faulkner: A Critical Interpretation* (Baton Rouge: Louisiana State University Press, 1959), 84–102; Porter, *Seeing and Being,* 242. Cleanth Brooks writes that "*Absalom, Absalom!* does not merely tell the story of Thomas Sutpen, but dramatizes the process by which two young men of the twentieth century construct the character Thomas Sutpen." *William Faulkner: The Yoknapatawpha Country* (New Haven: Yale University Press, 1963), 309. Further demonstrating the critical paradigm that seeks to credit the "individual" worker for the labors of many, Millgate writes that ultimately "the burden of recreation, interpretation, and suffering falls inexorably on Quentin." *Achievement,* 154.

18. Bordwell, Staiger, and Thompson, *Classical Hollywood Cinema,* 313.

19. Faulkner to Samuel Marx, 12 October 1949, *Selected Letters,* 293.

20. For more of this history, see Bordwell, Staiger, and Thompson, *Classical Hollywood Cinema,* 311–19.

21. Carnegie, *Empire of Business,* 17; Henry Ford, with Samuel Crowther, *My Life and Work* (Garden City, N.Y.: Doubleday, Page, 1922), 40, 51, 119–20; Andrew Carnegie, *Autobiography of Andrew Carnegie* (1920; repr., Boston: Houghton Mifflin, 1948), 84.

22. Cobb, *Selling of the South,* 5, 7–8.

23. Ibid., 33.

24. Hodges, *New Deal,* 37.

25. And as subsequent labor history suggests, the introduction of "right to work" legislation in the 1940s served as an opportunity for these arguments to be reformulated when, once again, the doctrine of states' rights was used to limit workers' rights to be represented by union negotiators. A CIO publication from 1955 observes, for example, that the phrase "'States' Rights' . . . is used as a cloak, or disguise, for anti-labor measures that really have nothing to do with 'State's Rights'" (10). *The Case against "Right to Work" Laws,* Joint Publication of the Legislative Department, Legal Department, and the Education and Research Department of the Congress of Industrial Organizations.

26. See Philip S. Foner, *Women and the American Labor Movement: From World War I to the Present* (New York: Free Press, 1980), esp. 225–43; Susan Lehrer, *Origins of Protective Labor Legislation for Women, 1905–1925* (Albany: State University of New York Press, 1987), 183.

27. Godden, *Fictions of Capital,* 139–42.

28. Quoted in the introduction to *Faulkner's MGM Screenplays,* ed. Bruce F. Kawin (Knoxville: University of Tennessee Press, 1982), xxx.

29. George Tindall quotes the complaint of Georgia Representative Eugene Cox, for instance, during congressional debate over the Wagner Act, that the act proposed to use the "commerce clause of the Constitution . . . to the extent of ultimately striking down and destroying completely all State sovereignty." Quoted in *Emergence of the New South*, 513. Southern representatives were especially interested in keeping the federal government out of labor relations because of the region's successes in the 1920s and 1930s in luring northern industry with promises of low wages, surplus labor, and an antiunion environment.

4. Ethnographic Allegory and *The Hamlet*

1. James Clifford, "On Ethnographic Allegory," in *Writing Culture: The Poetics and Politics of Ethnography*, ed. James Clifford and George E. Marcus (Berkeley: University of California Press, 1986), 103. Respectively, see Morris and Morris, *Reading Faulkner*, 124–32; James Snead, *Figures of Division: William Faulkner's Major Novels* (New York: Methuen, 1986), 140–79; and Matthews, *Play of Faulkner's Language*, 162–211.

2. Faulkner's critics have avoided this direct comparison between *The Hamlet* and the ethnographic "turn" of the 1920s ever since Cleanth Brooks stated categorically that "the narrator of *The Hamlet* has . . . scarcely a hint of the modern anthropologist investigating the customs of the Trobriand Islanders" (*Yoknapatawpha Country*, 174). Morris and Morris call for an examination of Faulkner's "narrative of narrative" in *The Hamlet*, but despite their further goal to ground "the act of southern narration in the immediate and material conditions of present southern experience," they generalize about the traditions of southwestern storytelling as the only pertinent context (*Reading Faulkner*, 125). Grimwood situates *The Hamlet* within a context of sociological study of the South. In arguing that Faulkner's novels reflect the author's inner conflicts over competing literary and agrarian sympathies, Grimwood places *The Hamlet* within a southern dialogue about poverty that pits the Nashville Agrarians against a school of sociologists headed by Howard Odum at the University of North Carolina at Chapel Hill. Although our readings of *The Hamlet* overlap in certain areas—as when he writes that "*The Hamlet* achieves its meaning in the context of the Southern dialogue" (*Heart in Conflict*, 167)—where Grimwood argues that *The Hamlet*'s "two principle voices are those of Ratliff and the omniscient narrator, close relatives of 'Mr. Faulkner' and Ernest V. Trueblood," I will argue that both Faulkner's and the novel's conflicting voices speak from a splintered subjectivity within anthropological discourse, one that is available to Faulkner (and to us) only because of the introduction of the ethnographic method (*Heart in Conflict*, 172).

3. George E. Marcus and Michael M. J. Fischer, *Anthropology as Cultural Critique: An Experimental Moment in the Human Sciences* (Chicago: University of Chicago Press, 1986), 17; James Clifford, *The Predicament of Culture: Twentieth-Century Ethnography, Literature, and Art* (Cambridge: Harvard University Press, 1988), 34.

4. Foucault, "Discourse on Language," 218, 219, 224.

5. Mary Louise Pratt, "Fieldwork in Common Places," in *Writing Culture: The Poetics and Politics of Ethnography*, ed. James Clifford and George E. Marcus (Berkeley: University of California Press, 1986), 32.

6. Michael Grimwood (*Heart in Conflict*) has written most extensively on Faulkner's parody of conventions of pastoral and romance in the section on Ike and Houston's cow. For Grimwood, Faulkner's exaggeration of the pastoral performs two functions: first, by drawing attention to pastoral literature's use of language in ways that could not be understood by its provincial subjects, it interferes with pastoral literature's ideological effect of maintaining privileges enjoyed by the ruling (educated) class; second, Faulkner's exaggeration of the pastoral helps him resolve his inner conflict over competing agrarian and literary sympathies, a conflict that Grimwood believes is central to Faulkner's career.

7. Indeed, Marcus and Fischer refer to Hayden White's analysis of three modes of nineteenth-century European historiographical practices (troped by White as romance, tragedy, and comedy) in order to indicate broad affinities between the "discursive" histories of anthropology and historiography (*Anthropology as Cultural Critique*, 12–16). While it would be difficult precisely to locate Faulkner's parody of nineteenth-century pastoral traditions within the framework of White's analysis, I will argue that we can understand these three disciplinary discourses (historiographical, anthropological, literary) as converging in a moment of hardened irony in the early decades of the twentieth century.

8. Ibid., 17; Clifford, "On Ethnographic Allegory," 113.

9. More generally, the metaphor of "salvage" is signified in the long history of Faulkner criticism when critics, notably Cleanth Brooks, have sought evidence in *The Hamlet* of Faulkner's concern over the passing of an authentic or "organic" way of life, and the emergence of a (corrupted) modern society (signaled by the rise of the Snopeses).

10. Moreland, *Faulkner and Modernism*, 138.

11. Marcus and Fischer, *Anthropology as Cultural Critique*, 14.

12. Pratt, "Fieldwork in Common Places," 32. Without overtly recognizing the parallel between his language and that motivating the ethnographic project, Millgate writes that "Ratliff, as he appears in *The Hamlet*, is *in* the world of Frenchman's Bend but by no means entirely *of* it." *Achievement*, 197. Snead, too, observes that Ratliff "is both an 'internal' and an 'external' observer, included in the hamlet and foreign to it" (*Figures of Division*, 156).

13. John Dollard, *Caste and Class in a Southern Town* (1937; repr., New York: Doubleday, 1957), 32–33.

14. Identified as such in the *Encyclopedia of Southern Culture*, ed. Charles Reagan Wilson and William Ferris (Chapel Hill: University of North Carolina Press, 1989), 1102.

15. William Faulkner, "Barn Burning," *Collected Stories*, 11.

16. Renato Rosaldo, "From the Door of His Tent: The Fieldworker and the Inquisitor," in *Writing Culture: The Poetics and Politics of Ethnography*, ed. James Clifford and George E. Marcus (Berkeley: University of California Press, 1986), 81, 91.

17. Wesley Morris and Barbara Alverson Morris discuss this scene in terms of Ratliff's "credentials" within the traditions of southwestern storytelling. *Reading Faulkner*, 127.

18. William Faulkner, "Lizards in Jamshyd's Courtyard," *Uncollected Stories*, 148.

19. Marcus and Fischer, *Anthropology as Cultural Critique*, 21–22; Dollard, *Caste and Class*, 22, 30, 37.

20. Allison Davis, Burleigh Gardner, and Mary Gardner, *Deep South: A Social Anthropological Study of Caste and Class* (Chicago: University of Chicago Press, 1941), 63–71, 208.

21. Snead, *Figures of Division*, 161.

22. W. T. Couch, ed. and author of preface to *These Are Our Lives* (Chapel Hill: University of North Carolina Press, 1939), ix, x, xii, 37, 411.

23. Catherine Belsey, *Critical Practice* (New York: Methuen, 1980), 57, 65.

24. See Pete Daniel, "Command Performances: Photography from the United States Department of Agriculture," in *Official Images: New Deal Photography* (Washington, D.C.: Smithsonian Institution Press, 1987), 36–65.

25. Ibid., 40. See Maren Stange, "'The Record Itself': Farm Security Administration Photography and the Transformation of Rural Life," in *Official Images: New Deal Photography* (Washington, D.C.: Smithsonian Institution Press, 1987), esp. 1–5.

26. William Stott, *Documentary Expression and Thirties America* (New York: Oxford University Press, 1973), 60.

27. Ibid., 218; Daniel, "Command Performances," 38.

5. Race Fantasies: The Filming of *Intruder in the Dust*

1. "Negro Lynched by Mob," *Oxford Eagle*, 17 September 1908. The story gives "Lawson" as Patton's proper name. The spelling of the female victim's surname differs in the various discussions of this case, further evidence, to me, that the particulars were of less importance than the formula these events reproduced.

2. For answers to some, but not all, of these questions, see John B. Cullen, *Old Times in the Faulkner Country* (Chapel Hill: University of North Carolina Press, 1961), 89–98.

3. This is a reformulation of Žižek's discussion of the ideological figure of the Jew in *The Sublime Object of Ideology* (New York: Verso, 1989), 43, 45, 48.

4. For an analysis of film as fantasy-construction, see Timothy Murray, *Like a Film: Ideological Fantasy on Screen, Camera, and Canvas* (New York: Routledge, 1993). Žižek provides numerous readings of film, desire, and ideology in *Looking Awry: An Introduction to Jacques Lacan through Popular Culture* (Cambridge, Mass.: MIT Press, 1991).

5. Dudley Andrew, *Concepts in Film Theory* (New York: Oxford University Press, 1984), 23.

6. On the representation of slavery in American historiography, see Smith, *Old Creed for the New South*. For a detailed analysis of white appropriation, and subsequent scorn, of black culture, see Eric Lott, *Love and Theft* (New York: Oxford University Press, 1993).

7. The relation between minstrel stereotypes of the nineteenth century and the development of the American film industry is the subject of Donald Bogle, *Toms, Coons, Mulattoes, Mammies, and Bucks: An Interpretive History of Blacks in American Films* (1973; repr., New York: Continuum, 1989), and Edward Campbell, *The Celluloid South: Hollywood and the Southern Myth* (Knoxville: University of Tennessee Press, 1981).

8. For example, "Three Movies about the South," a Brandt's Mayfair advertisement in the *New York Times*, proclaims the following: "*The Birth of a Nation* created a sensation in 1915; *Gone with the Wind* did the same in 1939; *Intruder in the Dust* gives the dramatic answer in 1949." *New York Times*, 21 November 1949: 29.

9. "These Lafayette Scenes to Become Movie Sets," *Oxford Eagle*, 17 February 1949.

10. On Faulkner and black migration, see Cheryl Lester, "Racial Awareness and

Arrested Development: *The Sound and the Fury* and the Great Migration," in *The Cambridge Companion to Faulkner,* ed. Philip Weinstein (New York: Cambridge University Press, 1995), 123–45. Emigration from Mississippi slowed during the 1930s, but by the 1940s it had regained its pre-Depression pace. The 1950 census recorded a black population in Mississippi of 986,494, down 8.2 percent compared to 1940, according to Donald B. Dodd, *Historical Statistics of the States of the United States: Two Centuries of the Census, 1790–1990* (Westport, Conn.: Greenwood Press, 1993), 50.

11. Marc Ferro, for instance, writes that "unlike a work of history, which necessarily changes with distance and analytical developments, a work of art becomes permanent, unchanging." *Cinema and History,* trans. Naomi Greene (Detroit, Mich.: Wayne State University Press, 1988), 159.

12. Trevor Whittock, *Metaphor and Film* (New York: Cambridge University Press, 1990), 59; Blotner, *Biography,* 1284, 1277; "MGM Seeking More Local Actors as Movie Progresses," *Oxford Eagle,* 17 March 1949.

13. Žižek, *Sublime Object of Ideology,* 43.

14. Felix S. Cohen, *Handbook of Federal Indian Law* (1941; repr., Washington, D.C.: U.S. Government Printing Office, 1945), 83.

15. Weinstein, *Faulkner's Subject,* 77.

16. "In Most Any Newspaper in the Country, May Appear Something about Oxford," *Oxford Eagle,* 6 October 1949; Snead, *Figures of Division,* 197.

17. Edmund Wilson, "William Faulkner's Reply to the Civil-Rights Program," review of *Intruder in the Dust,* by William Faulkner, *New Yorker,* 23 October 1948: 120.

18. Irwin Ross, *The Loneliest Campaign: The Truman Victory of 1948* (New York: New American Library, 1968), 121, 122.

19. Indeed, one reason Walter White of the NAACP worked the Democratic Convention as thoroughly as he did was the pressure southern members of Congress exerted upon Senate and House committees earlier that spring to write weak antilynching legislation. See Robert L. Zangrando, *The NAACP Crusade against Lynching, 1909–1950* (Philadelphia: Temple University Press, 1980), 192–94.

20. Ross, *Loneliest Campaign,* 132.

21. For the history of this and other antilynching organizations, see Jacquelyn Dowd Hall, *Revolt against Chivalry: Jesse Daniel Ames and the Women's Campaign against Lynching* (New York: Columbia University Press, 1993).

22. W. E. B. Du Bois, *The Souls of Black Folk* (1903; repr., New York: Dover Publications, 1994), 7.

23. In his *New Yorker* review, Edmund Wilson "interpolates" the proposed exchange in this way: "Let the white man give the Negro his rights, and the Negro teach the white man his endurance." As the following discussion of the possible senses of "reversion" will make clear, my interpretation of Gavin's proposal is quite different.

24. *Oxford English Dictionary,* 1989 ed., s.v. "reversion."

25. Ibid.

26. Blotner, *Biography,* 1277; "Negro Star Was Well Liked, Well Respected in Town," *Oxford Eagle,* 6 October 1949; "Movie Folk Enthused over Oxford: Expect Film Start Early in March," *Oxford Eagle,* 10 February 1949.

27. "From This Small City Will Be Launched National Campaign for Oxford's Own Picture," *Oxford Eagle,* 6 October 1949; "Waiting to See Oxford's Own Picture Almost Over, Big Night Monday," *Oxford Eagle,* 6 October 1949.

28. "In Most Any Newspaper in the Country, May Appear Something about Oxford," *Oxford Eagle,* 6 October 1949.

29. Ibid.

30. "A New Star Is Born!" *Oxford Eagle,* 21 April 1949.

31. Cullen, *Old Times,* 97. See the "Weeping Willie" letters in James B. Meriwether, ed., *Essays, Speeches, and Public Letters by William Faulkner* (New York: Random House, 1965), 93–94.

Epilogue: Rethinking Revision: "Zones of Contact" in Faulkner

1. Bakhtin says of the novel: "Since it is constructed in a zone of contact with the incomplete events of a particular present, the novel often crosses the boundary of what we strictly call fictional literature—making use first of a moral confession, then of a philosophical tract, then of manifestos that are openly political. . . . These phenomena are precisely what characterize the novel as a developing genre. After all, the boundaries between fiction and nonfiction, between literature and nonliterature and so forth are not laid up in heaven. Every specific situation is historical. And the growth of literature is not merely development and change within fixed boundaries of any given definition; the boundaries themselves are constantly changing" (*DI,* 33).

2. Faulkner, *Selected Letters,* 84; Grimwood, *Heart in Conflict,* 214.

BIBLIOGRAPHY

Agar, Herbert, and Allen Tate, eds. *Who Owns America? A New Declaration of Independence.* New York: Houghton Mifflin, 1936.

Allen, James S. *Reconstruction: The Battle for Democracy, 1865–1876.* 1937. Reprint, New York: International Publishers, 1955.

Andrew, Dudley. *Concepts in Film Theory.* New York: Oxford University Press, 1984.

Bakhtin, Mikhail. *The Dialogic Imagination.* Edited by Michael Holquist. Translated by Caryl Emerson and Michael Holquist. Austin: University of Texas Press, 1981.

Belsey, Catherine. *Critical Practice.* New York: Methuen, 1980.

Blotner, Joseph. *Faulkner: A Biography.* New York: Vintage, 1991.

Bogle, Donald. *Toms, Coons, Mulattoes, Mammies, and Bucks: An Interpretive History of Blacks in American Films.* 1973. Reprint, New York: Continuum, 1989.

Bordwell, David, Janet Staiger, and Kristin Thompson. *The Classical Hollywood Cinema: Film Style and Mode of Production to 1960.* New York: Columbia University Press, 1985.

Bové, Paul. "Agriculture and Academe: America's Southern Question," *Boundary 2* 14 (1986): 169–95.

Brooks, Cleanth. *William Faulkner: The Yoknapatawpha Country.* New Haven: Yale University Press, 1963.

Byerly, Victoria. *Hard Times Cotton Mill Girls: Personal Histories of Womanhood and Poverty in the South.* Ithaca: ILR Press, 1986.

Carnegie, Andrew. *Autobiography of Andrew Carnegie.* 1920. Reprint, Boston: Houghton Mifflin, 1948.

———. *The Empire of Business.* New York: Doubleday, Page, 1902.

Cawelti, John G. *Adventure, Mystery, and Romance: Formula Stories as Art and Popular Culture.* Chicago: The University of Chicago Press, 1976.

Chandler, Raymond. *The Raymond Chandler Omnibus.* New York: Knopf, 1964.

Clifford, James. "On Ethnographic Allegory." In *Writing Culture: The Poetics and Politics of Ethnography,* edited by James Clifford and George E. Marcus. Berkeley: University of California Press, 1986.

————. *The Predicament of Culture: Twentieth-Century Ethnography, Literature, and Art.* Cambridge: Harvard University Press, 1988.

Cobb, James C. *The Selling of the South: The Southern Crusade for Industrial Development, 1936–1980.* Baton Rouge: Louisiana State University Press, 1982.

Cohen, Felix S. *Handbook of Federal Indian Law.* 1941. Reprint, Washington, D.C.: U.S. Government Printing Office, 1945.

Couch, W. T., comp. and author of preface to *These Are Our Lives.* Chapel Hill: University of North Carolina Press, 1939.

Cowley, Malcolm. *The Faulkner-Cowley File: Letters and Memories, 1944–1962.* New York: Viking, 1966.

————, comp. Introduction to *The Portable Faulkner,* by William Faulkner. 1946. Reprint, New York: Viking, 1974.

Creighton, Joanne. *William Faulkner's Craft of Revision: The Snopes Trilogy, "The Unvanquished," and "Go Down, Moses."* Detroit: Wayne State University Press, 1977.

Cullen, John B. *Old Times in the Faulkner Country.* Chapel Hill: University of North Carolina Press, 1961.

Daniel, Pete. "Command Performances: Photography from the United States Department of Agriculture." In *Official Images: New Deal Photography.* Washington, D.C.: Smithsonian Institution Press, 1987.

Davis, Allison, Burleigh Gardner, and Mary Gardner. *Deep South: A Social Anthropological Study of Caste and Class.* Chicago: University of Chicago Press, 1941.

Dodd, Donald B. *Historical Statistics of the States of the United States: Two Centuries of the Census, 1790–1990.* Westport, Conn.: Greenwood Press, 1993.

Dollard, John. *Caste and Class in a Southern Town.* 1937. Reprint, New York: Doubleday, 1957.

Du Bois, W. E. B. *Black Reconstruction in America, 1860–1880.* 1935. Reprint, New York: Athenaeum, 1992.

————. *The Souls of Black Folk.* 1903. Reprint, New York: Dover, 1994.

Faulkner, William. *Absalom, Absalom!* 1936. Reprint, New York: Vintage International, 1990.

————. *Collected Stories of William Faulkner.* 1950. Reprint, New York: Vintage International, 1995.

————. *Flags in the Dust.* 1929. Reprint, New York: Vintage, 1974.

————. *Go Down, Moses.* 1942. Reprint, New York: Vintage International, 1991.

————. *The Hamlet.* 1940. Reprint, New York: Vintage International, 1990.

————. *"Helen: A Courtship" and "Mississippi Poems."* Oxford, Miss., and New Orleans, La.: Yoknapatawpha Press and Tulane University Press, 1981.

————. *Intruder in the Dust.* 1948. Reprint, New York: Vintage International, 1991.

————. *Knight's Gambit.* 1949. Reprint, New York: Vintage, 1977.

————. *Selected Letters of William Faulkner.* Edited by Joseph Blotner. New York: Random House, 1977.

————. *Soldier's Pay.* 1926. Reprint, New York: Liveright, 1997.

————. *The Town.* 1957. Reprint, New York: Random House, 1973.

————. *Uncollected Stories of William Faulkner.* Edited by Joseph Blotner. New York: Vintage, 1981.

————. *The Unvanquished.* 1938. Reprint, New York: Vintage, 1991.

Ferro, Marc. *Cinema and History.* Translated by Naomi Greene. Detroit: Wayne State University Press, 1988.

Foner, Philip S. *Women and the American Labor Movement: From World War I to the Present.* New York: Free Press, 1980.

Ford, Henry. *My Life and Work.* Garden City, N.Y.: Doubleday, Page and Company, 1922.

Foucault, Michel. *The Archaeology of Knowledge.* Translated by A. M. Sheridan Smith. New York: Pantheon, 1972.

————. "Nietzsche, Genealogy, and History." In *Language, Counter-Memory, Practice: Selected Essays and Interviews,* edited by Donald Bouchard. Ithaca: Cornell University Press, 1977.

————. *Power/Knowledge: Selected Interviews and Other Writings, 1972–1977.* Edited by Colin Gordon. New York: Pantheon, 1980.

Garner, James Wilford. *Reconstruction in Mississippi.* New York: Macmillan, 1901.

Godden, Richard. *"Absalom, Absalom!* Haiti and Labor History: Reading Unreadable Revolutions." *ELH* 61 (1994): 685–720.

————. *Fictions of Capital: The American Novel from James to Mailer.* New York: Cambridge University Press, 1990.

Goodrich, Peter. *Legal Discourse.* New York: St. Martin's, 1987.

Graham, Howard Jay. "The 'Conspiracy Theory' of the Fourteenth Amendment." In *Reconstruction: An Anthology of Revisionist Writings,* edited by Kenneth M. Stampp and Leon F. Litwack. Baton Rouge: Louisiana State University Press, 1969. First published in *Yale Law Journal* 47 (1938): 371–404.

Gray, Richard. *The Life of William Faulkner: A Critical Biography.* Cambridge, Mass.: Blackwell, 1994.

Grimwood, Michael. *Heart in Conflict: Faulkner's Struggles with Vocation.* Athens: University of Georgia Press, 1987.

Hall, Jacquelyn Dowd. *Revolt against Chivalry: Jesse Daniel Ames and the Women's Campaign against Lynching.* New York: Columbia University Press, 1993.

Hartsough, Denise. "Crime Pays: The Studios' Labor Deals in the 1930s." In *The Studio System,* edited by Janet Staiger. New Brunswick, N.J.: Rutgers University Press.

Hodges, James. *New Deal Labor Policy and the Southern Cotton Textile Industry.* Knoxville: University of Tennessee Press, 1986.

Holmes, Oliver Wendell. *The Essential Holmes.* Edited by Richard A. Posner. Chicago: University of Chicago Press, 1992.

Irwin, John T. "*Knight's Gambit:* Poe, Faulkner, and the Tradition of the Detective Story." *Arizona Quarterly* 46.4 (1990): 95–116.

Johnson, John W. *American Legal Culture, 1908–1940.* Contributions in Legal Studies 16. Westport, Conn.: Greenwood Press, 1981.

Kawin, Bruce F., ed. *Faulkner's MGM Screenplays.* Knoxville: University of Tennessee Press, 1982.

Kelsen, Hans. "The Pure Theory of the Law: Its Methods and Fundamental Concepts." *Law Quarterly Review* 50 (1934): 474–98.

Kirwan, Albert. *Revolt of the Rednecks: Mississippi Politics, 1876–1925.* Lexington: University of Kentucky Press, 1951.

Lehrer, Susan. *Origins of Protective Labor Legislation for Women, 1905–1925.* Albany: State University of New York Press, 1987.

Lester, Cheryl. "Racial Awareness and Arrested Development: *The Sound and the Fury* and the Great Migration." In *The Cambridge Companion to Faulkner,* edited by Philip Weinstein. New York: Cambridge University Press, 1995.

Lewis, David. Introduction to *Black Reconstruction in America, 1860–1880.* 1935. Reprint, New York: Athenaeum, 1992.

Lincoln, Abraham. *Selected Writings of Abraham Lincoln.* New York: Bantam, 1992.

Llewellyn, Karl. "Some Realism about Realism—Responding to Dean Pound." *Harvard Law Review* 44 (1931): 1222–63.

Lott, Eric. *Love and Theft.* New York: Oxford University Press, 1993.

Marcus, George E., and Michael M. J. Fischer. *Anthropology as Cultural Critique: An Experimental Moment in the Human Sciences.* Chicago: University of Chicago Press, 1986.

Marx, Karl. "The Civil War in the United States." In *The Civil War in the United States,* Works of Marxism-Leninism 30. New York: International Publishers, 1937.

Matthews, John T. "*As I Lay Dying* in the Machine Age." *Boundary 2* (1992): 69–94.

———. "Faulkner and the Culture Industry." In *The Cambridge Companion to*

William Faulkner, edited by Philip Weinstein. New York: Cambridge University Press, 1995.

———. *The Play of Faulkner's Language*. Ithaca: Cornell University Press, 1982.

Meriwether, James B., ed. *Essays, Speeches, and Public Letters by William Faulkner*. New York: Random House, 1965.

Millgate, Michael. *The Achievement of William Faulkner*. 1963. Reprint, Athens, Ga.: Brown Thrasher, 1989.

Minter, David. *William Faulkner: His Life and Work*. Baltimore, Md.: Johns Hopkins University Press, 1980.

Moreland, Richard. *Faulkner and Modernism: Rereading and Rewriting*. Madison: University of Wisconsin Press, 1990.

Morris, Wesley, and Barbara Alverson Morris. *Reading Faulkner*. Madison: University of Wisconsin Press, 1989.

Murray, Timothy. *Like a Film: Ideological Fantasy on Screen, Camera, and Canvas*. New York: Routledge, 1993.

Owsley, Frank Lawrence. "The Irrepressible Conflict." In *I'll Take My Stand: The South and the Agrarian Tradition*, by Twelve Southerners. 1930. Reprint, Baton Rouge: Louisiana State University Press, 1983.

Oxford Eagle, 17 September 1908 and 10 February–6 October 1949.

Polk, Noel. *Children of the Dark House: Text and Context in Faulkner*. Jackson: University Press of Mississippi, 1996.

Porter, Carolyn. *Seeing and Being: The Plight of the Participant Observer in Emerson, James, Adams, and Faulkner*. Middletown, Conn.: Wesleyan University Press, 1981.

Pound, Roscoe. "The Need for a Sociological Jurisprudence." *Green Bag* 19 (1907): 607–15.

———. "The Scope and Purpose of Sociological Jurisprudence." *Harvard Law Review* 25 (1912): 140–68, 489–516.

Pratt, Mary Louise. "Fieldwork in Common Places." In *Writing Culture: The Poetics and Politics of Ethnography*, edited by James Clifford and George E. Marcus. Berkeley: University of California Press, 1986.

Rosaldo, Renato. "From the Door of His Tent: The Fieldworker and the Inquisitor." In *Writing Culture: The Poetics and Politics of Ethnography*, edited by James Clifford and George E. Marcus. Berkeley: University of California Press, 1986.

Ross, Irwin. *The Loneliest Campaign: The Truman Victory of 1948*. New York: New American Library, 1968.

Ross, Murray. *Stars and Strikes: The Unionization of Hollywood*. New York: Columbia University Press, 1941.

Ross, Stephen. "Close Reading and Discursive Practice: A Review-Essay on

Faulkner." Review of *Reading Faulkner,* by Wesley Morris and Barbara Alverson Morris. *Mississippi Quarterly* 43.3 (1990): 431–45.

———. *Fiction's Inexhaustible Voice: Speech and Writing in Faulkner.* Athens: University of Georgia Press, 1989.

Rumble, Wilfred E. *American Legal Realism: Skepticism, Reform, and the Judicial Process.* Ithaca: Cornell University Press, 1968.

Saunders, Rebecca. "On Lamentation and the Redistribution of Possessions: Faulkner's *Absalom, Absalom!* and the New South." *Modern Fiction Studies* 42 (1996): 730–62.

Schwartz, Lawrence. *Creating Faulkner's Reputation: The Politics of Modern Literary Criticism.* Knoxville: University of Tennessee Press, 1988.

Shumway, David. *Michel Foucault.* Boston: Twayne Publishers, 1989.

Smith, John David. *An Old Creed for the New South: Proslavery Ideology and Historiography, 1865–1918.* Athens: University of Georgia Press, 1991.

Smith, Paul. *Discerning the Subject.* Minneapolis: University of Minnesota Press, 1988.

Snead, James. *Figures of Division: William Faulkner's Major Novels.* New York: Methuen, 1986.

Snell, Susan. *Phil Stone of Oxford: A Vicarious Life.* Athens: University of Georgia Press, 1991.

Stange, Maren. " 'The Record Itself': Farm Security Administration Photography and the Transformation of Rural Life." In *Official Images: New Deal Photography.* Washington, D.C.: Smithsonian Institution Press, 1987.

Stott, William. *Documentary Expression and Thirties America.* New York: Oxford University Press, 1973.

"Three Movies about the South." Advertisement. *New York Times,* 21 November 1949: 29.

Tindall, George. *The Emergence of the New South, 1913–1945.* Baton Rouge: Louisiana State University Press, 1967.

Urgo, Joseph. "*Absalom, Absalom!* The Movie." *American Literature* 62 (1990): 56–73.

Vickery, Olga. *The Novels of William Faulkner: A Critical Interpretation.* Baton Rouge: Louisiana State University Press, 1959.

Watson, Jay. *Forensic Fictions: The Lawyer Figure in Faulkner.* Athens: University of Georgia Press, 1993.

Weinstein, Philip. *Faulkner's Subject: A Cosmos No One Owns.* New York: Cambridge University Press, 1992.

Whittock, Trevor. *Metaphor and Film.* New York: Cambridge University Press, 1990.

Wilson, Edmund. "William Faulkner's Reply to the Civil-Rights Program." Review of *Intruder in the Dust,* by William Faulkner. *New Yorker* 23 October 1948: 120.

Woodward, C. Vann. *The Burden of Southern History.* Baton Rouge: Louisiana State University Press, 1960.

Zangrando, Robert L. *The NAACP Crusade against Lynching, 1909–1950.* Philadelphia: Temple University Press, 1980.

Žižek, Slavoj. *Looking Awry: An Introduction to Jacques Lacan through Popular Culture.* Cambridge, Mass.: MIT Press, 1991.

———. *The Sublime Object of Ideology.* New York: Verso, 1989.

INDEX

Absalom, Absalom! (Faulkner): family in, 21, 22; and historiography, 21, 22, 23; labor in, 76–104; storytelling in, 76–78, 81, 82, 102–3, 171*n*2; Sutpen's story in, 76–78, 81, 84–85, 89–90, 102–3, 171*n*2; and cotton mill workers, 81–82; and Hollywood film industry, 82–85, 87; Sutpen's Hundred in, 86–87, 92; fictions of labor and capital in, 87–103; contract obligations in, 88, 94–98, 100–101; entrepreneurship in, 88–94, 100; Sutpen's labor identities in, 90, 92–95, 98–103; women's labor in, 96–98; women's reproductive function in, 97–98, 100–101; subjectivity and fictions of labor and capital in, 98–103, 171*n*2; map in, 128; irony in, 171*n*7

AFL, 97

African Americans. *See* Civil rights for blacks; Lynching and near-lynching; Race; Segregation; Slavery; *and headings beginning with Black*

Agrarians, 24–25, 33–35, 39–43, 45–46, 49, 151, 169*n*18, 173*n*2

Agricultural Adjustment Administration (AAA), 64

Agriculture, 39–40, 42–49, 76, 122–23, 128, 151, 153

Agriculture Department, U.S., 122–23

Alabama, 144

Allen, James S., 23, 42, 45, 168*n*14

Althusser, Louis, 123, 133

"Ambuscade" (Faulkner), 23–24, 26–34, 35–38, 41, 167*n*3

American Gothic (Wood), 141

Anthropology: ethnographic method in, 104–7, 109, 110–17, 119–22, 129, 161; and *The Hamlet*, 104–30, 160, 173*n*2; objectifying description in, 106–7, 108, 121, 129; personal narrative in, 106–7, 120–21; "salvage" metaphor in, 109, 111, 174*n*9; bias in information gathering in, 111–12, 115–17; "politics of domination" in ethnography, 113–14; "life histories" project during Depression, 120–21

Anti-Communism, 68–69, 170*n*9

Antilynching legislation, 143, 144–45, 176*n*9. *See also* Lynching and near-lynching

The Archaeology of Knowledge (Foucault), 12, 13–14

Argonauts of the Western Pacific (Malinowski), 105

Association of Southern Women for the Prevention of Lynching, 145

Bakhtin, Mikhail: on *heteroglossia*, 2, 158–59; and novelistic language, 2, 158–60, 166*n*18; and theory of dialogics, 2, 16–17; on epic genres, 3, 4, 158, 162; on laughter as novelistic trope, 5, 161; on ideologemes, 7; and authorship, 11; on ideological development, 121; on everyday speech, 128; and zones of contact, 157–62, 177*n*1; and theory of the novel, 158–62